China's Social Credit

This book analyses credit crisis issues in China from the aspect of individuals, enterprises, and government through investigations of six Chinese urban and rural areas.

After China's reform and opening up in the 1970s, a slew of new problems involving integrity, trust, and credit appeared with the establishment of a market economy and the creation of new business opportunities. To track these phenomena down to their very origins and to explore the theoretical principles underlying them through a truly holistic sociology, this book highlights a native Chinese perspective when dissecting and analysing the characteristics of their origins, mechanisms, and manifestations.

The book will be of great interest to students and scholars of economic sociology, Chinese studies, and those who are interested in the sociology of credibility in general.

Professor Zhai Xuewei is the Director of Sociology Department at Nanjing University, China. His research interests include the localisation of sociology and social psychology. He is also Yangtze River Distinguished Professor at the Ministry of Education.

Huang Xiaoye is Professor at the School of Marxism of Hohai University, Nanjing, China, with a PhD in management.

China Perspectives

The *China Perspectives* series focuses on translating and publishing works by leading Chinese scholars, writing about both global topics and China-related themes. It covers Humanities & Social Sciences, Education, Media and Psychology, as well as many interdisciplinary themes.

This is the first time any of these books have been published in English for international readers. The series aims to put forward a Chinese perspective, give insights into cutting-edge academic thinking in China, and inspire researchers globally.

To submit proposals, please contact the Taylor & Francis Publisher for China Publishing Programme, Lian Sun (Lian.Sun@informa.com)

Titles in sociology currently include:

Family Burden Coefficient in China
Exploratory Research and Application
Tian Feng

The Relationship Between Trust and Social Capital of China's Urban Residents
Zou Yuchun

Constructing Space
A Longitudinal Study of Immigrants from Wenzhou in Paris
Wang Chunguang

Structural Change and Evolution of China's Internet Society
Liu Shaojie

Two-Dimensional People
Lives, Desires, and Social Attitudes in a Changing Chinese Village
Tan Tongxue

China's Social Credit
Theoretical, Empirical Research, and Countermeasures
Zhai Xuewei, Huang Xiaoye

For more information, please visit https://www.routledge.com/China-Perspectives/book-series/CPH

China's Social Credit

Theoretical, Empirical Research, and Countermeasures

Zhai Xuewei and Huang Xiaoye

Translated by Wang Weichao and Wu Zhongxiu

Routledge
Taylor & Francis Group
LONDON AND NEW YORK

中国社会科学出版社
CHINA SOCIAL SCIENCES PRESS

Sponsored by Chinese Fund for the Humanities and Social Sciences.

First published in English 2023
by Routledge
4 Park Square, Milton Park, Abingdon, Oxon OX14 4RN

and by Routledge
605 Third Avenue, New York, NY 10158

Routledge is an imprint of the Taylor & Francis Group, an informa business

Translated by Wang Weichao and Wu Zhongxiu

British Library Cataloguing-in-Publication Data
A catalogue record for this book is available from the British Library

Library of Congress Cataloging-in-Publication Data
Names: Zhai, Xuewei, 1960- author. | Huang, Xiaoye, 1971- author.
Title: China's Social Credit : Theoretical, Empirical Research, and Countermeasures / Xuewei Zhai, Xiaoye Huang ; translated by Wang Weichao and Wu Zhongxiu.
Other titles: Zhongguo she hui xin yong. English
Description: New York : Routledge, 2023. | Series: China perspectives | Includes bibliographical references and index. |
Identifiers: LCCN 2022053854 (print) | LCCN 2022053855 (ebook) | ISBN 9781032450599 (hardback) | ISBN 9781032451404 (paperback) | ISBN 9781003375579 (ebook)
Subjects: LCSH: Social credit--China. | Credit--China. | Trust--Economic aspects--China. | Economics--Moral and ethical aspects.
Classification: LCC HG359.C6 Z4313 2023 (print) | LCC HG359.C6 (ebook) | DDC 332.560951/eng/20230103--dcundefined
LC record available at https://lccn.loc.gov/2022053854
LC ebook record available at https://lccn.loc.gov/2022053855

ISBN: 978-1-032-45059-9 (hbk)
ISBN: 978-1-032-45140-4 (pbk)
ISBN: 978-1-003-37557-9 (eBook)

DOI: 10.4324/9781003375579

Typeset in Times New Roman
by Deanta Global Publishing Services, Chennai, India

Contents

List of figures *vi*
List of tables *vii*

Synopsis 1

Introduction 4

1 Clarification of Concepts and Theoretical Exploration 15

2 The History and Tradition of China's Social Credit 45

3 The Status Quo of China's Social Credit 68

4 Humanity and Morality 101

5 Institution and Trust 110

6 Social Credit: Relationship or Social Capital 127

7 Social Credit in China in the Internet Era 161

8 Funnelling Theory 182

Afterword 200

Appendix 1: Questionnaire for the "Study of China's social credit system" (city version) *203*
Index *216*

Figures

1.1 History of China's social credit 29
1.2 Summary of piracy situation 38
1.3 Changes in the quantity of regular higher educational graduate 40
3.1 Performance credit of interviewees of different levels of education 78
3.2 Performance credit of interviewees of different political status 80
3.3 Performance credit of interviewees between the city and the countryside 80
3.4 Average values of institution credit (%) 81
3.5 Trust in government agencies by interviewees of different levels of education 81
3.6 Trust in government agencies by interviewees with different political status 82
3.7 Trust in government agencies by urban and rural dwellers 82
3.8 Effective percentage of personnel credit 83
3.9 Mean value of personnel credit (percentage) 85
3.10 Crosstabs analysis of product quality credit between the city and the countryside 87
3.11 Crosstabs analysis between vocation and product quality credit 87
3.12 Crosstabs analysis between education level and product quality credit 88
3.13 Differences of credit between the city and the countryside 91
3.14 Influences of differences of education background on personal credit 92
7.1 The most credible information channel on the Japanese nuclear radiation incident 168
7.2 The most credible information channel on the July 23 rear-end accident 168
7.3 Trust model in the internet era 173

Tables

3.1	Distribution of interviewees in city and countryside	74
3.2	Geographical distribution of interviewees	74
3.3	Age distribution of interviewees	75
3.4	Gender distribution of interviewees	75
3.5	Marriage status distribution of interviewees	75
3.6	Ethnicity distribution of interviewees	75
3.7	Religious distribution of interviewees	76
3.8	Distribution in city and countryside of interviewees	76
3.9	Income distribution of interviewees	76
3.10	Political status distribution of interviewees	77
3.11	Effective percentage of performance credit	79
3.12	Effective percentage of personnel credit	84
3.13	Overall situation of China's social credit	85
3.14	Overall situation of symbol credit	86
3.15	Symbol credit by groups of different educational backgrounds	86
3.16	Symbol credit by groups of different political status	86
3.17	Overall situation of product service credit	88
3.18	Overall brand credit situation	88
3.19	Overall credit situation of advertisements	89
3.20	Basic situation of charity organisation credit	89
3.21	Credit of different modes of donation	89
3.22	Credit situation of the process and result of charity operation	90
3.23	Result of factor analysis of personal credit	91
3.24	Description of variables of level of trust in social relationships (city samples)	92
3.25	Description of variables of level of trust in social relationships (rural questionnaire)	93
3.26	Situation description of social-organisation participation (city samples)	94
3.27	Situation description of social-organisation participation (countryside samples)	94

3.28 Situation description of social-activity participation (city samples) 95
3.29 Situation description of social-activity participation (countryside samples) 96
6.1 Conceptual dimensions of social capital 131
6.2 Descriptive statistics of the social participation variable (city sample) 133
6.3 Social participation (urban sample): factor loading after rotation 134
6.4 Descriptive statistic of social participation variable (rural samples) 136
6.5 Social participation (rural sample): factor loading after rotation 137
6.6 Descriptive statistics of interpersonal trust (urban sample) 138
6.7 Interpersonal trust (urban sample): factor loading after rotation 140
6.8 Descriptive statistic of interpersonal trust (rural sample) 141
6.9 Interpersonal trust (rural sample): factor loading after rotation 141
6.10 Universal concept of trust (urban sample): factor loading after rotation 145
6.11 Universal concept of trust (rural sample): factor loading after rotation 146
6.12 Influence of social capital on universal trust 147
6.13 Trust in government by the rural and urban residents 149
6.14 Impact of social capital on the trust in government 150
7.1 The first channel for urban residents to learn about current affairs (N = 3138) 166
7.2 The first channel for rural residents to learn about current affairs (N = 2158) 167
7.3 December 2013–June 2014 utilisation rate of various internet applications among Chinese internet users 170

Synopsis

After China's reform and opening up, there appeared two parallel socio-economic phenomena that coincided with the establishment of a market economy and the creation of many new business opportunities. On the one hand, the rapid and sustained growth of China's economy was breath-taking to behold; on the other, a slew of new problems involving integrity, trust, and credit were equally unmistakable. At the beginning, these problems were mainly economic in nature, but later they spread to other areas of society, proliferating to varying degrees in politics, culture, education, and everyday social behaviour. Some of these behaviours have since breached the bottom lines of morality, incurring immeasurable losses to the state and to the individuals involved. As a result, China's so-called credit crisis came into being.

Obviously, it is inadequate to research these problems from the perspective of a single discipline. More specifically, these problems could not have been explained via any currently available Western theories. In order to track these phenomena down to their very origins and to explore the theoretical principles underlying them through a truly holistic sociology, this book highlights a native Chinese perspective when dissecting and analysing the characteristics of their origins, mechanisms, and manifestations. The goal of this study is that such findings may ultimately be translated into policy proposals.

By adopting both the sociological stance and the native perspective, this book is able to approach three distinct social elements at the same time: the government, the market and individual, and the transition from the traditional to the modern. In this way, a full view of contemporary China's social credit may be offered. In order to grasp the synchronic and diachronic dimensions of the problem, and also to integrate issues of dishonesty from various fields into one unified research framework, this book first examines concepts such as integrity, trust, and credit, pointing out that, unlike the situation under Western knowledge regimes where trust and credit often belong to different fields, China's idea of social credit comes with the characteristics of coherent thought. The concept of integrity comes first, and next comes trust followed by credit. In other words, if there is no integrity, then there is no trust and ultimately no credit. This is due to the fact that, under the influence of Confucian concepts (cultivating the person, regulating the family, governing the state, and bringing universal peace to the kingdom), the Chinese treat these concepts as a continuous progressive relationship that interconnect several

DOI: 10.4324/9781003375579-1

social levels (the individual, the family, the society). Of course, by judging based on a small-scale, agricultural society defined by blood relationships and geographical relationships, it could be seen that the "staggered pattern" has some degree of rationality; however, with the modernisation and scale expansion of society, the efficacy of this pattern is gradually attenuated, eventually leading to the need for the maintenance of social credit to revert to morality and ethics in terms of institution construction. This is the basis for contemporary China's credit system and the reason for discussing its social control in a sociological way.

By interpreting the Chinese social tradition in the context of the individual, the market, and government behaviour, and by combining that interpretation with thoughts on the research on China's modern systems of credit, this book constructs a pair of sociological theories: homogeneous and heterogenous society. Regarding the appearance of the credit crisis in contemporary China, the overall assumption of this study is that Chinese society is highly homogeneous in all areas of society. The crux is that the Chinese tend to homogenise their social products through different means of homogenisation, but those means come from the law of the jungle as derived from the biological theory of evolution, which ultimately obliterates all differentiation in all aspects of society. In order to verify this hypothesis, the authors conducted an indoor questionnaire survey in six cities and areas in China (Tianjin, Nanjing, Chongqing, Lanzhou, Ningxia, and Shenzhen) and took into consideration differences between the city and the countryside. The survey discovered that the more an area was modernised (or the higher the education of the people in the area and the higher the social status of the individual) the more distrustful the people became towards contemporary society. Thus, the credibility of the government in the public's eyes dwindled in a cascade from the central to the local, and chaos reigned in market credit. This conclusion has also reinforced the received wisdom that claims that there is a lack of social participation among Chinese; they still resort to "relationship" to maintain trust. What's more, there is a great deal of data supporting the notion that the social products of China feature a tendency towards homogenisation.

Based on the situation discussed above, this book carries out theoretical explorations on realms that include human nature and morality, trust and institution, internet and credit. The purpose is to return to the real environments, to the real social conditions, and the real motivations of real Chinese in order to evaluate the challenges that have faced Chinese society over the past 40 years.

The authors believe that, because China has made progressive improvements to its legal systems and its credit reporting systems over this period, the social-credit crisis has been somewhat mitigated. Still, the price and cost paid for this crisis have been excessively high with no substantial effects. On the one hand, the improvement of social credit in China illustrates the country's ability to adjust to the impacts of a transformative process of modernisation; on the other hand, it also shows that duplicating Western models or focusing solely on market finance or personal credit reporting is far from enough. Therefore, this book advances the "funnelling theory" as an overarching framework for understanding social credit. The underlying view is that, prior to the completion of the individual's socialisation, the individual must undergo normative learning, including the practice of knowledge transmission, moral improvement, and the effects of punishment. Society, by contrast, arranges corresponding forms of socialisation and regulation when individuals proceed to enter the various institutions, levels, and vocations of society. Of course, these types of developmental work are first and foremost conducted under the auspices of school education, and ultimately only schools can improve the systems of social credit.

Introduction

For over 40 years since the introduction of the reform and opening-up policy, China's economy has maintained a healthy growth momentum. Up to now, China has gradually realised her grand vision of a national renaissance in terms of overall national strength. Meanwhile, in both the market and in broader society, the demands for social credit have been growing. However, such demands have not prompted effective credit mechanisms to be built in China. A slew of dishonesty continues to spread across various social realms. Although governments, social organisations, and other organisations at all levels have launched many measures to check the irregularities of credit entities, these measures have failed to effectively check the occurrence of dishonesty. Thus, the "credit crisis" still lurks and ferments in China. These conditions compel us to frame the following questions: What has happened to social credit in China? Why is the social credit crisis so prevalent? How can a sound credit system be built? Naturally, these questions lead into other areas, including cultural tradition, social evolution, and public mentality. Moreover, these questions require us to put forward theoretical speculation and a great deal of empirical research.

I.1 Problem and Problem Awareness

To understand the credit issue, one must first place it against the grand background of China's social change. From the founding of the People's Republic of China (PRC) to the implementation of the reform and opening-up policy, China transformed from a highly centralised economic system to a market economic system featuring competition at many levels. Particularly after the reform and opening up, the everyday life of the people of China has required drastic readjustment and undergone change in areas that include overall economic structure, social structure, cultural concepts, and the urban and rural relationship. Accordingly, the ideas of integrity, trust, and credit have undergone changes. It is acknowledged that the concept of credit is forever related to the stability of certain norms, but this transformative period had already rendered many previously stable norms unstable. What's more, the establishment of a market economy has made pursuit of profit a core social interest. When new norms fail to take form or are unable to take form, dishonesty becomes an inevitable phenomenon – and at times a deliberate action.[1]

DOI: 10.4324/9781003375579-2

Regarding the social credit system, some scholars have definitively pointed out that the absence of social credit harms the economy, increases transaction costs between individuals and enterprises, reduces benefits, wastes social resources, and hampers the healthy growth of private investment and the private sector.[2] The chaos of credit makes it impossible for the government to receive due responses to its policies, which hinders the sound operation of the national economy and retards the marketisation process of China. In addition to these economic risks, "the spread of dishonest conducts leads to grave moral risk and aggravates the unfair distribution of social wealth."[3] When a fundamental moral norm like honesty or integrity is abandoned by most members of society, the result is a degradation of social credit and the introduction of disorder and suspicion among people. Such a fundamental loss may even bring forth discontent with the government, which may jeopardise the stability of society as a whole. Therefore, investigating the causes of the collapse of social credit and working out solutions for the social credit crisis have become top priorities recently.

Of course, with respect to global socio-economic growth in general, the weakening of social credit is closely related to the characteristics of modern society. Indeed, the social credit crisis may be said to originate in the "uncertainty" of modern society.[4] Uncertainty results in social risk, and social risk renders the original social credit unstable. Obviously, The relationship that exists between the characteristics of the times, social risks, and social trust is a causal correlation mechanism. A problem occurring in any link of this chain would produce effects on other aspects and would ultimately reshape our state of living. Therefore, it could be said that the study of China's social credit in China has both a modernising context and the specific transformational features of the Chinese society. The focus of this book lies in the social credit issue generated by specific modernisation processes in China and not by the more abstract idea of modernity explored by Western sociologists.

The laser-sharp focus of the Communist Party and the Chinese Government has never for a moment been removed from these problems. The Communist Party has made clear the direction and objective of the social credit system as established by the Sixteenth National Congress of the Communist Party of China (CPC) and the Third Plenary Session of the Sixteenth Central Committee of the CPC. The 11th five-year plan proposed to accelerate the construction of a social credit system by focusing on improving the credit records, tax payment, contract performance and product quality. The 2007 National Financial Work Conference further proposed to promote the building of the social credit system in a comprehensive way by placing emphasis on the establishment of a credit-reporting system and by speeding up the establishment of the basic framework and operation mechanism for the social credit system to correspond to the level of social development of China. In 2011, the Sixth Plenary Session of the 11th CPC Central Committee proposed to separate social credit from the financial system, expanding it into an independent system. Hence, credit building would be placed in a prominent position in the overall social development programme. In this way, the plan for a nationwide social credit system was to be implemented. Under this plan, comprehensive coverage of social credit would be accomplished through a credit building programme centred in four principal areas, namely, the government, business, society, and the judiciary. A uniform platform incorporating elements from the financial, industrial, and commercial worlds involving issues of tax payments, social-security payments, traffic-violation payments, etc., would be established by 2017 to realise the objective of resource sharing.[5]

Why, then, have no significant results been achieved? If there are such clear directions and objectives – and there are so many supporting measures in place corresponding to every stage of implementation – why does there still exist such tremendous breaches of conduct regarding credit norms? Why is there still such an explosion of fraudulent conduct? Some scholars attempt to answer these questions by resorting to jurisprudence, economics, or ethics. They suggest either to perfect laws and regulations centred on intellectual property, or to make an enterprise's credit rating the starting point for a new system, or to improve the moral quality of society at large, etc. Despite some positive results, studies in this vein remain generally shallow, and the content under discussion comparatively narrow, for they have yet to conduct historical research on and empirical examination of the basics of the current realities and causes of contemporary China's social credit situation. Their simplistic copying of Western social credit systems also conceals the practical problems that China faces. Especially on the planes of human psychology and behaviour, the foregoing studies have so far failed to gain any understanding of the relationship between the Chinese people and society as a whole.

This book proposes that it would be better for anyone who wishes to study social credit to avoid any immediate decisions on disciplinary scope and theory. Rather, we should always be guided by an awareness of the particulars of whatever problem we are studying. Only when we have constructed a reasonable research approach and research framework should we then conduct empirical research and exploration. In proceeding this way, we hope that our research may break through the superficial slogans shouting "return to traditional Chinese culture!" or alternately "modernise now!" Instead, we hope to discover a route of exploration that raises theoretical speculations through our empirical research, speculations that ultimately form the basis for policy proposals on the issue of social credit.

I.2 Contending Views among Different Disciplines

It is clear that China's social credit problem has been advanced through major social events and through individual perception. Because the problem does not belong to any specific discipline, all disciplines have their respective explanations and remedies for it. Roughly speaking, the following are the prevailing views.

Firstly, the economist basically holds that the study of the social credit problem is mainly linked with the credit crisis of the 1990s. Scholars believe that credit is the expectation of a future loan repayment by the credit receiver in a loan relationship. Universally cited are transaction cost theory, game theory, reputation theory, the economics of information, and so on. These theories are based on the assumption of the rationality of the economic participant and hold that China's corporate credit crisis originates in its institutional arrangements as manifest in its credit mechanisms and its ideas of intellectual property. The credit crisis, or the prevalence of dishonest conduct in China's real economy, is due to faulty mechanisms of information transmission and improper credit incentives.[6] If, during the period of economic transformation, defective ideas of intellectual property restrained the positive effects of the market, thus creating low corporate credit levels,[7] then a clearly defined property rights system, or a "society–government" dual structure, could be established, making it possible to eliminate unnecessary supervision and to enhance enterprise liquidity. Alternatively, a credit assessment system or credit reference system could be established, in tandem with the improvement of relevant laws and regulations, so as to promote the better transmission of information during credit transactions.

Secondly, the ethicist holds that credit is a type of ethical relationship and that a code of ethics is what determines such relationships. A person's understanding of an unethical relationship and the application of its rules can affect the personality and virtue of the person; at a broader level, such an understanding also affects the moral level of society as a whole.[8] As markets have developed and the goal of profits has become more intense, many market entities have sought personal gain through illegal or irregular activity, which has in turn damaged market order and even the foundations of the market economy itself. Having investigated these problems, scholars have often concluded that contemporary economic transformations show that traditional notions of morality and conduct are incapable of restraining individuals in the modern age. Because new notions of morality and norms of conduct have yet to come into being, the result is a sort of chaos or disorder. Hence, reshaping social credit not only requires strengthening the government's intervention, enhancing the self-restraint of market entities, and establishing the rule of law, but it also requires the improvement of moral education to make people aware of the important roles that integrity and honesty continue to play in social harmony. But what direction should such education take? Some people have proposed that we should go back to traditional Chinese culture to nourish "honesty and integrity" or search Confucian teachings for an effective way of retrieving or re-establishing the moral quality of the Chinese citizen. On the other hand, other people think that ideas of personal trust founded on blood relationships are antithetical to the kind of social trust required by modern society,[9] thus requiring China to borrow from Western culture the "contract spirit" that matches its market economy.

Thirdly, the view of the lawyer. Legal scholars hold that a market economy should, properly speaking, be under the rule of law, for credit is founded on the basis of the legal system. China has so far conducted tremendous work in terms of stepping up legal protections. However, generally speaking, the rule of law in China has yet to be perfected, and the law has yet to make a powerful, protective impact in the operation of the credit economy. In some areas, there are no laws to abide by on many economic issues; in some areas, even though there may have been laws enacted, these laws have been left unobserved or unenforced. Hence, China must strengthen its legislation regarding relevant laws and regulations, and it must intensify its law enforcement and supervision. There are also scholars who hold the view that the root cause of the social credit crisis is the non-independent status of China's consumer rights and the fact that no emphasis has been attached to such rights; they believe that if consumers had their own rights, the situation would fundamentally improve.[10]

Fourthly, in the eyes of the researcher of politics and public policy, credit or government reputation is a convention of the client-proxy relationship between the government and the people. The smooth operation of credit entails an inherent covenant with credit entities. Government credit is a form of social credit, which mandates that the government, as a credit entity, also should abide by the covenant. However, the vague image, multi-dimensional structure, dominant position, and non-optional nature of the government deviate from the credit-entity covenant; they do not work harmoniously with such a covenant.[11] The credit of the government itself cannot be brought under effective supervision, and the ensuing dependence on "interest" relationships has created large-scale government credit issues and market credit issues,[12] which have in turn led to breaches of promise on the government side. Such breaches are primarily manifest in government abuses of state policy and its administrative function, disregard of the administrative vocational ethics of public servants, "behind-the-scenes" activities in government actions, rampant corruption of officials, etc. Meanwhile, in such relationships, there is a game between the government and local entities. And due to information asymmetry, one-sided guidance of the performance appraisal mechanism and weak supervision and control mechanisms, there are problems of changing policies and declining credibility. Therefore, the government should enhance its credit capability by improving the credit awareness of public servants, stringently restricting the government's manoeuvrability in matters of credit, vigorously pushing the disclosure of government information, and perfecting mechanisms to supervise and limit government credit.[13]

Lastly, on the sociological plane, there is the phenomenon of social anomie that appeared during China's transitional period. This phenomenon was caused by the rift between the social basis on which credit depends in social transformation and the institutional arrangements. Simply put, the original institutionalised and non-institutionalised social norms lost their justification and effectiveness. From the macro-perspective, the functions a normal social structure should have feature both distinction and complementarity. However, in our society, these functions are usually subsumed under one common core. The functions assumed by different structural bodies are converging to an extremely high degree, which leads to the distortion and deformation of such functions and the disorder of society.[14] From the micro-perspective, trust originates in the personal experience and the degree of familiarity of the interaction between the doer and others. In China's transformation from a traditional society to a modern one, due to changes in the dimension of time and familiar circumstances, the personal experience of the individual ceased to be the ground on which the future was derived, which in turn gave rise to doubts about interaction and engendered uncertainty, ultimately leading to issues of trust. The lopsided development of China's economy has not only failed to establish a new trust mechanism but has undermined trust. In its vigorous pursuit of a market economy, China did not pursue with equal vigour the trust mechanisms it needed for a modern society.[15] This led to the outbreak of the credit crisis.

Having conducted a comprehensive review, examination, and content analysis of social credit studies conducted by domestic scholars from various disciplines, we would say that, after roughly 20 years of development, some results of the investigations on China's social credit and its system have appeared. However, many views fall under the category of "emergency treatment." They are either topical or countermeasure studies, and it is difficult to sort out and give a more reasonable account of the context of China's social credit problems from a theoretical standpoint. Specific inadequacies are set out as follows.

Firstly, there is an uneven development among the various research dimensions of social credit. In the foregoing paragraphs, we pointed out that social credit could be roughly divided into three main dimensions: Individual (consumer) credit, corporate (market) credit, and government (political) credit. It is clear that the focus of study has been on the slow development of personal credit and corporate credit systems as dominated by the central bank; thus, relatively complete systems of evaluation, supervision, and management have taken shape. However, this arrangement places social credit primarily under the auspices of economic credit and financial credit, while failing to take the dominance of the government and its administrative role into consideration. As for Chinese society, government credit plays an important role in the development of the entire credit system. It assumes not only the identity of a credit entity but also that of a key establisher and supervisor of the credit system. Unfortunately, little discussion on the relationships and interactions between the three dimensions has taken place within academia thus far. Ignoring their interactive relationships will in practice lead to ignoring the foundation of the healthy operation of the social credit system, which will in turn lead to problems in understanding the multiple entities responsible for the causes and effects of the social credit crisis. Actually, the social credit problem that contemporary Chinese society experiences cannot be reduced to the problem of one specific entity. It requires examination and analysis from a perspective of interconnectedness and healthy interaction. Consequently, the authors of this book hold that the social credit system requires consideration from a holistic and inclusive standpoint, so that all the gaps of the credit problem may be plugged.

Secondly, the literature lacks a clear understanding of China's traditional culture and social structure. Developed Western countries have accumulated a tremendous amount of research experience; hence, the current credit system in China is largely examined by comparison to the practical experiences of Western economic theories and systems. This situation inevitably calls into question the degree of integration between the two. The practice of mechanically copying a Western social credit system also reflects the fact that Chinese scholars lack a continual understanding of the changes in China's traditional culture and social structures. Thus, scholars often graft worthwhile Western experiences onto Chinese society by applying these experiences out of context. As one of the authors of this book remarked,

> Modern society is a risk society, which entails a modern credit system to safeguard the security of man. However, whether a society can establish a modern credit mechanism concerns the cultural basis of the society. The cultural foundation of the Chinese society originates in the family life, and it restrains the scope of social credit. However, the lopsided development of China's economy has not only failed to establish a new trust mechanism, but has undermined its traditional ground; this is the root cause of China's credit crisis.[16]

A general examination of recent studies shows that there is virtually no in-depth examination of traditional Chinese credit culture and its interrelations with a real social structure, which in practice leads to empty talk about credit divorced from social reality: Such emptiness will render whatever policies and regulations are introduced ineffective. The authors of this book hold that the unique cultural tradition and current social structure in China are important background variables upon which the existence and continuation of social credit depend. Only when we first get down to the root of these problems can we correctly set our objectives and discover the crux of the credit problem – which has practical significance for China – and in turn propose an appropriate solution.

Lastly, the perspectives and methods that considerable research on social credit has employed have lacked variety. So far, most of the research by domestic scholars has taken the perspective of economics. These scholars have explored the absence of social credit by looking almost exclusively at the relationship between the debtor and the creditor, which has left the research unable to approach all aspects of social credit in a holistic manner. Consequently, most scholars have employed qualitative research methods, or even engaged in a simple discussion of tackling strategies, all of which have lacked the support of large-scale social surveys and quantitative research. In addition, many scholars have engaged in conducting low-level duplicative work or in running similar studies with minor, superficial changes.

In short, we believe that problems behind the various issues uncovered in the study of contemporary credit can be summarised as follows.

1. It seems that the various disciplines are all discussing "credit"; however, each researcher has his or her own understanding and use of the concept. Due to the vagueness of the concepts and the arbitrariness of their use, in tandem with the very limited interaction between the different academic disciplines, the result is a deepening chaos and fragmentation of the relevant research. If such a chaotic situation is not corrected, it will be very difficult for us to focus on the crux of the issue. If we cannot make cumulative research possible, then the result will likely be research dealing with China's credit problem just marking time.
2. Theories are divorced from reality. Viewed in a detached way, the practical credit problem is getting increasingly more serious; many complicated social, economic, cultural, psychological, and practical institutional factors contribute to this situation. However, the fact that academics have failed to address this crisis effectively is one major cause of its continued fermentation. We should

acknowledge that, in the last 150 years of social evolution, Chinese society has undergone radical change and development. Indeed, such tremendous change is unprecedented in China's long history and has rarely been seen in the history of the world. Especially during the 40 years after the inception of the reform and opening-up policy, the rapid growth of China's economy has rendered theoretical explanation of it by contemporary social sciences inadequate. The current demarcation and segmentation of the social sciences in exploration of the credit issue only reinforce the current barriers between the different disciplines, making it difficult for us to get down to the nature of the problem. According to our examination, academic exchange usually occurs only within a discipline or within a relatively closed academic community; within their respective communities, scholars each indulge in their own academic worlds. Even without a proper definition of key concepts, scholars who confine their research to their closed academic communities will only communicate with their colleagues – and thus they will fail to see they are actually using different meanings for key concepts. What is more, they will find it impossible to engage in interdisciplinary debates.

3. There is tension between Western theories and the Chinese problem. Due to their wide-ranging nature, the academic exploration of the issues of integrity, trust, and credit will naturally be subject to the methods of the many different branches within academia. However, this implies the introduction of Western academic concepts, academic discipline division, and analytical frameworks into a Chinese context, which in turn leads to the neglect of the Chinese social phenomenon under investigation.
4. Appearance of interlocking rings. Due to their institutional differences, each discipline indulges in its own respective narratives; collectively, such narratives ultimately lead to an interlocking situation.[17] Figuratively, this may be likened to building a house. If the house were judged as substandard, how would we evaluate the situation? Of course, experts from different fields would find different problems. Some would say that the contract was not clearly defined, others would claim that there were loopholes in the contract, still others would point to information asymmetry, and some might even refer to a lack of supervision. In this fault-finding process, an interlocking situation of explanation comes into being. Firstly, there are the substandard products used by the unit in charge of construction, and the reason for the substandard products used by the unit in charge of construction lies in the fact that the construction unit has not honoured the contract. The reason that the construction unit has not honoured the contract lies in the fact that the construction unit does not exercise good faith in contract performance, and the reason that the construction unit does not exercise good faith in contract performance lies in the fact that the construction unit is of poor quality, and the reason that it is of poor quality lies in the fact that its personnel have not received a proper education. The reason that the construction-unit personnel have not received a proper education lies in the fact that education in China has failed to keep up with the changing situation, and the reason that education in China has failed to keep up with the changing situation

lies in the fact that education itself has not received proper public attention. The reason that education has not received proper public attention lies in the fact that education does not produce instant effects. While placing an emphasis on education is a slow process, in the short term, exercising proper supervision is an answer, but that brings to the forefront the issue of inadequate supervision. Inadequate supervision can be ascribed to imperfect laws and regulations, but that then requires the improvement of laws and regulations. When laws and regulations are perfected, there then surface issues such as the failure to abide by such laws and regulations and the failure to strictly enforce such laws and regulations. The failure to abide by such laws and regulations and the failure to strictly enforce such laws and regulations can be ascribed to the inferior quality of law enforcement, which once again necessitates the improvement of education. Lastly, improving education requires increasing investment in education, while increasing investment in education requires building houses – but alas, the house being built is still substandard.

Considering the foregoing mini summary, it can be seen that if substantial progress is to be made in the research of China's social credit, the researcher must first have an awareness of the real problems involved and then he or she must make theoretical clarifications, seeking the interrelationships among the concepts. Finally, he or she may hope to arrive at understanding by employing a comparatively reasonable interpretative analytical framework.

Notes

1 Ye Tan, *Start Building Government Credit to Build a Social Credit System, No. 136 Commentary of Ifeng.com, May 7, 2014*, http://news.ifeng.com/opinion/wangping/detail_2014_05/07/36191511_0.shtml?_114sobiaoqian.
2 Liu Ke, Wang Pingang, Sun Qunying, Establishing the Perfection of the Social Credit System, *Technical Economy* 2002(1); Zhao Wenlong, Feng Xianfen, The Current State and Regulation of Social Credit during China's Transition, *Journal of Xi'an Jiaotong University* 2002(2); Li Jizi, Analysis and Study of the Ills and Causes of the Lack of "Social Credit," *Science-Technology and Management* 2003(2); Zhang Rui, Wang Jianzhan, Social Credit Crisis in Modern Times, *Journal of Hebei Institute of Technology* 2003(2); Shen Guigen, Song Yuxian, Thoughts on Establishing Social Credit System, *Theoretical Exploration* 2004(4).
3 Ke, Pingang, Qunying, Establishing the Perfection of the Social Credit System.
4 Zygmunt Bauman, *Liquid Modernity*, translated by Ouyang Jinggen, Shanghai Sanlian Bookstore Press, 2002, p. 250.
5 Fang Jiaxi, *A Framework for the Establishment of National Credit System to Be Published, May 5, 2014*.
6 Yu Li, Yu Zuo, Ding Ning, Credit, Information and Regulation – an Economic Analysis of Honesty and Dishonesty, *China Industrial Economics* 2002(6); Zhang Weiying, *Property Right, Government and Reputation*, SDX Joint Publishing Company, 2001; Zhang Weiying, *Information, Trust and Law*, SDX Joint Publishing Company, 2003; Shang Qingjun, *Credit System Construction in Transitional Period*, Shanghai Sanlian Bookstore, 2011.
7 Zhang Weiying, *Property Right, Government and Credibility*, SDX Joint Publishing Company, 2001.

8 Zheng Yefu, Peng Siqing et al., *Trust in Chinese Society*, China City Press, 2003; Chen Xuxin, A Credit Perspective Interpretation of the Institutional Effective Function and the Ethical Value of its Promise, *Social Science Research* 2007(1).
9 Ibid.
10 See Zhai Xuewei, The Social Cause of Credit Crisis, *Jiangsu Social Science* 2014(1).
11 Nie Yanqing, Zhang Wei, On the Antinomy of "Credit – Government" in Government Credit, *Journal of Tianshui Institute of Administration* 2007(4).
12 Shen Yi, A Comparative Sociological Analysis of the Credit Problem – A Shift of Research Perspective from Vocational Ethics to Corporate Body, *Jianghai Academic Journal* 2011(2).
13 Wu Jingmei, On the Supervisory Mechanism of Government Credit, *Qiushi Theory* 2004(3).
14 Sun Liping, A Sociological Analysis of Moral Decline, *Journal of China Youth University of Political Studies* 2001(5).
15 Zhai Xuewei, Trust and Social Risk – Western Theories and China's Problems, *Social Science Research* 2008(4).
16 Ibid.
17 Xuewei, The Social Cause of Credit Crisis.

References

Bauman, Z. (2002). *Liquid modernity* (J. Ouyang, Trans.). Shanghai Sanlian Bookstore Press.

Chen, X. (2007). A credit perspective interpretation of the institutional effective function and the ethical value of its promise. *Social Science Research*, *1*, 152–159.

Fang, J. (2014, May 5). A framework for the establishment of national credit system to be announced. *Economic Information*. http://dz.jjckb.cn/www/pages/webpage2009/html/2014-05/05/content_89756.htm?div=-1

Li, J. (2003). Analysis and study of the ills and causes of the lack of "social credit". *Science-Technology and Management*, *2*, 100–103. https://doi.org/10.16315/j.stm.2003.02.035

Liu, K., Wang, P., & Sun, Q. (2002). Establishing the perfection of the social credit system. *Technical Economy*, *1*, 24–26.

Nie, Y., & Zhang, W. (2007). On the antinomy of "credit – government" in government credit. *Journal of Tianshui Institute of Administration*, *4*, 39–42.

Shang, Q. (2011). *Credit system construction in transitional period*. Shanghai Sanlian Bookstore.

Shen, G., & Song, Y. (2004). Thoughts on establishing social credit system. *Theoretical Exploration*, *4*, 49–50.

Shen, Y. (2011). A comparative sociological analysis of the credit problem: A shift of research perspective from vocational ethics to corporate body. *Jianghai Academic Journal*, *2*, 121–127+239.

Sun, L. (2001). A sociological analysis of moral decline. *Journal of China Youth University of Political Studies*, *5*, 65–69. https://doi.org/10.16034/j.cnki.10-1318/c.2001.05.019

Wu, J. (2004). On the supervisory mechanism of government credit. *Qiushi Theory*, *3*, 70–72.

Ye, T. (2014, May 7). Start building government credit to build a social credit system. *Commentary of Ifeng.com*. http://news.ifeng.com/opinion/wangping/detail_2014_05/07/36191511_0.shtml?114sobiaoqian

Yu, L., Zuo, D., & Ding, N. (2002). Credit, Information and regulation: An economic analysis of honesty and dishonesty. *China Industrial Economics*, *6*, 65–70. https://doi.org/10.19581/j.cnki.ciejournal.2002.06.009

Zhai, X. (2008). Trust and social risk: Western theories and China's problems. *Social Science Research*, *4*, 123–128.
Zhai, X. (2014). The social cause of credit crisis. *Jiangsu Social Science*, *1*, 85–96. https://doi.org/10.13858/j.cnki.cn32-1312/c.2014.01.030
Zhang, R., & Wang, J. (2003). Social credit crisis in modern times. *Journal of Hebei Institute of Technology*, *2*, 9–11+21.
Zhang, W. (2001). *Property right, government and credibility*. SDX Joint Publishing Company.
Zhang, W. (2003). *Information, trust and law*. SDX Joint Publishing Company.
Zhao, W., & Feng, X. (2002). The current state and regulation of social credit during China's transition. *Journal of Xi'an Jiaotong University*, *2*, 90–92.
Zheng, Y., & Peng, S. (2003). *Trust in Chinese society*. China City Press.

1 Clarification of Concepts and Theoretical Exploration

In different contexts, the Chinese character XIN has different meanings, and, in the modern social sciences, its different meanings can only be dismembered and studied under different disciplinary realms. This is the breaking-the-whole-into-pieces research approach so often engaged by modern scientific research. This approach also exists because the researcher needs to determine which aspect of XIN his study concerns, or which discipline his study of XIN should fall under. We have to acknowledge that such a research approach does have the advantage of deepening our understanding of XIN in some respects; however, its insufficiency is also plain to see. On one hand, as we differentiate XIN's many meanings, we lose sight of the possibility of connecting them back together and gaining a holistic understanding of them; on the other, we also see that we may have lost the chance to construct a research framework more appropriate to XIN. In other words, this chapter will show that, compared with the partitioned investigation of XIN under different disciplines, "social credit" is an overarching and general concept within the Chinese academic context. Its study may not be confined to an internal debate within the realms of sociology, political sciences, psychology, and economics. In order to make this point clear, an investigation must be first conducted on XIN itself. We must first make clear through this investigation what a more feasible – and enriching – research framework on XIN would look like.

1.1 Clarification of Concepts

1.1.1 Native Explanation of XIN

XIN has long been a core issue of common interest to various schools examining the history of Chinese thought. Discussions about it can be retrieved from the thoughts and classics of the Confucianist, the Mohist, the Taoist, the Legalist, and so on. In ancient thoughts and classics, the meanings of XIN vary considerably. As a part of speech, there are verbal uses, such as "friends **believed** it" (*the Analects of Confucius – GONGYE CHANG*), there are also adverbial and adjectival uses, and there are many instances (indeed, too many to enumerate) in which XIN refers to a virtue. Morphologically, XIN is a character coined via associative compounding. It associates two radicals, REN (man) and YAN (words, speech): "man honouring his words is XIN (honesty, being truthful)," which means that one's words should

DOI: 10.4324/9781003375579-3

be dependable. In other words, man should not make groundless claims; he should be honest and honour his promises. The meanings of the term thus include "honesty," "promising-keeping," "trust," and "credit," all of which are derived from the original coinage. XIN on many occasions refers to important personal qualities and extends to interpersonal commitments and promise-keeping activities. XIN may also constitute the foundation on which a country is founded as well as the way its ruler rules that country. For instance, *Lv Shi Chun Qiu: GUI XIN* (literal translation: *The Annals of Lv Buwei: Valuing Integrity*) treats XIN as the ethical canon to be universally observed across the world. It is no wonder, then, that Mencius placed XIN at a height equal to that of his ideal, "goodness."

If we replace XIN in Chinese classics with modern concepts, we must remember that in ancient China, XIN refers to personal integrity, trust, and reliance between individuals, including officials and businessmen; it also refers to the reputation of the government and the state as well as the values, beliefs, etc., that the country must support. Clearly, the single Chinese character XIN may be interpreted in multiple ways from multiple perspectives.

What is more, in traditional thinking, the meanings of XIN mentioned above are often mixed with concepts like "sincerity," "allegiance," and "righteousness." The meanings embodied in the use of XIN by the ancients can be obtained through their reciprocating definitions with "sincerity," "allegiance," and "righteousness." The reciprocating definitions of "sincerity," "allegiance," "righteousness," and XIN focus on the inherent connections and unity among them. As important virtues of man, "honesty" and XIN both denote a state of realness and freedom from delirium; their meanings are close and each could be employed in the definition of the other. In contrast, "sincerity" reveals the nature of the world; that is, the ancient Chinese believed that all things show their appearance because of their "sincerity." If a person is sincere, his behaviour will display "faithfulness." It could thus be deduced that "sincerity" is the internal motivation of "faithfulness," whereas "faithfulness" is the external manifestation of "sincerity." Conversely, when a person keeps his promise, it can indicate his inner honesty. "Allegiance" and "XIN" also constitute a pair relationship. Sometimes allegiance and sincerity are of equivalent meanings, and the combination of the two constitutes a two-character phrase also denoting allegiance. However, "allegiance" refers more to inner sentiments and beliefs, and its meaning is not as broad as that of "sincerity." When applied to non-human entities, "faithfulness" also denotes the accord of inner sentiments with speech and conduct. Another difference between allegiance and faithfulness lies in the fact that faithfulness is often directed to a specific matter, whereas allegiance is always directed to an overall situation. For instance, to promise someone to do something for him is faithfulness, while assisting somebody and dedicating one's life to him is allegiance. The definition of "faithfulness" by the ancients does not stay on the surface of the concept. In other words, in using "faithfulness," they do not dwell exclusively on keeping promises and commitments but pay equal attention to the legitimacy and righteousness of such conduct. This is the relationship between faithfulness and righteousness. The Chinese thinker holds that "righteousness" is the basis and prerequisite for the performance of "faithfulness." Only when a commitment conforms to "righteousness" can it have the moral requirements for performance; otherwise, one may refuse to perform a "not-righteous" commitment. A promise must be "righteous" to be legitimate; only then can it be performed and honoured. Hence, it could be deduced that, under the concept of virtue, which is one traditional category of China's construction of XIN, "faithfulness" must be guided by "righteousness." What "faithfulness" follows is the moral principle – that is, faithfulness follows the way of righteousness. If a person keeps a promise for profit, such faithfulness is not commendable. "Practising faithfulness" is always accompanied by "valuing justice," while "treachery" is forever connected to "discarding justice."

In a word, in the traditional study of virtue, the meaning of some Chinese character combinations has a mutually reinforcing character, which results in a great differentiation among philosophical ideas, ideas of social morality, and ethical normative systems. For instance, as stated in the foregoing elaboration, faithfulness, allegiance, righteousness, etc., all derive from "sincerity." In the eyes of the Confucianist, "sincerity" is the primordial essence of all things, the universe and nature. "Faithfulness," as a purely human item of virtue, comes exclusively from one characteristic of the evolution of the universe and nature, so naturally it does not occupy as decisive a position as "sincerity." It can only have a subordinate position. Meanwhile, the mixed use of "sincerity" with "allegiance," "righteousness," etc., is an attempt to show that there are also meanings, including human sentiments, values, beliefs, and moral principles, underneath "allegiance," all of which bring forth a richer variety and more tension from the practice of "faithfulness." Of course, due to the fact that the meaning of the former is itself of great vagueness, the meaning of XIN should also be determined by the researcher according to the topic and the context under discussion.

Confucianism's discussion of "faithfulness" runs across various stipulations on aspects including personal cultivation, interpersonal interaction, and state governance. According to Confucius, honouring one's promise is not only the code of conduct one must conform to, it is also the fundamental issue concerning personal conduct, personal accomplishments, and state governance, which is the foundation upon which the ideal of "cultivating the person, putting the family in order, governing the state, and bringing universal peace to the empire" could be realised. Under the logical and theoretical framework of Confucianist thought, personal performance relates to the empire. That is to say, if the individual is faithful, there will be trust in the relationship; and when there is trust in the relationship, there will be credit. This is the foundation upon which the empire can be properly governed. It can be seen that XIN takes the sincerity of the person as the starting point, proceeds to derive the XIN of relationship and the XIN of society from the XIN of the person, and expands ultimately to the XIN of the entire empire.

The foregoing characteristics lead to the many definitions of XIN. Different contexts and situations bring about a multitude of interpretations of XIN.

1.1.2 Establishing the Relevant Conceptual Relations

Having examined the relevant concepts, we found that there are no XIN-like terms that denote such wide-ranging meanings and cut across so many different domains in the English lexicon. Etymologically, the English terms (e.g., belief, trust, information, reputation, credit, distrust, etc.) corresponding to the Chinese XIN-related terms do not evolve from the same root. Comparison of the morphological structures of terms in the two languages reveals that there is the common character XIN in all of these Chinese terms, which demonstrates either that they are extensions in different social domains of the same character, or that the meaning of XIN has been extended to different areas of society. Apart from the fact that in English the Latin root for "credit" inherently denotes trust, most of the other related terms have their different fields of application and denote differently in their respective fields. In other words, the implied content of "trust" in these English words could only be obtained through examination, whereas in Chinese the trust content is directly expressed. Therefore, when translating SHEHUI XINYONG (society credit) into English, should we say "social credit" or "social trust"? If we are discussing CHENGXIN WEIJI (integrity crisis), should we say "the crisis of honesty," "credit crisis," or "trust crisis"? These discussions demonstrate the problems arising from same-field applications and different-field applications.

Having differentiated the credit-related terms between Chinese and English, now let's return to the modern sciences to determine, according to a Western disciplinary approach, what will happen when the concepts constituted by XIN, which evolved from China's traditional culture, are classified in accordance with the current disciplinary classification. It seems that these concepts can be roughly classified into three different disciplinary clusters. The first cluster involves aspects of individual psychology and behaviour, such as integrity, self-confidence, confidence, belief, that is, entities relating to disciplines which are related to the individual, such as psychology, ethics (morality), jurisprudence, and religious studies (theology). The second cluster involves aspects of social relationships, social interaction, and market transactions, such as information, trust, reputation, trust fund, credit loan, and courier. They can be classified into disciplines related to social relations, such as sociology, social psychology, economics, management, and political studies. The third cluster has a somewhat special meaning, for it usually covers the uses of XIN, which can be considered as "the use of XIN" "the application of XIN," or "the state of promise-keeping," etc. It could also be interpreted as "the total quantity of XIN (credit or promise-kept) performed in society," "the quantity of social credit," "a medium of exchange," and so on. Such being the case, it could only be investigated under the social and behavioural sciences. Of course, sociology might be the most appropriate discipline to conduct a comprehensive discussion of the topic.

Along with the simplistic understanding of XIN in Chinese, according to definitions by Chinese dictionaries, XIN has two aspects of meaning in its most popular sense in Chinese society. The first refers to "integrity, honesty," that is, the consistency and agreement between the idea, the mind, the behaviour, the words, and the corresponding results, which is demonstrated in the saying "a promise is to be kept, and a deed effected." In plain language, it means "do not lie, do not cheat." The second sense refers to "reliance" or "dependence," that is, a situation in which any person or group is sure of or entertains no doubt about the words and conducts of the other party in a social relation or social interaction. In folk terms, it means the "reliability and dependability of the other party." Having these two basic clues in mind, we will discover that many disputes about the concept are not issues that actually arise from cumulative study but are rather issues that derive from isolated research, disciplinary demarcation, and differences of understanding outside academic dialogue.[1]

In order to place this confounding medley of isolated discussions into a relatively symphonic analytical framework, we hereby construct a theoretical perspective fit for investigating Chinese social credit by combing through the evolution of the Chinese character XIN itself, for it must be remembered that the Chinese discussion of XIN runs across sub-concepts including personal cultivation, interpersonal interaction, state governance, and supreme harmony over the empire. Proceeding from there, it can be concluded that the Chinese concept of XIN follows a thinking process that originates from a single focal point and burgeons into an array of areas. It requires us to follow a path of expansion that scales up from the small, running through "the person" and on to "the relation, the community, the state, and the empire." Specifically, according to Chinese thinking, "integrity" corresponds to morality or personality appeal, "trust" corresponds to social relations, "reputation" corresponds to relations with organisations or the public, and "credit" corresponds to relations with the government and the market. Such an expansionist analytical framework is built on the following Chinese assumption: If everybody keeps their promises, their interactions will generate social credit, and the overall credit situation of the whole country will thrive. This statement coincides perfectly with the mentality underlying the modern Chinese slogans "Responsible behaviour now starts from me" (or "The buck stops here") and "So long as everybody loves the world a little bit more, it will turn into a paradise on earth." It also conforms with the Chinese preference for running a pilot project before rolling the project out across the country. When we view integrity, trust, and credit as a continuum of relations, then the medley of Chinese statements about crisis becomes quite clear to us; hence, the so-called "integrity crisis" denotes the degradation of social relations, whereas the so-called "credit crisis" stresses that there are problems in the mechanisms and systems of Chinese society. So why do the three sometimes get confused? As the continuum demonstrates, these three elements stand in a mutually compatible relationship, and as a result they sometimes get confused.

When the relationships among integrity, trust, and credit constitute a continuum, we can then relatively truthfully reconstruct the Chinese understanding and its use of XIN. Firstly, the Chinese discussion of XIN remains largely undetached from the backdrop of the native community; in other words, traditional Chinese thoughts are embedded in the acquaintance society. The relative closeness of the native community and the immobility of the populace result in the establishment of a self-reliant and self-sufficient XIN. This concept largely satisfies the needs for subsistence and development of community members, and it has a fundamental impact on the entire Chinese landscape, involving politics, markets, transactions, commerce, and the military. In discussing the issue of XIN, the Confucianist realises that, on the one hand, blood relationships and geographical relationships form the natural basis for XIN; he is also aware, on the other hand, of the peril of building a trust relationship based on non-blood relationships and non-geographical relationships. Such being the case, how could the Confucianist, who originated in an agricultural civilisation, defuse the situation and shift from a blood-based relationship to a non-blood-based relationship? The answer relates to what the Confucianist calls "allegiance and forbearance," which extends the concept of XIN by way of analogy (extending). This analogical process likens a friendly relationship to a brotherly relationship, likens the monarch-and-subject relationship to the father-and-son relationship, and concludes that supreme harmony of the empire will be brought forth by combining "allegiance," "righteousness," and "integrity." Leafing through Chinese classics, time and again one comes across instances of the Confucianist pushing concepts of "filial piety" into social domains such as "allegiance and integrity" or "integrity and righteousness." However, the industrialisation and urbanisation China has undergone since the inception of modern society have broken apart the community life of traditional Chinese society and the trust network on which it was built. In particular, the market economy that developed out of the 30-plus years of the reform and opening up has created a situation in which most interactions are conducted with strangers, which renders inoperable the traditional mentality of extending from personal cultivation all the way to supreme harmony of the empire.

Due to the fact that each discipline has its own research orientation and problem, Western academia tends not to treat these problems as a wide-ranging social phenomenon. If we simplistically replicate the Western concepts and analytic framework in the analysis of China's credit problem, we in essence break apart the wholeness, heterogeneity, and continuum of the concept, and thus we can only conduct our study in a local, meticulous, and self-contained manner. Currently, under the influence of discipline partition, a great number of papers seem to have found their way to address the situation. For instance, the ethicist holds that credit is an ethical and moral issue, and activities relating to credit are restrained by morality; thus, he advocates for uplifting the moral character of society through propaganda and moralisation. Similarly, the economist proceeds from the basic assumption that man is a rational being: The doer is considered a man who operates in the rational pursuit of maximising his personal interests. He thus concludes that credit-related activities are interest-driven phenomena and the outcomes of rational choice. Gains or losses in transaction costs, the presence or absence of information symmetry, and the effectiveness of reward-and-punishment measures will collectively affect the behavioural choice of members of society. Therefore, establishing an effective information transmission mechanism to conduct "information screening" may reduce the potential increase of promise-breaking behaviour arising from information asymmetry. By the same token, establishing various credit systems to increase the cost of opportunistic behaviour and to reduce the gains obtained therefrom may prevent such opportunistic behaviour. The sociologist believes that credit behaviour is influenced and restrained by culture and social structure and that the credit crisis is an "anomaly" resulting more from a change and disruption in the social structure. Consequently, he advocates conducting cultural developments and carrying out changes and improvements in the social structure. By contrast, due to the fact that the government and the people are on unequal footing in certain fields, the political scientist sees the government as both a game player and a legislator of social interaction rules, so there is always the possibility that the government will not honour its promises. Therefore, he proposes to develop independent, autonomous social organisations, making them a force to fight, influence, and check government conduct.

Are these views and proposals right? Yes, we may say that each and every piece of them is right. Nonetheless, such correctness does little to help us to deepen our exploration of China's social credit. Many improved methods are nothing but "politically correctness" or "armchair strategies," for they fail to help us see through and understand the relationship between the operation mechanism and credit in China's society. Therefore, setting up a more appropriate research perspective that helps us better understand the credit issue and ultimately helps us put forward a strategy to tackle it is the main task of this book.

1.1.3 Research Perspective

The tradition of sociological study views society as a whole entity in its investigation. By contrast, trust is considered by the sociologist as a phenomenon associated with social structure or social scenario. As Niklas Luhmann aptly put it,

> Under all circumstances, trust has always been a social relationship, social relationship is itself subordinate to a special rule system. Trust is generated from an interactive framework, such interaction is under both the influences of psychology and social relationship, and no exclusive relationship may be established unilaterally with any one of the two.[2]

Therefore, to the sociologist, the formation and operation of a trust research mechanism can always be explicated through the relationship between the social structure and the action of the individual. Hence, based on sociology and grounded in the cultural connotations of XIN in China, we have attempted to construct a native perspective of sociological study.

The so-called native perspective does not mean reverting to a traditional, Chinese academic research system (i.e., the study of Chinese classics) to understand society, history, culture, economy, institutions, and so on, nor does it mean that researchers should pin their hopes of solving China's problems via transforming Western academic theories. The study contained herein attempts to find another perspective from outstanding sociological research perspectives fit for China's social setup and configuration, with the aim of arriving at a reasonable explanation of China's credit issue. Using this native perspective and analytical framework, we expect to demonstrate the historical evolution and cultural mode of social credit and to describe and analyse how China's social backgrounds and specific situation have modelled our attitudes and behaviours. At the same time, we would also like to construct our own theories and strategies with a specific objective in mind under the same perspective and analytical framework.

In order to examine China's credit problem, the researcher must first acquaint himself thoroughly with the various outstanding theoretical methods of Western academics and their respective research limitations. The researcher needs to recognise to what extent and limit Western theories and methods "can" or "cannot" explain the problems related to the Chinese and Chinese society. As researchers of China's issues, we should not only learn from certain Western academic traditions but, more importantly, foster a mentality for initiating a dialogue between the two on an equal footing. Only when we have arrived at a comparable understanding of the various Western approaches and inspected the problems in accordance with the social characteristics of China, can we find the crux of the problem in the collision or communication between them.

From the foregoing discussion of conceptual relationships related to XIN, we have already obtained a continuous perspective; that is, honesty, trust, and credit correspond to the individual, the relationship, and the institution respectively, and they also denote morality, reliance, and evaluation systems respectively. Of course, it should be pointed out that, after all, the so-called continuous perspective is only a path of thinking close to the Confucianist mentality; it has its own aspect of reasonableness, however, in its operation in large-scale society, for it also reveals society's blind spots. In other words, discussing the differences in social scale helps us to gain a more favourable analytical perspective. For instance, when we imagine an individual, a family, a village, and a region, we do indeed engage in continuous thinking; however, its limitation lies in the fact that when the object of our thought scales up from region to cross-region and country, our mode of thinking changes. That is, in the governance mode of the Confucianist "cultivating the person, regulating the family, governing the state and bringing universal peace to the kingdom," cultivating the person can indeed regulate the family; however, whether regulating the family can help us govern the state remains in doubt. There is a hurdle from properly regulating the family to properly governing the empire. In the domain of a family, it seems plausible to infer that when one properly cultivates his person, the family can then be properly regulated; however, when the family is properly regulated, this hardly implies anything about proper governance of the country. The relationships contained here are rather complex. The most obvious issue is that once scaled up, the energy generated from the relationship ceases to have any effect because, in a small living unit of a family, it is totally possible to ensure each member properly conducts himself. However, as a large-scale government entity, the country, on the one hand, cannot assume every living unit is properly regulated, especially given natural disasters, man-made calamities, poverty, illness, international disputes, and so on. None of these issues can be resolved on the individual level; on the other hand, even if all families are properly regulated, it does not follow that the state system (the government) itself will do well, too. What can be inferred is only that the folk customs and the basis of state governance are sound. Hence, a qualitative change in the quantity of social trust is involved here, which means a simple scaling up from the individual will not work. Instead, we need a system framework to reasonably constrain and assess the performance of the various individuals, namely, the so-called credit system and its corresponding assessment system. Therefore, there emerges a kind of transmutation within the model. For instance, originally, the incremental promotion from integrity to trust is initiated and extended from the plane of the individual; however, once such promotion gets hindered, it can only be reverted to the plane of the individual from the perspective of institutional establishment. Specifically, when we inspect the system of XIN from the perspective of the individual, we focus on the inference of integrity and honesty; however, when we inspect the system of XIN from the perspective of the institution, our focus shifts to the constraints placed on the individual by the credit system. Even if the case involves only oral agreement between individuals, such should still be approached and understood from the plane of the institution. Actually, investigating China's "system of XIN" via the mode of transmutation between the two poles is a discussion of the transmutation relationship between the conduct and the institution, which includes the transmutation between policy and tackling strategy, between conduct and structure, as well as between issues of expediency and adaptation. In other words, on the practical plane, establishing a trust network based on the integrity and character of the individual is plausible. However, the issue of formality will bob up when transforming the trust network into the state credit system. Of course, establishing a state credit system requires the establishment of a social network; however, this kind of top-down formal network differs from the social network that has taken form among the folk. For instance, bank loans and private loans belong to two different credit networks; the operation of the two is sometimes complementary, sometimes confrontational, and sometimes parallel.

Similar circumstances also occur in another area: On one hand, the Chinese want very much to improve their credit situation through the cultivation of personal integrity, but, on the other, there is a very real need to establish a rigid regulatory system on the plane of the system due to the pressures brought forth by reality, i.e., by various major practical, social, political or economic events. When a social credit crisis takes place, an overwhelming call from the public is heard. It calls for stepping up supervision of all aspects of social credit. Obviously, the unspoken underlying assumption is that any attempt to solve the crisis by focusing exclusively on cultivating personal integrity is doomed to failure; but whenever a social credit situation improves, public opinion then shifts its focus to moral cultivation. Actually, building a social credit system involves not only the issue of system establishment, not only the issue of improving the morality of the person, and not only the issue of remodelling interpersonal interaction. It involves a game between the man and the institution and the possibility of transmutation between the two. Only when this point is made clear can we lift ourselves out of the oblivion created by the duality and reciprocal causality of establishing a social credit system by returning to integrity.

Of course, campaigning for the adoption of the native perspective requires not only a disciplinary investigation corresponding to the various phrases of XIN in

Chinese; it also requires a discussion that incorporates the aforementioned perspective and modern sociology. The disciplinary nature of sociology manifests in a comprehensiveness (i.e., its integratedness) that does not exclude other disciplines. After all, from the sociological perspective, the discussion of the macrostructure and microstructure can integrate many discrete, local issues. But when we view credit through isolated disciplines like economics, management studies, ethics, or political science, we can easily arrive at a side view of the issue. There are already some specific research results, a fact that has been borne out both by our literature review conducted in the foregoing chapters and by the fact that many governmental agencies have been stepping up efforts in formulating policy regulations in many areas. The authors adopt a (native) sociological perspective, with the aim of conducting the study by combining "integrity," "trust," and "credit" with their social background, culture, and structure.

1.2 Theoretical Exploration

1.2.1 Evolution of China's Social Credit

From the perspective of human history as a whole, social change across the globe is largely a modernisation process whereby nations and countries originally situated in different natural and human geographies have been swept up together. Undoubtedly, Chinese society has been engulfed by this modernisation process. This process has transformed an agricultural country into an industrial country, a small-scale peasant economy into a market economy, and a rural culture into an urban culture. In order to accommodate these transformations, China's economic system, together with its political, social, and cultural systems, has changed accordingly. Naturally, the nature of integrity, trust, and credit embedded therein have undergone corresponding changes. However, such changes have not been obvious, nor have they been deliberate or planned by the people. Over the long history of China, because the original social credit was presumed to be self-reliant but only reversely constructed after the fact, people were generally unaware of its existence. Not until they encountered problems of the modernisation process did this issue come to light. Therefore, we will first discuss the self-reliance of traditional China's social credit and then discuss how the problems related to it emerged.

We argue that the social credit of traditional Chinese society is relatively self-reliant. Why would we make such a claim? Traditional pre-industrial Chinese society can generally be considered an agricultural society. A prominent feature of China's agricultural society was a small peasant economy of family-based production units; its basic characteristic was self-reliance. Absent war, famine, or state migration policy, the people would usually hold fast to their native land and homes, where they would live for generations without end. Even if they left, they would ultimately return to their hometowns, like fallen leaves returning to their roots. It may be seen, then, that the holding-fast-to-homeland mentality confined the scope of life for the overwhelming majority of Chinese to a limited geographic range: namely, from the family to the clan, then to the entire village, and at most to the town. Of course, from the perspective of politics, a small number of people would find their way into the state bureaucratic agencies via taking the various levels of imperial examinations, which constituted another form of social credit (allegiance to the monarch); however, the latter would still retain an unbroken relationship with the former. As a continuum of social relationships, the Chinese adopted a cover term, "hometown," to refer to the village that had been expanded from the family. Accordingly, the people living in the family-expanded village were fellow villagers. Sociologically, the hometown was subsumed under the concept of "community," also known as Shequ (literal meaning: a section or partition of a society). The aspect where a community differs from a "society" lies in the close relationship among the people living within it.[3] Such close relationships could usually lead to the formation of a relationship network, which was also known as an acquaintance society. Especially in rural China, the reason acquaintances had closer relationships lies in the fact that many neighbours and fellow villagers were quite likely descendants of the same ancestor or clan; hence, such acquaintance relationships to some degree also mimic a relationship network.

Compared to other societies or market networks, the network within the community remained relatively closed and permanent. Distinctive features of such networks usually included surname, land boundaries, and linguistic varieties. Of course, hometown life with relatively closed blood and geographical ties could largely satisfy the living needs of the members of a community; however, when it came to the plane of the state, such an existence appeared rather rudimentary. Hence, there was a need for the state to institute a highly integrated political framework – a centralised system – over the social communities distributed over the vast expanse of land where people lived in compact clusters. The state needed to facilitate the handling of administrative affairs from the state to the local, including the issuance of currency, the operations of national security, and the systematic arrangement of human resources. Under such a mode of governance, officials presumed to be credible would be appointed to supervise the various areas ranging from high-ranking positions all the way down to the county level in the administrative hierarchy, while the people exercised autonomy in towns and villages below the county level. Thus, it may be deduced that, for the vast majority of the people, the better part of their home and working lives were largely situated in the towns in which they lived and in the markets in which they traded for daily necessities; hence, there was no need for the purpose of specialised production, transportation and commercial transaction for them to set up a more mature and sound market or the credit system that might be derived from the same. That is to say, the trust that originated in a so-called acquaintance society reflected the tight-knit interpersonal relationship. It, at most, involved country customs and conventions. But it did not reflect a formal, systematic relationship between the person and the state. In this sense, integrity and trust appeared more important; it sufficed to understand credit as a gentlemen's verbal agreement vouched for by the character of the person.

Within a community, the trust relationships established between and by the people could be called a credit network. Whether such a network could operate independently depended to a great extent on the governance of a state.[4] We hold that the traditional Chinese credit network had in itself all the conditions for operating on its own; it was not, then, an isolation strategy adopted in response to external pressures as Western scholars have claimed in their study of credit networks.[5] Rather than restraining or isolating the local trust network by wielding state political means (at most requiring that an official may not govern in his native place), the centralised system that was established in traditional China's agricultural society made certain the local trust network that had penetrated state bureaucracy, for instance, in the form of a town fellowship, a student fellowship, the fellowship of passing the imperial examinations, the fellowship of a clique, etc. At the same time, traditional Chinese military groups, business groups, private money shops, exchange shops, and the like were similarly established alongside such trust networks. Then, what were the characteristics of the trust developed through family relationships? The two most critical features were the intense sense of affiliation and the sense of omniscience. That is to say, thanks to the intimacy displayed in the community, the fellow villager group placed far more emphasis on the communication of sentiments and human relations than did members of an industrial organisation. The people were united not because of work or cooperative requirements owing to the division of labour, but because they needed to look after and protect each other as members of the same business and community. As is well known, an organisational relationship is something that can be rescinded or walked back; but a community relationship is a kinship, and it can never be rescinded or walked back. If it were impossible for a trust network to be walked away from, then such a network would not break apart. The establishment of such trust was also implicit and self-reliant; it tolerated no questioning and did not need to be guarded against. On the other hand, due to the fact that trust was established on the basis of omniscience, such a trust system eliminated the need for providing formal personal information as a guarantee. Viewed from the relationship between trust and information, in the operation of trust, the less information provided, the greater the suspicion; accordingly, the more information, the less suspicion. There was an entire life of interaction within the community that allowed its members to get to know each other and to accumulate information over several generations. One view that could verify the foregoing theory comes from the so-called "teaching fidelity between friends" by Mencius. The question we would like to raise here is, why did Mencius not claim that there should also be fidelity between father and son, husband and wife, and between brothers? Instead, he only mentions fidelity between friends. Viewed from the perspective of our theoretical assumptions, we conclude that the trust among the above-mentioned relationships is self-reliant, while the relationships between monarch and subject and between friends are neither of affiliation nor of omniscience. Hence, when the affiliation nature goes, the omniscience nature goes, and the self-reliance of good faith would go accordingly. Proceeding from such a mentality, we argue that the issue of trust looms more prominently in an environment outside the community, or among strangers. Of course, the Confucianist emphasises greatly personal cultivation; naturally, he would like to apply the virtues of *benevolence, righteousness, courtesy, wisdom,* and *trust* as requirements for all in the abstract sense. Such requirements tend not to go wrong inside the trust network. In other words, if we are to examine whether a person is a man of integrity, we usually could not find the truth inside the kinship environment. Only when we step outside the kinship network can we discover the true character of such a person. Hence, it could be seen that the concept of the gentleman (variously translated as the illustrious man, the virtuous man, the superior man, etc.) is one that transcends the everyday trust network: It requires a virtue of benevolence and righteousness on all circumstances in man, which is manifested in the remarks "the mind of the gentleman is conversant with righteousness, the mind of the mean man is conversant with gain." So, why couldn't the character of the gentleman be translated into the character of the average person? One reason is that it does not fit the situation of China's agricultural society. It is also due to the fact that such character is an impractical requirement; it is more of an expectation of scholars who entertain aspirational ideals of bringing universal peace to the empire and serving the country on a grander platform. In discussing traditional Chinese character, some scholars elevated the social status of Confucianism groundlessly; they may have been convinced that man could attain integrity by invoking the education of Confucianist thought.[6] That is a very naïve view. It is also the main reason the Chinese ultimately failed in their present-day effort to rescue integrity by pinning their hopes on moralisation and ethical indoctrination. Based on the foregoing discussion, we can see that once trust undergoes a crisis on the state level, it will be very difficult to reconstruct the same within the individual. Such a situation could only be addressed by applying regulations and constraints from the outside.

However, since China entered modern times, processes of industrialisation and urbanisation broke the community life of China's traditional society and the trust networks established therein. Due to the market economy that grew out of the 30-year period of reform and opening up, most people interacted with strangers, a situation that virtually wiped out China's original trust constraints. Though industrialisation and urbanisation had already started during the time of the planned economy, China more or less maintained the trust relationships established in traditional society, despite problems of various natures that were already present in such relationships.[7] Then the state adopted the urban-rural dual structure of social management, which on the one hand tied peasants to their own lands and, on the other hand, developed a unit system for the city-dweller. The dual system made it possible to maintain the community system of the former, while the new unit system made it possible for personnel records to guarantee the information assessment that activated personnel movement (which was another form of a restrictive tie-down system). Implementation of the dual system sustained the original affiliation and omniscience of rural society. At the inception of the reform and opening up, the state abandoned the omnipotent government model, and, at the same time, shifted its focus from the pursuit of an ideal social form to the pursuit of GDP growth. The introduction of market mechanisms brought forth the disintegration of China's acquaintance society and its unit system. Once the urban-rural dual relationship had been dismantled, it was theoretically possible for almost anyone to lack affiliations with any group, network, unit, or other forms of organisation. Population migration was once an effective way of breaking the rural-urban boundaries and eliminating the defects of the unit system. Particularly over the last 20 years, as peasants could migrate freely to the city in pursuit of work, they constituted a tremendous army of migrant workers. Further still, for a city-dweller, an individual could join an organisation or enterprise, and he could also freely switch roles, join another company, or leave the company without handing in his resignation, which ultimately rendered the personnel record system ineffective. Especially when it came to talent movement or personnel movement, the personnel record system ceased to work as a guarantor of reputation (barring public servants).

When individuals could move about in China with only an identification card (which might be fake, borrowed, or stolen from someone else) with neither a personal record, nor any affiliation; when a self-employed individual or production group could engage in production activities, business operations, or transaction activities without a corresponding credit record or credit assessment, and especially when they could run underground workshops or conduct unlicensed business activity or when local governments could engage in local protectionism to further local interests. How could we possibly demand integrity or morality from such individuals or organisations, or demand the trust of others when such individuals or organisations were conducting business? By then, morality and public opinion had ceased to have a constraining power on personal character. A more effective means could only be to establish a framework to re-assess the credit of members of society by incorporating all the trust networks that had been originally classified under the category of morality and trust networks. In other words, in an industrialised and urbanised society, the focus of institution-building could no longer be to repair past trust networks. Instead, it was to ensure the presence of integrity and trust in members of society by invoking external laws and social mechanisms, with punishment measures implemented accordingly. Of course, we all hope that the more ideal and harmonious solution remains in finding a way to restore morality and trust in modern society under the present system.

All in all, the trust network established by agricultural civilisation was self-reliant in itself. It largely satisfied the need for the sustenance and development of community members. With the inception of the planned economy, a substantial amount of people had left their hometown communities and worked in urban unit organisations; nevertheless, the personnel record system still maintained their original trust relationships. However, when the market economy came on the scene, the state failed to make timely changes to accommodate the development of the credit situation, which resulted on the one hand in the absence of a new credit system, and, on the other hand, in the occurrence of heart-wrenching or even hideously vicious events owing to the disintegration of the original trust networks and the personnel record system. In order to illustrate the foregoing theoretical points, see Figure 1.1.

This figure largely outlines the transformation of China's society from trust building to credit crisis. On the one hand, it reflects the systematic transition Chinese society underwent during the modernisation process and the focus on the credit system; on the other hand, it also reveals the inapplicability of the credit system already in place to accommodate such dramatic social change. It specifically highlights the characteristics of the corporate-style operations present in various

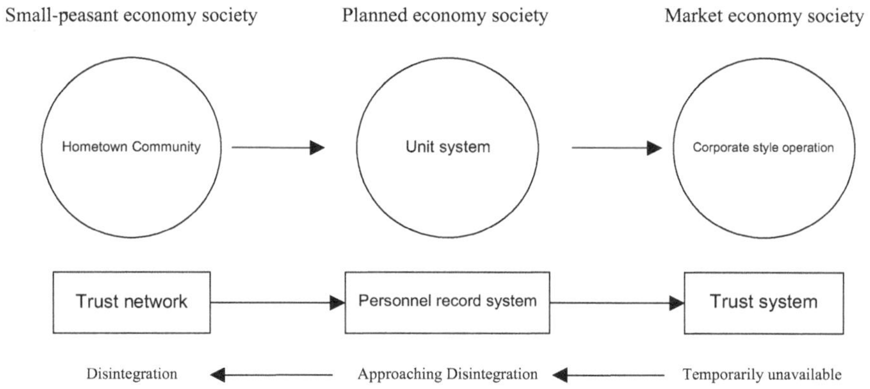

Figure 1.1 History of China's social credit

organisations, including local governments, supervisory agencies, public institutions, and industries in the contemporary market economy driven by profit. This profit-driven tendency features clear selfishness, which is highly likely to induce all society members to conduct themselves based on the interests of their personal or small-unit needs, which become the starting point for social operation, rather than basing their conduct on what's best for their larger organisation as the starting point of social operation. Ultimately, this dynamic has prevented China's credit system from taking root.

1.2.2 The Theory of Evolution and China's Secular Philosophy

Obviously, the evolution of China's social credit involves a transition from its original agricultural society to its current market society. As is known, the focus of Confucianism hinges on stabilising family relationships and the hierarchical relationship between superior and subordinate; that is to say, Confucianist thought aspires to a relatively static society. However, once a society finds that it is in need of revolution, it would be highly likely for such a thought to be replaced by a new one, a more dynamic thought for struggle. Indeed, there was a radical change in in Chinese social thought since modern times, and to some extent a critique and abandonment of Confucianism, in the form of Huxley and Spencer's theory of social evolution. When social evolutionism was introduced to China, it seemed that the gravely enervated and destitute situation of a China battered by foreign bullies had found a theoretical explanation. At that time, Chinese scholars finally abandoned the Confucian tradition, which had been held in high esteem for a long time, and began to borrow this theory to re-examine their own civilisation, and in doing so sought a more radical path: from evolution to revolution.

The term Social Darwinism was introduced into China by Yan Fu at the close of the Qing Dynasty. Under Yan Fu's rendition, the fundamental principle of the theory of evolution could be summarised into the phrases "competition of the species" and "selection by nature." The so-called

> Taking the theory of evolution as the body, to which two functions are attached: namely, competition of species, and selection by nature. This principle works on all things on earth and is particularly prominent among living creatures. The so-called competition of species refers to the situation wherein all things compete for survival. When one species competes with other species, it may survive or perish, while natural selection has the final say. The so-called selection by nature refers to the sole survival of a species in the competition with other species. The fact that one species survives lies in that it has something that makes it necessarily survive, its survival necessarily attributes to the collective working of its natural endowment, the utmost application of its effort, the environment, and the time it happens to be in, as well as the external forces outside itself.[8]

This thesis brought immeasurable excitement to Chinese scholars of the time. In remembrance of the scene at that time, Hu Shi said,

> After the publication of *Evolution*, within a few years, it had swept the country, so much so that it had entered middle school textbooks. Few people reading the book could have imagined the contribution of Huxley to the history of science and thought. What these theses drove home was primarily the significance of the formula "survival of the fittest" in the arena of international politics. After repeated defeats, and especially the burning shame of the 1990 Boxer Indemnities, this "survival of the fittest" formula was no less than a rude awakening, one that immensely stimulated numerous Chinese. In a few years, this idea spread like wildfire and scorched the minds and boiled the blood of many youths. Terms such as "natural selection", "competition of the species", "elimination", and "evolution" gradually became fixtures in newspapers, and became the "catch phrases" of patriots. And many loved to use the terms for the names of themselves or their offspring … my own name is also a souvenir from that atmosphere.[9]

Now that the theory of evolution was so deeply rooted, it is necessary to first explore what it means to be evolutionary, as relayed by Yan Fu. In his day, Yan Fu valued Darwin's theory of evolution, but it was Huxley's Evolution and Ethics that he translated. The reason for his choice lay in the fact that the book by Huxley not only concisely expounded Darwin's idea of natural selection but also discussed human-related thoughts. This aspect of the book immensely excited Yan Fu. However, due to the fact that Yan Fu had been under the influence of Spencer's The Principles of Sociology, his explanation of the theory of evolution is Darwinian instead of Huxleyan. What distinguishes the latter from the former lies in the interpretation of "ethics." That is to say, Huxley holds that the evolution of human society should be constrained by ethics. However, the purpose of Yan Fu in translating Western thoughts was to find a path to national "prosperity." Therefore, he did not need to introduce Huxley's thought in its entirety and accurately; instead, he engaged in a liberal translation and played down Huxley's theorisation of ethics, placing his emphasis on the theory of natural selection.[10] Yan Fu linked the theory with Spencer's thought because Spencer proposed the social-organism theory, which both contains analogies to natural selection and conforms to Confucianism in that it demonstrates human desires by resorting to natural principles. However, if differences are to be found between the former and the latter, they are in the way the two handle the relationship between the individual and the state. The Confucian pursues a path of suppressing the person, whereas the West takes the path of pursuing individual freedom and liberation. Though this point had harassed and agonised Yan Fu in his translation and introduction, the current affairs of China at the time diverted his focus more to enlightening folk intelligence and enhancing national strength.

Of course, relating the Western theory of evolution by incorporating his grasp of current domestic affairs instead of engaging in a faithful translation has led Yan Fu's work to reinterpretation,[11] which has made this work more accessible to Chinese who may resort to their own culture to understand it. Then, if we are to re-examine and understand the theory of competition or struggle by way of Chinese wisdom, who would be the "fittest" and who would be favoured by "natural selection"? For instance, there is an old saying in Chinese, "when enemies run into each other head on, the brave one prevails." Who would be the brave? In the eyes of Yan Fu, the brave were those who had received the baptism of Western civilisation, the nations or peoples who were wiser, more powerful, and more civilised, rather than the peoples who were benighted, underdeveloped, barbaric, and savage. However, in the eyes of the Chinese, strength and high-level civilisation were of course important, but they were issues to be addressed through a grand-century programme. In terms of contemporaneity and effect, however, nothing worked better than being irrational, opting for surprise manoeuvres, making trouble, using imitation, and engaging in fraud. This mentality came from the stratagems of China's art of war, i.e., "the only rule is to ditch the rule."[12] Imagine, an unarmed man confronted by a man with a weapon – what reason can he still resort to? He has no way but to give up resistance. By analogy, similar conclusions may be drawn from "the gentleman argues, the mean man shoves," "a scholar is always wrong when he is in front of a gunman," "while the timid goes starving, the bold gets stuffed," "the barefooted scares the shod, and is scared of those who risk their lives," "a gentle horse gets mounted, and a gentle man gets bullied," "a tree withers if its bark is done away with, but a man will be invincible if he does away with his sense of shame." The foregoing sayings or idioms all convey one meaning in common: The civilised may not necessarily prevail over the savage. If we amplify these rules of everyday life and extend them to the macro-level, then the failure of China's modernisation before the founding of the People's Republic of China could then be restated as, however refulgent the Chinese civilisation of the past five millennia might have been, it was still no match for Westerners with modern weapons (therefore Yan Fu held in high regard the "military" stage of the three stages of development advanced by Spencer). That is the historical background for the appeal of the Darwinian theory of evolution to the Chinese.

The foregoing thought was then more vividly restated by Wu Zhihui during the May 4th Movement: "if I'm shot at by others with a machine gun, I'll fight back with a machine gun."[13] The unsaid lines are, the current debate over the thread-bound book and the eight-legged essay is meaningless; when you are barehanded, your "empty high-sounding reason" will bring you nowhere, but a rifle will more than suffice to bring you out of your dilemma.[14] To resort to force is an embodiment of power politics; it encourages more people to resort to "bully tactics" and "teleological" arguments. Some insightful people, well informed in current affairs, might argue that when discussing the weapon in the hands of Westerners, we should not confine ourselves to the weapon itself; instead, we should see through the savage conduct of Westerners and find a great civilisation behind the weapons. Of course, such an argument is not wrong. However, another layer of reason might win easier recognition; that is, an unarmed man is no match for a man with a "rock" in hand. Obviously, there is no so-called great civilisation behind the rock, there is only the difference between whether one would try to win by engaging in "argument" or by "thrashing his opponent," by "word" or by "weapon," through "reason" or through "bullying," through a "shod tactic" or through a "barefooted tactic," by being "kinder" or by being "more wicked," by being "reserved" or by "life-risking," by "maintaining the sense of shame" or by "ditching the sense of shame." Of course, it must be pointed out that the reason that the uncivilised defeat the civilised lies in the effective exploitation of the rule by the one who refuses to conform to such rules instead of combat between one non-conformist to the rule against another non-conformist, or of fighting evil with evil, or of overcoming poison with poison, so it is far less a trial of real strengths. The foregoing widely accepted reason can be ultimately reduced to two layers of secular philosophical propositions. One layer of meaning is that "honest dealing always ends up in being taken advantage of," "honest dealing can never bring prosperity," or "none of those who have made it are engaged in honest dealing"; the other layer of meaning is that "the end justifies the means" or "the means mean little, but the end ends final."

Though the way of success on this plane has departed far away from the theory of social evolution, it is still included in the principle of "natural selection" and "survival of the fittest." Competition should naturally be ethical, fair, and justifiable in human society. When immoral, unfair, and unjustified competition becomes the social norm, the "nothing but profit mentality" and the ethic of "unscrupulous growth" are the only ways for individuals, enterprises, and regions to pursue development or defeat rivals. Such a law of survival of the fittest might also bring China its own characteristics in the civilisation process of Chinese society.

1.2.3 Social Credit and Social Control

Through the foregoing review of the theory of evolution's introduction to China and its integration with China's secular philosophy, we argue that the current credit crisis in Chinese society is the inevitable manifestation of the various problems accumulated over the social evolution and mutation of modern China; in other words, it had been fermenting for quite a long time. However, due to the necessity to rescue China from subjugation and to dramatic events like the great revolution and the cultural revolution, the crisis had yet to find an opportunity to surface distinctly – and it may also be said to have remained below the surface thanks to a series of protective measures. But along with the advent of the market economy, the foregoing crises converged at this time and came to a head. The various mechanisms that had originally maintained cultural stability were rendered virtually inoperable such that the people and even social institutions actively or passively reverted to pursuing self-interest. The protective zone of the original trust network, the original system of social values, and many institutions under the former unit system and so on had been discarded by the market economy. The naked law of the jungle held sway. Faced with the interest-driven situation of individuals trapped within this jungle, sociological investigators had to locate the structural control mechanisms of society.

From the foregoing cultural explanation of XIN, it may be seen that the XIN anticipated by Confucianists was rooted in "sincerity" and that this type of XIN should have arisen without the precondition of an external constraining mechanism. Rather, it should have originated in the kindness of human nature with the internal integrity of the person being built from an innate conscience, such that a relationship of mutual trust between people could also be built. Under this model of inference, obviously, the logical starting point rests on the personal morality of the individual; therefore, so long as the personal morality issue could be solved through education, all other ensuing problems could then be solved without a hitch. There seems nothing wrong from a purely logical perspective with this assumption. The only problem is with the foregoing discussion of social scalability, that is, not everyone can be expected to possess integrity. In other words, the smaller the scale of a society, the greater the possibility such integrity may appear, for instance, between two persons or within a family, or within intimate relationships such as a circle of friends. However, the greater the social scale, the lower the possibility such integrity may appear. As society cannot assume that everyone is sincere in their treatment of others, it would then enter a credit-constraining model that deliberately invokes foreign force (non-spontaneous).

Treating the credit problem through the same logic, it is not difficult to see that large-scale social operations actually depend to a still greater degree on social control, while endogenous credit is not necessarily a must. A large-scale society may or may not have credit – but so long as there is the presence of restraining mechanisms, the contractual nature of this society would naturally still function. In other words, the mandatory measures of society will force its members to follow the norms of conduct. However, we see that most societies do not go to the length of counting on stringent social controls to constrain their people, despite the fact that they still advocate integrity and the establishment of trust itself. Social control necessarily carries tremendous operational costs. However, if a society relinquishes its efforts to maintain social control and functions according to personal integrity alone, then it can only revert to a primitive community. Therefore, most societies, so long as they attain a certain scale, reduce operational costs by expecting their people to develop credit on their own. That said, these societies still need to establish social-control systems to prevent and punish dishonest conduct. The question that remains, however, is just this: What is a reasonable social-constraint mechanism?

From the context of Chinese history, there have been many different opinions about the most effective means of maintaining social control. The Taoist almost completely relinquished social control. He wanted society to remain small; otherwise, it might "lose the Way." As Lao Zi remarked,

> Therefore, virtue comes after the loss of Tao (the Way); benevolence comes after the loss of virtue; justice comes after the loss of benevolence; rites come after the loss of justice. Thus rites result from the lack of loyalty and good faith, and function as the beginning of great disorder.[15]

The contention between the Confucianist and the Legalist manifests in the two social-control mechanisms they opted for: "rule of virtue" and "rule of law." Faced with the collapse and ruin of rites and music in social life, the Confucianist emphasised "the rule of virtue," conducting social control by means of morality education. In the eyes of Confucius, it is necessary to establish social institutions (the institution of rites). However, the biggest problem with the institution of rites lies in that it regulates the conduct of people but fails to constrain the mind; therefore, there should be superimposed on the institution of rites some sort of mental constraint. Only in this way would people conduct themselves in accordance with the requirements of the institution of rites of their own accord, instead of fearing punishment or pursuing material gain. Exactly on this point, Confucius proposed his key concept, "benevolence." Benevolence in combination with rites, one from the inside and one from the outside, together demonstrate that institutions and norms should be grounded in morality, that is, the so-called "rule of virtue." The Legalist represented by Han Fei Zi simply employed "the law" as a means of social control. The Legalist argues that "benevolence may not be employed in governance," for moral education would do evil rather than good: "while power and influence can check violence, profound virtue may not put an end to unrest."[16] Ergo, Han proposed that "one should subject people with force," that is, he advocated the role of law (institution) backed by state violence, thus unifying the mind and conduct of the people with laws, decrees and mandates. However, it should be pointed out that Legalist thought was occasioned by its times – times in which the empire was disintegrating and society was in great chaos; it failed to play much of a role in maintaining and promoting the development of society. On the other hand, "the rule of virtue" of the Confucianists became the main theory expounding social control; it has had a deep and lasting influence up to the present.

The revelation of the foregoing review is twofold: First, integrity boils down to sheer conscience or intuitive knowledge, and, second, because society does not guarantee that each individual possesses such goodness, trust and credit must operate on the basis of external constraint. Taking the scales of acquaintance society and regular society into consideration, the so-called trust zone is actually a middle ground which is objectively indefinite and must be subjectively defined. The safest part of this trust zone is the blood-relationship zone, which does not require any social-control mechanisms, for morality, kinship, or intimacy are its guarantors. However, if a society lacks such guarantors, then constraining mechanisms must come into force. However, along with the strengthening of the restraining mechanisms, the cost of social credit grows, as its operation can only be affected by the most stringent supervision and the threat of punishment. It follows that the effective operation of social credit falls to the middle ground, but the situation on both ends of the continuum works in exactly opposite ways. On one end are the people who are totally unsuspecting; it is a zone wherein the life or existential security of a person depends. By contrast, the other end teems with suspicions, frauds, and perfidies; if stringent measures are not adopted, it will become a place of panic and social disintegration. Hence, society will introduce stringent means of control and build up systems of social sanction so as to bring people back to a zone where they may rest assured. What this dynamic tells us is that credit can only work under a conditional, constrained, and doubtful environment.

One judgement we can infer from the foregoing theoretical assumptions is that contemporary Chinese society has arrived at a situation where only through the exertion of stringent control can its credit be guaranteed; that is, there is actually widespread social anomie. When the original morality, relationship networks, and unit system fail to maintain modern social credit, society is in urgent need of new constraining mechanisms. Unfortunately, such mechanisms have so far not been fully established. The breakdown of the original social-control mechanisms during the social transition and the absence of credit-control mechanisms centred upon institutions exacerbated the social risks. In the eyes of Niklas Luhmann, familiarity is the prerequisite of trust. People live in a familiar environment and share a common world outlook, such that the mode of acquaintance embodies the self-evident characteristics of familiarity and the existent. Even if we sense similar problems of immorality or difference of identity in real life in society, they have lost the importance of differentiation in the world of meaning wherein consensus has been arrived at; therefore, they would not engender doubt and uncertainty in personal experience.[17] Two types of uncertainty create two different paths: One is that society re-establishes an effective credit system; the other is that when people are unable to find, or refuse to seek, a constraining mechanism, they seek shelter in family relationship networks, hoping to ground their security in an original point of familiarity. We can see that, even when they find work in the city, migrant workers transfer or duplicate their original network. For instance, people from Henan province vividly refer to this process as "pulling vines," and pulling one vine may drag out scores of vines.[18] One man leads to scores of people; these people often derive from very complicated relative relationships, and they maintain these extremely complex relationships even when they are removed from their native land. If they could, they would completely replicate their village mode of life in the city, thus retaining an acquaintance society. This phenomenon takes place not only in China but has also spread abroad; consider, for instance, the circle of Wenzhou merchants.

In real life, be it for seeking a job, seeing a doctor, going to school, or conducting business, the presence of "relationship" can be seen almost everywhere.

The "relationship" the small-scale society counted on plays such an important role that it makes the grass-root social life or the real social life divorced from the social credit system, the establishment of which has been repeatedly called for by society. In other words, if the acquaintance relationship network remains the foundation of social credit, then such a system either would exist in name only for lack of public credibility or would not be people's first choice. It might even be discarded due to uncertainty in various aspects of society despite the fact that it may have a certain public credibility. However, in the contemporary market economy, does the relationship network retain its original positive restraining function? Actually, its constraining power has been greatly reduced. The popular mobility of society has afforded people the opportunity to discard their contractual obligations and dodge their responsibilities. Indeed, people might even default on their obligations and make a comeback and defraud their acquaintances; this is the so-called "fleecing acquaintance." Nowadays, in a time during which relationship plays a key role while it is getting rapidly instrumentalised, the relationship network has on the one hand illustrated how essential it is to establish a social credit system and, on the other hand, it has greatly strengthened the self-profiting characteristics of society. That is, it has made most members place their personal and group interests, such as the small unit to which they belong, as the starting point for social operation, while it has simultaneously relinquished any expectation of the establishment of a macro social credit system or even the restoration of social control of credit. Finally, either the operation of relationship shelves the credit system or people transgress the system by availing themselves of "relationship" for the pursuit of personal gain, which gives rise to a broad transitional zone between system and non-system, social control and social anomie. In such a zone, phenomena such as faking, paying lip service, defrauding, frivolousness, and the separation of name and reality constitute the representation of contemporary credit problems. What's more, there is also the operation of power behind it. Once relationships combine with power in practice, they together give rise to a protective umbrella that leads to a decrease in the public's credibility in the government.

1.2.4 Overall Research Assumption

From small-scale society to large-scale society, the inner complexity changes; how shall we express such complexity? We proceed from the sociological perspective, working according to the differences of performance in social operation, abstracting a pair of concepts of the characteristics of culture – society and economy – that is, "homogeneous society" and "heterogeneous society."

We hold that there are two tendencies in understanding the overall characteristics of the modernisation process (industrialisation, marketisation, technicalisation): One is the homogeneous tendency and the other the heterogeneous tendency. So, how should we understand homogeneity and heterogeneity? "Homogeneity" refers to a situation in which there is a strong urge to move towards the same standards in society, though this may prove difficult to accomplish in practice; "heterogeneity" refers to a situation in which a continual diversification and pluralisation of social tastes and standards come into existence. Distinguishing the homogenisation of society from its heterogenisation means inspecting society's degree of purification in any aspect or on any plane. We will first make a theoretical assumption here: Any plane or any aspect of modern society is already complete with a unit quality necessary for the establishment of itself. Unit differentiation refers to the difference from other unit qualities by comparison, and unit purity refers to that which sustains its own quality. Suppose the differentiation and purity of the various units on the various planes or in the various aspects of a society are maximally maintained, then that society will be of greater overall differentiation and a higher degree of heterogeneity; whereas if it is difficult for the differentiation of the various units on the various planes or in the various aspects of a society to be maintained, then the society will be of lesser overall differentiation and a higher degree of homogeneity. In order to reinforce our understanding of the pair of concepts, we may try the following example: Suppose there is a wealth disparity in society such that the rich buy high-end products and the poor buy low-priced products; such a society is heterogeneous. But suppose also that there is a wealth disparity in a society such that the rich buy high-end products and the poor buy imitations of high-end products (for the sake of face); such a society is homogeneous. Comparatively, the former society manifests individuality, focuses on niche, on professional and personal taste, and each end of society spends according to their financial strength; the latter society, by contrast, embodies collectivity and emphasises the masses, face, and trend following. Having compared these concepts, the overall assumption for the present study is, regardless of motivation and purpose, the heterogeneity of China's society is disappearing. With the marketisation process, Chinese society has become a society showing a high degree of homogeneity. In this regard, the most crucial assumption is that it has achieved this end by following the exact secular principles that guided the Chinese adaptation of the theory of social evolution discussed above.

In what follows, we will, pursuant to whatever materials are available, randomly select different forms of unit quality in Chinese society and inspect their situation in terms of homogeneity and heterogeneity. Firstly, let's take the example of the publishing industry in China (see Figure 1.2).

From the perspective of social demands, it is clear that the Chinese are in strong need of roughly similar fine-quality products or hot-sale products with the lowest possible prices, which means that pirated products and counterfeits provide the optimal way of satisfying the demand. Rampant piracy activities have thus directly impacted the creation, production, and sales of cultural products in China. For instance, some China-produced movies won acclaim but met with poor box-office income; some musicians produced very popular songs but the records did not sell; some novels made quite a sensation but only sold a few copies. It can be seen from Figure 1.2 that the total number of products pirated annually stayed above 40 million pieces over the decade; during the period 2005–2006, the number of articles pirated annually reached 100 million but then receded to 40 million after 2007. Upon analysis, this phenomenon was clearly attributable to the Chinese government's energetic preparation for the Beijing Olympics. A more effective crackdown on piracy commenced in 2009; however, piracy activities remained substantial thereafter. Still, we have seen reports like that from the Ministry of Public Security, which in 2011 continued organising its nationwide "Drawing Sword" campaign to crack down on 16 criminal activities, including the production of counterfeit and sham products, counterfeit trademarks, and counterfeit patents; the production and sale of foods failing to satisfy sanitation standards; the production and sale of substandard medical equipment; the production and sale of inferior pesticides, veterinary drugs, fertilisers, and seeds; and the production and sale of cosmetics that fail to satisfy hygiene standards. By November of the year, the "Drawing Sword" campaign had solved over 28,000 cases, locating over 22,000 hideouts that had engaged in counterfeiting and the sale of counterfeit products, and destroying over 6,700 criminal rings engaged in the sale of counterfeit and substandard products with a value surpassing 18 billion yuan.[19] However different the foregoing illegal activities may have been, their essential characteristics remained the same: Their sole purpose was to seek maximum gain through unfair, low-cost means that disturbed the market and brought into existence a situation in which the authority of the law was held in contempt, and human life was taken lightly.

As a shared mentality, homogeneity itself does not tolerate the social operation of heterogeneity (i.e., the high degree of differentiation and purity). Exactly for this reason, there sprouted a fuller neutral concept in China, namely, "Shanzhai" (faking, copycat). Shanzhai products originally came from the IT industry. However, if we define Shanzhai products as those that encroach on patents, as clones, as imitations, the term can only approximate its full meaning, which is incomplete here, as there are also Shanzhai products that make some superficial changes in the original product, creating pieced-together products or products that create a visual misconception. The appearance of "Shanzhai" products triggered hot debates among the public, with some regarding them as a byword for counterfeit, for inferiority, and for the encroachment on intellectual property. However, others held them as a private industry, spawned domestically, which embodied the grassroots nature and creativity of the Chinese people. So long

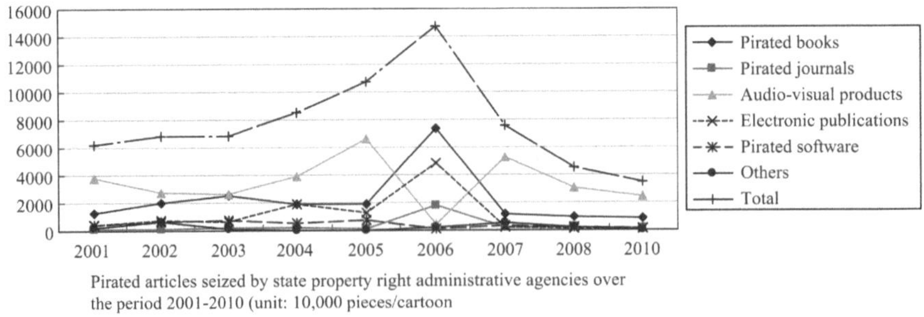

Figure 1.2 Summary of piracy situation

as protection and support were in place, the industry grew bigger and stronger. What here merits special attention is that the appearance of the term "Shanzhai" quickly kindled the enthusiasm of the Chinese people, bringing 2008 the name "Year of Shanzhai." This zeal quickly spread from the field of mobile phones and other electronic apparatuses to almost every field of social life, ultimately creating a Shanzhai culture. From apparel, medicine, food, and everyday basics to advertisements, internet addresses, movies and videos, the Spring Festival Gala, universities, etc. there was no area untouched by Shanzhai culture. Generally, the Chinese people are tolerant of this Shanzhai culture. Even though some raised opposing voices – including powerful members of the Committee of the Chinese People's Political Consultative Conference, which proposed certain boycotts in condemning this culture – the persistence of Shanzai culture should suffice to demonstrate Chinese society's toleration of and identification with the phenomenon of homogeneity.

Perhaps it is believed that the existence of objective standards gives rise to the possibility of imitating, faking, counterfeiting, and cloning. Could the social or cultural unit quality (identity, qualification, level, psyche, character, etc.) of an entity be homogenised? Let's first examine an incident that took place in 2012. The media reported a press conference held by the State Public Security, the event disclosed a crackdown on a hideout for making fake certificates by the police. The hideout made fake certificates of up to 44 categories, covering eight fields ranging from construction and medical treatment to finance and so on, and hacked up to 73 government personnel websites at the provincial and municipal levels. They combined illegal activities such as creating illegal search links, tampering with official databases, hacking and selling personal data materials, and making fake certificates in their counterfeiting efforts. In this case, the police arrested 165 people and seized over 7,100 fake certificates of various categories and over 10,000 fake seals. Judging from the electronic evidence seized in the investigation process, the 185 government websites hacked by the criminal ring involved 30 provinces, municipalities, and autonomous regions. From the database seized, it could be seen that over 30,000 people had successfully obtained fake certificates of various categories, with transactions valuing over 300 million yuan, and that the data materials involved in the hacking and selling amounted to over 3 million pieces.[20] What does this piece of news mean? It means that fake qualifications could be "verified" on government websites and then used as genuine ones. Actually, this is but one major case; if we are to view similar matters as discrete, spreading sporadically across the country, then any Chinese can easily find ads marketing fake certificates with mobile phone numbers attached on bus stops, pavements, electricity poles, and walls. Many a little makes a mickle. We are unable to find out how many more hideouts engaging in the production of fake certificates remain at large and how many more people are "benefiting" from such irregular activities.

Having examined the issue so far, the data we have presented here are still within the criminal range. In fact, "Shanzhai" activities are dancing on the edge of legality; however, this is still not the most serious issue. What merits special attention is that some planes or aspects of society itself are becoming gravely homogenised.

The following is an examination of education, which illustrates the situation of enrolment and graduation at institutions of higher education.

Based on the ratio of four-year degree student enrolment and graduation published on the website of the Ministry of Education of the People's Republic of China, we plotted Figure 1.3, which clearly shows that the ratio of irregular graduates stays at about 10% of four-year degree graduates nationally, while irregular graduation includes graduation from a course study, suspension of schooling, dropout, expulsion, death, and/or transfer. If such is set as the basis to infer the passing rate of China's college students, one may assume the following: Except for good reason, students enrolled in a common college will almost all graduate. This mode of education is termed "closed-door enrolment" as compared with the "open-door enrolment" of the West. Higher education conducted on the mode of closed-door enrolment will necessarily lead to the homogenisation of college-student education. That is to say, so long as one can get enrolled in an institution of higher education, one can basically pass the tests and graduate. Perhaps, we may assume, that college enrolment tests at least distinguish between those who can get enrolled in college and those who cannot. However, the truth is that students who might otherwise have had little chance of getting enrolled have already gotten enrolled in some pretty fine colleges, occupying a slew of programmes including adult education, internet undergraduate programmes, and the EMBA at the postgraduate level, not to mention a variety of training programmes that exploit legal loopholes and make the college diploma an easily available certificate. Of course, energetically developing higher education and benefiting more people is itself not a problem. The problem is that regardless of the mode, the internal property and external property of the various modes of higher education have become rapidly homogenised. Let's examine another phenomenon prevalent in China, that is, awards, selection,

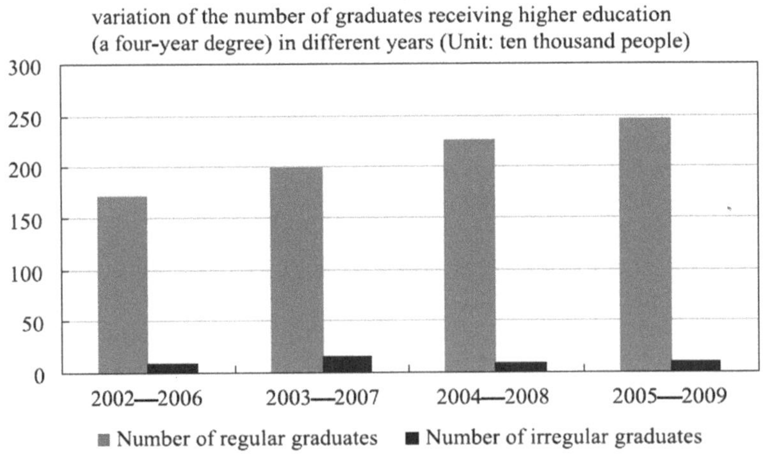

Figure 1.3 Changes in the quantity of regular higher educational graduate. Source: statistics from the portal of the Ministry of Education of the People's Republic of China.

and qualification activities of great variety in all industries and organisations of varying natures. The original purpose of staging such activities is to increase the distinctiveness and purity of the unit quality and the properties of the product or service involved; however, even with so many awards, nothing can be proved: These awards are either distributed according to the number of participants, rotated among participants, purchased, obtained through string-pulling, or even awarded by the participants themselves.[21] Also coming out frequently are reports of government offices being sold by public servants, stories of officials getting promoted based on adulterated statistical numbers, and accounts of officials ordering that statistical numbers be tampered with.[22] Briefly, the manifestation in society of so-called homogenisation would be that the society recognises a social unit in terms of its value and incentive mechanism so long as it finally achieves its objective, regardless of the means, mode, and method employed in the process.

The phenomena described above also bear out our definitional setting that construes homogeneity through the characteristics of "any social plane or aspect." Of course, the society with the highest credit might also be one of homogeneity. Its typical form in the traditional sense is a small-scale rural community. If one is to ask how the homogeneous operation of a modern society could produce dysfunction, the answer lies in exactly how we maintain the homogeneity of the society. When the law of bad money driving out good money prevails in the market, dysfunction comes into existence. As to the determination of the positive and negative functions of a homogeneous society, it depends on how the society creates its system of reward and punishment according to the grand objective and overall direction of said society. For instance, when a society defines private business ownership as a racketeering activity, all private commercial activities will be subjected to punishment by that society, and when a society looks the other way and allows illegal business conduct to go unpunished so as to increase that society's wealth, the idea of getting rich through honest labour gets suppressed.

Besides, in itself, the growth of a market economy does not result in the appearance of social homogeneity; in other words, homogeneity is a culture issue, not a market issue. According to Western sociologists, the main basis for its differentiation lies in the vocational group or legal person group.[23] However, due to the dearth of functional effects of such organisations in China's market economy, supervision and monitoring of unit differentiation and purity come more from the various departments and agencies instituted by the state; while many departments and agencies engage in inaction in many respects, or wait for the initiation of a major event or the inception of a movement, and, in the process, the reparation of social credit may really have to resort to a social movement. When this mode has been discarded by society itself, or ceases working, or even when some departments or agencies strike a scheme with the racketeers, then wealth becomes the exclusive criterion of differentiation for society, and all other differences vanish. Regarding wealth, the criterion for differentiating wealth is money, but money is ineffective in determining the differentiation and purity of social units. In other words, money is the most powerful weapon for shattering social differentiation. When money can purchase everything in society, society can no longer display its differences. Of course, superficially, the amount of money a society member has can indicate differences in quality and taste in life. However, deep down, such differences are mainly manifest in differences within homogeneity; they do not manifest in heterogeneity. For instance, the rich use expensive products, and the poor use fake products; the rich purchase genuine products, and the poor smuggled ones. When the views "money makes the mare go" and "there is nothing that money cannot buy" become the universal values of society, people will sell their conscience or engage in desperate activities, stopping at nothing.

Back to the traditional Chinese local community: Its internal homogeneity comes from its shared culture and customs, and the differentiation between different communities is also based on culture and customs as well as dialects. Later, differentiation is further determined on the basis of administrative rank under the supply system. When society gets marketised, huge population migration is made possible and the concept of the pursuit of money prevails, causing all differentiation and purity to vanish into thin air.

Notes

1 Zhai Xuewei, Integrity, Trust and Credit: Clarification and Historical Evolution of Concepts, 2011(5), pp.107-114.
2 Niklas Luhmann, *Trust: The Reduction Mechanism of Social Complexity*, translated by Qu Tiepeng, Li Qiang, Shanghai People's Publishing House, 2005, pp. 6–7.
3 Ferdinand Tönnies, *Gemeinschaft und Gesellschaft (Community and Society)*, translated by Lin Rongyuan, The Commercial Press, 1999, pp. 65–66.
4 Charles Tilly, *Trust and Rule*, translated by Hu Weijun, Shanghai People's Publishing House, 2010, pp. 64–65.
5 Ibid., p. 7.
6 Ma Deyong, Trust, Its Origin and Evolution, *Opening Times* 2008(4), pp72-86.
7 Hong Mei, Interpreting the Causes of Social Credit Crisis in China's Transformation Period, *Shanghai Economic Study* 2009(8).
8 Yan Fu, *Evolution and Ethics, appeared in China's Modern Academic Classics – Yan Fu*, Hebei Education Press, 1993, p. 13.
9 Hu Shi, *Account of Myself at Forty, appeared in New Issue of Old Books*, Yuelu Press, 1988, p. 40.
10 See *In Search of Wealth and Power: Yen Fu and the West*, translated by Ye Meifeng, Jiangsu People's Press, 1996, pp. 87–94.
11 James Reeve Pusey, *China and Charles Darwin*, translated by Qian Yongqiang, Jiangsu People's Press, 2008, pp. 57–65.
12 Li Ling, *A Glass of Wine under Flowering Shrubs*, Tongxin Press, 2005, p. 124.
13 Luo Zhitian, Machine Gun and Thread Bound Chinese Books: A Look at the Intensity Relationship between the Science and the Study of Chinese Ancient Civilization from the Debate of the "Catalogue of the Study of Chinese Ancient Civilization," *Journal of Sichuan University* 2002(6).
14 Lu Xun held the same view, see It Hit on Me (10–11), Supplementary Notes, appeared in Unlucky Star, The Complete Works of Lu Xun – Volume 3, *The People's Literature Publishing House* 1981, p. 96, pp. 100–101.
15 Tao-Te Ching, Chapter 38.
16 *The Collation and Annotation Team of Han Fei Zi, Han Fei Zi*, Jiangsu People's Press, 1982, p. 691.
17 Niklas Luhmann, *Trust: A Simplification Mechanism of Social Complexity*, translated by Qu Tipeng, Li Qiang, Shanghai People's Press, 2005, p. 24.

18 Liang Hong, *Notes of Exiting Liang – Details and Experience of China*, Huacheng Publishing House, 2013, p. 120.
19 Liu Mengyu, Safeguarding the Peace of China: The Top Ten Awesome Public Security Campaigns across the Country in 2011, *China Report* 2012(3).
20 Their Fake Certificates Could Be "Validated" in Government Websites, *Jinling Evening*, 27 July 2012, p. A09.
21 Awards of the various industries, agencies, governments, and societies in China are of great variety, with complex inside stories and behaviour barely known to outsiders. Here we could only illustrate with a published case; there is no possibility of having any statistical data describing the issue. Please refer to the book compiled by Chen Ping, *Change of New China's Integrity: Phenomena and Speculation*, published by Sun Yat-sen University Press in 2010, pp. 166–169; Wei Xin, Bo Yang's, *Integrity Crisis*, published in 2003 by China Social Sciences Press, p. 194. For further stories see Li Song's, *Crisis Investigation of China's Social Integrity*, published in 2011 by China Commercial Publishing House, pp. 286–290.
22 Please refer to Ping, *Change of New China's Integrity*; Song, *Crisis Investigation of China's Social Integrity*, pp. 246–250.
23 [France] Emile Durkheim. *The Division of Labor in Society*, translated by Qu Dong, SDX Joint Publishing Company, 2000, p. 130, pp. 260–261.

References

Chen, P. (2010). *Change of new China's integrity: Phenomena and speculation*. Sun Yat-sen University Press.

Durkheim, E. (2000). *The division of labor in society* (D. Qu, Trans.). SDX Joint Publishing Company.

Hong, M. (2009). Interpreting the causes of social credit crisis in China's transformation period. *Shanghai Economic Study*, *8*, 57–64. https://doi.org/10.19626/j.cnki.cn31-1163/f.2009.08.008.

Hu, S. (1998). *Account of myself at forty, appeared in new issue of old books*. Yuelu Press.

James, R. P. (2008). *China and Charles Darwin* (Y. Qian, Trans.). Jiangsu People's Press.

Lao, T. (2021). *Tao-Te Ching, Chapter 38*. China Publishing House.

Li, L. (2005). *A glass of wine under flowering shrubs*. Tongxin Press.

Li, S. (2011). *Crisis investigation of China's social integrity*. China Commercial Publishing House.

Liang, H. (2013). *Notes of exiting liang: Details and experience of China*. Huacheng Publishing House.

Liu, M. (2012). Safeguarding the peace of China: The top ten awesome public security campaigns across the country in 2011. *China Report*, *3*, 34–39.

Lu, X. (1981). *The complete works of Lu Xun, – Volume 3*. The People's Literature Publishing House.

Luhmann, N. (2005). *Trust: The reduction mechanism of social complexity* (T. Qu & Q. Li, Trans.). Shanghai People's Publishing House.

Luo, Z. (2002). Machine gun and thread bound Chinese books: A look at the intensity relationship between the science and the study of Chinese ancient civilization from the debate of the "catalogue of the study of Chinese ancient civilization". *Journal of Sichuan University*, *6*, 84–101.

Ma, D. (2008). Trust, its origin and evolution. *Opening Times*, *4*, 72–86.

The Collation and Annotation Team of Han Fei Zi. (1982). *Han Fei Zi*. Jiangsu People's Press.

Tilly, C. (2010). *Trust and rule* (W. Hu, Trans.). Shanghai People's Publishing House.
Tönnies, F. (1999). *Gemeinschaft and gesellschaft (Community and society)* (R. Lin, Trans.). The Commercial Press.
Yan, F. (1996). *Evolution and ethics, appeared in China's modern academic classics*. Hebei Education Press.
Ye, M. (1996). *In search of wealth and power: Yan Fu and the West*. Jiangsu People's Press.
Zhai, X. (2011). Integrity, trust and credit: Clarification and historical evolution of concepts. *Jianghai Academic Journal, 05*, 107–114+239.

2 The History and Tradition of China's Social Credit

The so-called "credit" of China's traditional agricultural society refers more to interpersonal trust, whereas the business credit of the market manifests is more in line with China's traditional credit, because the covenant nature and temporality of interpersonal trust in agricultural culture are rather vague, whereas they are much more definite in business activities. It follows that discussion of these matters will, on one hand, help us examine the relationship between market credit and social credit in Chinese society and, on the other, help us determine what changes this relationship could undergo due to social modernisation. In other words, it will help us figure out under what circumstances Chinese business credit and social credit will generate a crisis.

2.1 Functions of Folk Covenant

Business credit originates in the economic exchange derived from the social division of labour. In human society, except for the on-the-spot settlement transaction mode of face-to-face trade, there are many situations where settlement cannot be made on the spot or where it is unnecessary to do so; this separation of commodity and currency in time and space necessarily leads to the birth of business credit. Usually, business credit is based on social activities. If a covenant is the norm in constraining economic exchange, then a huge amount of business credit is realised via covenant. However, it is inadequate to arrive at such an understanding because a covenant in the common sense always comes with formal documents and legal protections. However, because traditional Chinese society was based on social interaction, it had its own covenant form. Specifically, except in exceptional situations, there was little population migration in China's agricultural society, which led to multiple forms of credit constraint, including morality, habits, public opinion, exclusion, and so on.

Here lies an important concept: namely, the immobility of the population. One basic characteristic of a well-developed market economy is the mobility of merchants through commodity mobility; in other words, the basic characteristic of the merchant group is its mobility. This point seems incompatible with the population immobility of an agricultural society, so we will discuss the characteristics of Chinese merchants in what follows. We need first to understand the credit characteristics of an immobile population.

DOI: 10.4324/9781003375579-4

The use of folk covenants has a long history in China:

> the appearance of paper covenants in ancient China dated as far back as the closing period of primitive society. In the Western Zhou period, it had taken a primitive form, developed in the Qin and Han dynasties, matured in the Song and Yuan dynasties, and finalized in its form by the Ming and Qing dynasties.[1]

Some researchers even treated China's ancient folk covenant as a kind of law, however treating it as "a covenant code without being independent, with multi-party and ethical and moral constraints as its prominent features."[2] In China's traditional society, folk covenants are frequently employed in transactions such as land sales. In an agricultural society, land was not only the core issue in the operation of the political machine of traditional society, it played a still more important role in the life of the peasant: It was, indeed, the livelihood of the peasant. Therefore, regarding land, the most important living resource in China's traditional society, some culturally unique notions were formed, such as land not being considered the private property of the individual but a collective property of the clan. Thus, members of the same clan and their neighbours were given the right of first refusal when there was a sale of land. Understanding this point can afford us better understanding of the practices present in the deed title, which bears not only the fingerprints of the buyer and seller but of relevant clan members and neighbours. Actually, it is highly probable that this practice was instituted to prevent harm to the buyer by preventing nullification of the covenant due to any violation of customs allowing clan relations' pre-emptive buying rights, etc. In addition to deed titles relating to land, along with the development of a market economy and growing economic exchange activities, there appeared many private covenants in other economic activities, including big family break-ups and the division of family property, the buying and selling of houses, private loans, as well as social activities like buying and selling marriages. These all fall under the category of folk credit. What merits attention is that the folk covenant based on kinship resulted in the pursuit of the concept of "litigation-free" covenants by the Chinese. As noted by some scholars, the concept of "litigation-free" covenants in traditional Chinese society came from two areas: namely, the government's pursuit of a cessation of litigation and folk society's fear of litigation.[3] In traditional society, in the eyes of the government, folk matters such as deed titles for land, marriage covenants, and monetary and debt disputes belonged in the realm of trivial issues in the folk society domain. The government left the issues to be mediated by folk forces themselves and seldom intervened. The existence of the concept of "litigation-free" covenants created a situation wherein folk society engaged in stipulating spontaneous covenants to restrain themselves in various socio-economic transactional activities and resorted to informal norms within folk society to guarantee the execution of such covenants without invoking external coercive forces such as politics or the law.

In an immobile agricultural society, folk covenants can essentially play the role of a credit voucher. Business activities that grow out of such covenants require the credit of an intermediary to facilitate the deal because the transaction parties might not know each other, thus seeking to enter formal covenants instead. In Chinese society, the intermediary is mainly played by the broker house in feudal society and the broker's storehouse during the pre-liberation modern period of China. Since the Tang and Song dynasties, along with the development of the commodity economy, exchange activities required the mediation of brokers. As an intermediary for transactional activities, the broker is usually well informed in the business of its own brokerage, the situation of the seller and the buyer, as well as the prevailing market prices and so on. The duties of the broker and the broker house are basically limited to evaluating the products, assessing and fixing prices, presiding over the transaction, and facilitating and expediting the deal as an intermediary. In pre-liberation modern times, the development of the commodity economy led to the growing frequency of transactional activities in treaty ports; there appeared intermediaries like the broker's storehouses that played the role of a credit voucher.

> Regarding commodity transactions in trading hubs, as the buyer and the seller are from different places and not acquainted with the credit situation of the other party, they could not but trade on the basis of the credit of the brokerage.[4]

Hence, we believe that be it parties to a covenant relying on an intermediary to play the role of a credit voucher in folk society or the broker and brokerage playing the role of intermediary in a commercial society, all adequately manifest the characteristics of the covenant in traditional Chinese society. As has been noted by some scholars, the covenant in traditional Chinese society entailed the participation of a third party that provided it with authority. Regardless of the forms taken, this is the most prominent distinction between China's contractual spirit and the West's contractual spirit.[5] Why the necessity for third-party participation? It could be due to the lack of a universal and mandatory legal system constraining credit in traditional Chinese society. Therefore, folk society needed to invoke the mediation of an intermediary to forge social opinions, etc., for the sake of guaranteeing the performance of contracts. Again, why is the third party so crucial? The answer requires thinking in terms of the trust networks of traditional society.

2.2 The Trust Network

In the discourse of modern state governance and the free market, the Western scholar holds that China lacks direct regulation over commercial activities, and it also lacks institutions such as modern contracts, property rights, business law constraining market order, and the regulation of business credit. However, there was never any social credit crisis arising from the lack of those credit institutions of modern society in traditional Chinese society. Therefore, we need to situate the problem in a context unique to China's society. This context mainly refers to a situation wherein individual credit in traditional Chinese society was usually assumed by the community, including the family, extended families, and the clan instead of the individual himself. In Chinese folk society, resources for personal livelihood became embedded in the family community, and the individual could not exist detached from this community. From the point of constraining principles, it can be seen that this family-like community provided implicit joint responsibilities for the individual. The effectiveness of such a credit-constraining mode came from the normative force of the relationship network.

As is known, in a society where an agricultural economy is the dominant form of economy, land is the most fundamental production resource. Due to the immobile nature of land, people dependent on land for sustenance are bound to the land, while a small-peasant economy based on the family unit needed cooperation and mutual support for causes of irrigation, collective security, and so on. The most typical form of living in such a social unit would be living in a community based on family and blood relationships.

The socio-economic basis for living in a compact community of the clan reliant on cooperative living made it extremely easy for society to produce powerful credit constraints on the individual. In other words, if a member of the extended family committed any credit offence, the party sustaining the harm did not need to go to the offending party himself but could go instead to the offender's family for redress for the harm done to him. There is a famous saying in Chinese describing this situation: "the monk can run but not his temple." The primary purpose for living in the close quarters of a clan community was to find security among the collective and the community. Due to a shortage of resources for living – after all, agricultural harvests did not rely exclusively on human effort but also on the working of the climate and the change of weather – the cooperation and distribution of the community featured more prominently than extraordinary personal capability. Accordingly, the focus of such a culture was forever on cooperation, union, and coexistence. Therefore, internal cohesion, harmony, geographical relationships, and so on were all basic guarantees for the survival and development of the people. The spatial and temporal situation forced the individual to count on the social community for sustenance, while the most severe punishment that could ever be imposed on any individual was to be expelled and isolated from the community. What must be emphasised is that this relatively closed social structure manifested itself more in a kind of relationship network, which was markedly different from the religious organisation in a parish under Christian culture. There were no such concepts as joining a church or the eligibility for joining a church. The people were naturally born and grew up in a place and had no place to retreat to and no other recourse but to rely on the network to engage in various labour and business activities. We emphasise this networking nature instead of the organising nature because the boundaries were not as distinct as an organisation's; such boundaries were vague and extensible and not based on one binary division. Indeed, if some intermediaries were working in the process, such a network could be extended limitlessly. This is the socio-economic foundation of China's traditional credit operation.

Therefore, traditional credit is in essence a trust network or community credit. The basic principle of this type of credit can be summarised as follows: Community members were mutually acquainted and the full mobility of information made a breach of faith or fraudulent conduct hardly concealable. As there was full mobility of information among community members, any member failing to comply with folk custom and morality would be subject to public pressure in the form of gossip; furthermore, the cheating conduct of an individual would also implicate other related members, while these others, in order to avoid being implicated, would exert implicit constraints on the dishonest member. If any individual in a certain network really broke his promises, he would face condemnation and exclusion from within the community. If the entire society was composed of communities of varying sizes, then dishonest people would have no escape. Because escape from their native communities would mean they became foreigners, they would embark on a life adrift on the road. Based on all that, it follows that traditional communities could impose effective credit constraints on their members even in areas where the law was not involved. This is the primary operation principle for community credit.

Having discussed the agricultural social credit of an immobile society, let's examine business mobility within such a society. We might find that the purpose of such business operations was not to create another set of credit norms, but to carry on to great extent the credit mechanisms already inherent in the community. Especially in the Ming and Qing dynasties, along with the growth of the commodity economy and the expansion of commercial activities, cross-region commercial activities were increasingly frequent. In order to accommodate the mobility of commercial society, merchants living away from home had re-established merchant organisations and groups such as the guildhall, a merchant guild based on blood and geographical relationships. Its organising principle was no different from that of the merchants' clans or village communities. The merchants still relied on countryman fellowship, i.e., they still resorted to their countrymen for security when faced with the strangeness and insecurity of being away from home. Clearly, such mobile communities built away from home were actually displacements of the village community in space. They were built on the fundamental principles of mutual benefit and integrity. The informal norms generated from within these communities worked so effectively that they required no formal institutions to maintain credit. As all members were from the same village or clan community, such a community produced constraints far greater than external society was capable of producing. Durkheim had an explanation for this phenomenon:

> if a society is composed of a huge number of individuals, only when concentrated on monitoring a few individuals would any monitoring item implemented by the society look close, vigilant and effective. A man feels much less constrained in a jammed crowd than in a small circle.[6]

Fei Tsao Tung interpreted the phenomenon this way: "the rural society obtains trust from familiarity … the credit of the rural society does not lie in its emphasis on covenant, but in its offhand reliability when one is so versed in the rules of a conduct."[7] Therefore, compared with formal constraining institutions including law and the social credit systems of modern society, traditional Chinese society pays more attention to informal customs, conventions, and informal covenants.

The maintenance of a traditional trust network primarily depended on reputation, because in an immutable network of relationships, face and reputation were the symbols the merchant cherished the most. Its symbolic representation was manifest in the link between the individual's reputation with that of the community of which he was a member. Even if the individual engaged in business away from home, he still assumed the obligation and responsibility for the maintenance of the reputation of the community. The individual himself also aspired to make achievements so that he could not only bring honour to his community but also retire with glory. This mode of conduct is what is defined in Chinese culture as the "notion of face." As the co-author of this book has remarked elsewhere, as an informal constraint, the notion of face works both as a psychological pressure and a psychological motivation. On one hand, it originates in the melting into the society of which he is a member; on the other, it also originates in the expectations of society.[8] As informal social credit constraint mechanisms, face and reputation work only in interconnected and relatively closed network societies and circle societies. The structure of China's traditional society was exactly this type of relationship society and circle society.

2.3 Fundamental Principles of China's Traditional Credit Governance

The foregoing examination suggests that traditional credit control belongs more in the field of informal governance. Its fundamental principles can be summarised as follows.

2.3.1 The Principle of Combining Economic Punishment and Reputation Debasement

In rural society, punishment for contractual default and dishonest conduct entails neither mental compensation following the modern spirit of the law nor retaliatory punishment in accordance with traditional law. Instead, it follows the principle of combining economic punishment and reputation debasement. In immobile rural society, this kind of punishment principle gets intensively incarnated in folk conventions and covenants. If you are a defaulter, the whole village may slaughter your pig, ox, etc., to entertain all your fellow villagers. In addition, there are also corresponding incentive and punishment mechanisms established in this area. For example, anyone denouncing irregular conduct could be granted certain awards. On the other hand, anyone failing to denounce irregular conduct could be punished.[9] These measures greatly reduce the occurrence of irregular conduct. A further example concerns the mobile merchant community. The pursuit of gain gives rise to the competitive undercutting of prices, counterfeiting, taking in apprentices against guild stipulations, and so on; many guilds' punitive measures would involve ordering the wrongdoer to pay fines that would then be used to provide for a feast or entertainment for the people. Gathering the people to dine and entertain together would both render economic punishment on the wrongdoer and cause him some reputation debasement. The effects of such a mode of governance lie in the fact that the information about the irregular conduct gets spread among the circle via the banquet and entertainment, which disgraces the wrongdoer; meanwhile, these effects also work as a warning to those who participate in the banquet and entertainment.[10]

2.3.2 Principle of Combining Moral Self-Discipline and Collective Expulsion

China's traditional credit puts extraordinary emphasis on the inner moral strength of the subject. In this concept of integrity, the imperative to "be truthful to the heart on the inside, and get trusted by others on the outside" suffices to indicate the importance of the individual's moral self-discipline in maintaining credit. However, as is known, any form of morality is necessarily concrete and historical, and any moral consciousness is related to certain social structures, modes of production and living, and modes of association between people. The social immobility formed over the generations of settlement in a traditional society, bonded with blood and geographical relationships, gradually deposited and formed the moral notions and codes of conduct appropriate for such a society. Moral self-discipline exactly originates in the shaping of such collective life or community life; in other words, morality grows out of long-term collective life. For a society ruled by such norms, punishment was not reduced to moral condemnation alone. The other deterrent for violation of collective interests or violation of community morality was the potential for collective exclusion. For members of the village community, being expelled from the community literally obliterated the meaning of social life. For the merchant away from home, being expelled by a community of fellow merchants and guild was almost tantamount to cutting off his livelihood. Therefore, collective expulsion as a means of coercive isolation was an extremely powerful deterrent force. We can even assume that, in traditional credit governance, the moral strength of the system did not derive primarily from the inner self-discipline of the subject but more likely from the subject's fear of community expulsion.

2.3.3 Principle of Joint Liability

From the relationship between credit and information, the more symmetrical the information is, the easier it is for a breach of faith to be discovered, therefore lessening the possibility of a breach of faith. However, in terms of reducing information cost and governance costs, the difficulty and cost of conducting credit governance on countless individuals are definitely far greater than on a limited number of groups. Arranging individuals into an interlinking relationship reduces the difficulty and cost of governance. Some scholars have demonstrated this theory, concluding that collective punishment pivoted on blood relationships in ancient China such as the joint penalty system. The organisation mode of public power based on geographical relationships such as the institutional arrangement of the Bao-Jia system (a neighbourhood administrative system) is exactly such a mechanism of joint responsibility. Such a system can overcome information asymmetry and become an effective means of control.[11] For instance, in a closed village community, a villager with a family can borrow money more easily than a bachelor, because the family of the former assumes the role of a credit voucher. This is also the key reason for the continued existence of the concept of inheritance of the parent's debt by the son in China's folk society. In traditional society, there was the so-called system of recommendation and guarantee and Lin Bao (a system of guarantee by those on government subsidy) in the imperial examinations and government-office recruitment. According to textual research carried out by some scholars, the system of recommendation and guarantee originated in the Han dynasty, with the guarantor assuming lifelong responsibility for the recommended, which was called the joint recommendation and guarantee method. The method continued into the Qing dynasty, with a scholar needing first to secure an appropriate person to vouch for him before taking office. The system of Lin Bao was more developed, stipulating that anyone entering county-level imperial examinations had to join a union with five other co-examinees, who had to be vouched for by a scholar who lived on government grants.[12] Another example was in business-operation activities. For many men seeking to do business, the first stage they had to go through was to work as shop workers or apprentices. In many areas, an apprentice or shop worker had to be vouched for, with anyone vouching for the person assuming joint responsibility. The Anhui merchants and the Shanxi merchants stand out most prominently from among the top ten merchant groups in traditional China: The former bonded the community through blood relationships, whereas the latter expanded outward based on rural geographical relationships. Their apprentices and shop workers could not go into business without being vouched for by others. The Shanxi merchant community even stipulated that the wife and offspring of the person being vouched for could not leave their hometowns; this was a management style featuring a sort of hostage property. We can consider it as a form of joint-responsibility governance.

2.3.4 Principle of Intermediary Participation in Folk-Credit Governance

The person who goes between the covenant and the transaction activities was called an "intermediary." The intermediary took part in the folk-credit process, which was mainly manifest in folk-covenant relationships such as the buying and selling of land, lending and borrowing, leasing, and employing. According to the spirit of modern contract law, the folk contract is a civil action between the participants. Why the need for an intermediary? The sociological significance of intermediary participation lies in the fact that the participation of the intermediary could mitigate an otherwise extremely embarrassing event in an acquaintance society. As rural society was closed, once disputes arose from the many transactions that took place within the society, it was inevitable to hurt the feelings of both parties. Using an intermediary to mediate a dispute in a way in which both parties saved face was essential for folk-credit governance.[13] In traditional Chinese society, an appeal to gains or material benefits did not sound so justified, especially when it came to transaction activities involving direct material gain between acquaintances. And many transactions on many occasions were conducted between blood relations.

Without the office of an intermediary, it would be very hard to settle disputes when they arose. Therefore, intermediary participation and folk credit were related to the cultural psychology and economic ethics of a locality.

Some scholars believe that, in thousands of years of Chinese transactional activities, there was always an intermediary participating in the contract process, an intermediary who was required to affix a signature or a mark on a document so as to assume joint responsibility. Currently, this is a universal practice. A written contract that lacks the signature of an intermediary would be deemed null and void for lack of necessary conditions.[14] The intermediary usually is one who has a public identity from the same living area as the parties to the contract. Such an intermediary enjoys a certain degree of authority and reputation. In a rural society, legality was confirmed in an open environment. Especially in regard to transactional activities, they did not have the statutory force of law sanctioned by the government, so to guarantee the rights and interests of the parties, they relied on the presence of an intermediary. For instance, according to the regulations of the Qing dynasty, in the execution of deed titles involving land, a certain portion of the deed tax was paid to execute the transaction. However, to avoid paying the tax, the parties often bypassed the government, but in doing so, they were also worried that their rights and interests might not get secured. This situation spurred the appearance of the intermediary to vouch for the truthfulness and validity of the transaction and to forestall any possible future dispute. On the other hand, through the participation of the intermediary, the civil contract obtained public recognition, which helped bring the contract into force by invoking public opinion. Having examined the civil law of the Qing dynasty and the Republic of China prior to the founding of the PRC, Huang Zongzhi found that there were far more litigations arising from loans between close relatives and friends than from formal loans mediated by an intermediary. The use of an intermediary obviously helped reduce conflicts and resolve disputes.[15]

When looking at the participation of the intermediary in folk-credit governance from the perspective of social structure, we might observe that traditional society was an acquaintance one, featuring a sort of boundary in the acquaintance circle of acquaintances. However, the network of relationships in Chinese society was, in turn, highly retractable. As the scope of economic exchange expanded, there was an objective need for a credit-constraining mechanism to overcome transaction risk. The intermediary, who was familiar to both parties to the transaction, played the practical function of the credit voucher, helping to extend the scope of transaction activities.

2.3.5 Principle of Combining Holy Sanctity with Secular Authority

Authority is a recognised lawful force. It obtains mandatory force because it has been recognised. In traditional credit governance, punishment and sanction for breach of faith and irregular conduct require such a mandatory force. The mandatory force of traditional credit mainly counts on two authorities, holy sanctity and secular authority, which jointly participate in the control of traditional credit.

Merchants in traditional Chinese society lacked the commercial law and merchant tribunals to regulate commercial credit in the way of their Western counterparts; therefore, they spontaneously engaged in worshipping guild gods and offering sacrifices to effect credit governance. However, in a nation like China where faith and piety were lacking, this type of worship and sacrifice to guild gods might not always work as an effective credit constraint. Therefore, merchant communities of the same trade usually fostered the community spirit of the guild through a public space where they offered sacrifices and put on plays, reinforcing the interconnection of the members. For instance, in addition to forcing a wrongdoer to kneel before the memorial tablets of the guild god, the guild would also punish a wrongdoer by forcing him to throw banquets and stage plays. The belief was that trade credit would be safeguarded through banqueting and entertainment.

In addition to the authority of holy sanctity, secular authorities had an even more important impacts on the governance of traditional credit. Secular authority mainly came from two sources. One was social authority, or the social mandatory force; this authority originated primarily in the authoritative figure of the rural society and the public opinion formed via public review. Within a small group, as the wrongdoer violated the interests of the entire group, the punishment meted out would win social recognition, gaining the universally acknowledged authoritative effect of the public recognition of the community.[16] The second secular authority refers to government authority. In China's traditional society, government approval and support must be obtained for covenants, contracts, depositions, and so on entered into through folk activities such as clan mediation, neighbour mediation, and private settlement. Particularly when transactions involve large tracts of land, the government authority matters a great deal in supporting their lawfulness. This type of transaction not only requires a red seal (that is, a government red seal) to prove its legality, and it also requires payment of a transaction tax when transaction delivery is executed. The government usually did not interfere with folk transactions apart from land transactions, and it left as much as possible to self-regulation by folk forces. However, regarding those agreements and covenants that could hardly be resolved by folk forces, they were typically sent to the government for resolution, and any punishment would be meted out by invoking the power of the government. The authority of the government lay in the way its mandatory enforcement of a contract produced a deterrent effect. In this way, government authority was the authority of last resort in the folk-credit governance.

2.4 Historical Inheritance of China's Traditional Credit: Illustrated with Merchant Groups

In order to illustrate the internal logic of traditional credit or folk social credit, we have chosen several cases from the Anhui merchants, Shanxi merchants, and Ningbo merchants in pre-liberation times (before 1949), and the Wenzhou merchants in modern times, to highlight the characteristics of folk-credit operation.

2.4.1 The Birth and Operation Mechanisms of the Anhui and Shanxi Merchant Groups

Among China's traditional merchant groups (also called business groups), the Anhui merchants and the Shanxi merchants are typical. These two merchant groups not only attained tremendous business results but also formed a unique mechanism for the birth and operation of credit. This mechanism was effected through the following interconnected systems.

The first was the apprentice system. In the business-operation activities of the Anhui merchants and the Shanxi merchants, the apprentice system operated as a gateway to acquiring qualifications for practice in their trade, which in reality played the role of a credit constraint on the practitioner. Firstly, from the perspective of the apprentice selection process, all apprentices were selected from members of the same clan or the same locality. The rationale for this kind of selection process lay in its firm bonds based on blood relationships and geographical relationships, which rendered holistic information easily accessible. In a social network based on blood relationships and geographical relationships, information was almost totally open, thus overcoming the problem of information asymmetry; secondly, apprentice training involved a long process, especially in the training for apprentices in the exchange shops of the Shanxi merchants. In the first years of training, the apprentice seldom had access to the specific businesses of the exchange shop; instead, he mainly received training in customer service. Training of this sort was designed to shape the moral quality of the apprentice. Apprentices who failed to meet the standards would be weeded out and excluded from the business activities of the exchange shop, while those who met the standards would get promoted and entrusted with important businesses. The extended training process required a tremendous amount of sunk capital, which made successful apprentices cherish the hard-to-come-by opportunity that they enjoyed. Therefore, the apprentice system produced a credit-constraining function by shaping personal character and by fostering interpersonal relationships.

The second is the guarantee system. In China's traditional commercial activities, in order to avoid credit risk, merchant groups did more than just pay special attention to the moral quality of their practitioners. They also instituted corresponding credit systems, and the guarantee system was one such system. Take the Shanxi exchange shop for instance; though the apprentices were only selected from Shanxi locals, it was still hard for the proprietor of the exchange shop to have full confidence in those chosen, which made it necessary for an intermediary to recommend, guarantee, and assume corresponding joint liability. This kind of guarantee system worked not only in the selection of apprentices but also in the selection and appointment of managers. In addition to the guarantee by business firms of solid means, the family and family property of the manager naturally became security for the guarantee. What's more, to restrain the manager, the exchange shop proprietor usually stipulated that when he worked away from home, his family could not accompany him but had to stay at Taigu, Pingyao, or Qixian, the headquarters of the exchange shops. This was a hostage situation in disguised form.

The third mechanism was the reputation constraining mechanism. The traditional rural society was a closed circle society, which gave effective play to factors like traditional ethics, morality, and public opinion; such constraints are reputation constraints. Take, for instance, the Shanxi exchange shop. The managers and shop workers who acted as agents for the ticketing firms, and the principals, the Cai Dong, were in a principal-agent relationship, but because the circle of ticketing firms was relatively closed, any information about irregularities would be quickly transmitted within the circle, and fraudsters would not only be removed from the business of the ticketing firms by the proprietor and the boss but would also be ostracised collectively by the entire group of ticketing firms.[17] In the traditional business activities of China, a business operator's attention to reputation came not only from the mutual supervision of business operators of the same place and clan but also from the constraints imposed by the hometown community. Such constraints mainly emanated from judgement passed on a person by the hometown community. In traditional rural society, an upwardly mobile person usually won financial assistance from the clan community and thus high hopes were pinned on him. This situation worked both as a pressure and a motivation, prompting the outgoing person to be maximally dutiful in the hope that he might repay his hometown community through his success and bring honour to it. However, if he disgraced the clan through indiscretion, he would usually choose to conceal his identity or die in a strange land.[18] This dynamic reflects the fact that one's personal reputation was linked to that of the hometown community.

The fourth is risk sharing and mutual support. In traditional business-operation activities, merchants doing business in a strange land would usually construct a relationship network of fellow villagers in the hope of providing and supporting each other against external risks collectively. Take, for example, the Anhui merchants. Those well-capitalised merchants did not roam the business world single-handedly; rather, they entered into partnerships based on blood relationships and geographical relationships.[19] It would be difficult for irregularities and malpractices to emerge under this mode of cooperation, which also enabled rapid growth in the scale of businesses. This system of risk sharing and mutual support was even more widely applied by the Shanxi merchants. On one hand, these merchants maintained credit via merchant halls and trade guilds. For instance, the rules of the Shanxi Pingyao money exchange guild set out that guild affairs would be resolved by "a majority of votes" and that all businessmen would render mutual assistance and cooperation in business. If there was a major monetary project, "the shops shall offer inter-shop lending, no shop should worry too much about its balance with other shops at such time" – but when the event was over, "the borrower and the lender shall get together and settle the deposits and borrowings."[20] On the other hand, the Shanxi exchange shops had instituted a set of effective systems to handle risks through the shop communication system. The headquarters of the exchange shops was incorporated in the Shanxi hometown, with branches stationed across the country. There were intercommunications including the "report proper, report annex, prevailing market, feature report" that flowed between the headquarters and the branches and between different branches, for the purpose of "rewarding the successful and consolidating the poor performing, drawing from the sluggish and replenishing the quick turnovers." In this way, the shops rendered mutual assistance. This organisational system – at once flexible and rigid, not to mention grand – enabled the exchange shop the capability to "gather and distribute national financial strength, and make it smoothly run like a river running without end." Such a system substantially buttressed the credit of the exchange shop.[21]

In the sociological sense, the traditional credit constructed by traditional business groups like the Anhui merchants and the Shanxi merchants originated in the basic unit of the traditional community's social structure. The individual, even staying away from home in terms of social space, would still be under the psychological influence of the clan community. Especially in his self-identification and sense of belonging, he could not detach himself from the relationship network in which he was embedded. Effecting credit constraints by way of relationship networks was the fundamental way of the Anhui merchants and Shanxi merchants.

2.4.2 The Credit Generation and Operation Mechanism of the Ningbo Merchants

In pre-liberation modern times, the Ningbo Business Group no doubt eclipsed the business world. After the 1840s, the influence of traditional business groups including the Anhui merchants and the Shanxi merchants declined successively, while the Ningbo merchants, having undergone two transformations, became the biggest business group in China. In the first transformation, the Ningbo Business Group absorbed modern Western business management knowledge, assiduously expanded the scope of its operation, and worked intensively to involve traditional industries in international markets. The second transformation involved tremendous investment in the various fields of the early modern economy of China such as finance, industry, shipping, commerce, and insurance. The merchants successfully started a series of early modern enterprises and transformed into a modern capitalist industrial and commercial business group with prominent geographical features, becoming the dominant force of the Shanghai financial circle.[22] The successful transformation and upgrading of the Ningbo Business Group had everything to do with its unique mechanism for credit generation and operation. The mechanism can be summarised as follows.

The first characteristic of this mechanism is its emphasis on the union and mutual assistance of fellow countrymen. In China's traditional business culture, fellow countrymen freely entering into "business groups" was nothing but a natural phenomenon. Members of such business groups were mostly fellow countrymen as well as engaged in the same trade. The original purpose of their formation was to safeguard the groups' business interests.[23] These merchants from the same place were engaged in similar trades; this overlap of geographical background and business scope promoted unity and mutual assistance within the business group. Therefore, businessmen from the same place bonding together was a common feature of the survival and growth of a business group. One of the development models of the Ningbo Business Group is that most Ningbo entrepreneurs doing business in other places recruited apprentices and employees from their fellow countrymen.

Once an individual settled down in an area or took firm root in a certain industry, he would bring in more fellow countrymen through transmission, assistance, and guidance. This practice shaped a unique socio-economic phenomenon: A certain industry in a certain geographical location was usually dominated by Ningbo people from a certain geographical area. In some commercial metropolises, because of geographical identification factors such as similar dialects or customs, it was easier for businessmen engaging in industrial and commercial activities living away from home to unite and safeguard the collective reputation of the Ningbo Business Group. Consider the Siming Commercial Savings Bank. Incorporated with capital raised from Ningbo merchants, it was squeezed several times by foreign banks and foreign firms after it started operation in 1908. Whenever there was financial turbulence, these foreign banks and firms would press for silver dollars against the paper money issued by Siming. Actually, Siming Bank was not of solid financial means, but it managed the risks of multiple bank runs, mainly thanks to the union and mutual assistance rendered by fellow Ningbo countrymen. Whenever there was a run on the bank, the major department stores, money shops, and silver shops of Ningbo origin volunteered to redeem paper money on behalf of Siming Bank. Some vendors of Ningbo origin, when happening upon people queuing in front of Siming Bank, waiting to redeem their paper money, would produce silver dollars from their pockets in exchange for the paper money from these participants in the bank run. There were also Ningbo businessmen coming all the way from distant places to empty their purses to help the Siming Bank. Thanks to these activities, the squeezes soon quieted down.[24] In 1935, commerce and industry enterprises in Shanghai found themselves unable to repay loans due to widespread recession. Rumours surged, and Siming Bank experienced another squeeze. The Commercial Bank of China, operated by people from Ningbo, immediately stood up for the bank, publicly moving crate after crate of silver dollars into Siming Bank and offering redemptions without limit. Meanwhile, some money shops also offered redemption services on behalf of Siming; thus, this bank squeeze was also put down. By then, Shanghai citizens knew that Siming Bank had the power of the entire Ningbo group behind it. Their confidence in its paper money improved.[25] It was exactly this kind of union and mutual assistance that collectively safeguarded the credit and reputation of the Ningbo Business Group.

The second characteristic of this mechanism is the mutual support it created between the financial industry and industrial and commercial sectors. The financial industry was a pillar industry of the Ningbo Business Group. In the early stages of the Ningbo Business Group's development, the financial industry amounted primarily to traditional money shops. After the treaty ports opened, Ningbo people who had engaged in the traditional money-shop business began to dabble in the modern banking industry to a considerable scale. Unlike the Shanxi exchange shops' exclusive engagement in the financial industry, the financial industry of the Ningbo Business Group had close ties with commercial and industrial circles, and the two constituted a relationship of mutual support. In pre-liberation modern times, many Ningbo people engaged in running businesses in medicine, in foreign imports, in shipping and transportation, and so on. These industries had tremendous capital needs, and their operation expanded thanks to loans taken from money shops run by Ningbo people. For instance, Ningbo merchant Li Yeliang operated a river sand-shipping business and transported northern goods south and southern goods north; he had had the help of Zhao Puzhai, a money-shop business manager, and acquired substantial wealth because he could often obtain huge loans. In return, these businessmen usually deposited their idle cash in money shops, and some even conducted their own monetary businesses. This situation, wherein the industrial and commercial sectors and the money business covered for each other, produced a powerful economic force in commercial activities. After modern banks emerged, banks run by Ningbo people offered special care in terms of granting loans to businessmen from Ningbo, which helped the Ningbo Business Group overcome risks and grow strong. Consider Siming Bank's support of Yu Qiaqing, a Ningbo businessman and a major comprador in Shanghai. Siming Bank was incorporated by Ningbo businessmen in Shanghai. When the bank went into business, it spared no effort to help the Ningbo Business Group. The Sanbei Company started by Yu Qiaqing grew into the biggest shipping corporation in the lower Yangtze river and in the coastal area shipping industry, due to financial support from Siming Bank. Yu Qiaqing had many a time bought old ships and repainted them as security to take out loans in the name of new ships. And the loans so taken out were again used to purchase more old ships. This kind of revolving financing carried extremely high risk, and Yu Qiaqing's debt to Siming Bank amounted to 3 million silver dollars at the peak of his borrowing. Without such special treatment from Siming Bank, he would not only have found it very difficult to grow, he would have gone bankrupt at an early stage. When the Ningbo commercial and industrial entrepreneurs grew substantially in financial strength, they mostly became loyal shareholders of the financial institutions operated by the "Ningbo Business Group," becoming a solid base against the turbulences experienced by financial institutions such as the money shops and banks.[26] The development and expansion of industry and commerce, i.e., the real economy, could not be detached from financial support, whereas the financial industry also required the support of the real economy, especially during bank squeezes and financial turbulences when such support was crucial. The mutual support and mutual promotion between the financial industry and industry and commerce played an extremely important role in safeguarding the business credit of the Ningbo Business Group.

The third characteristic of this mechanism is the autonomous folk-governance mechanism. The other factor in forging the outstanding business credit of the Ningbo Business Group lay in the fact that they did not from the outset count on government authority as the major last resort; instead, they relied on the force of autonomous folk governance in society, gradually forming their own mechanism of autonomous governance. The autonomous folk-governance mechanism of the Ningbo Business Group was initially embodied as an ever-expanding network of fellow countrymen. Like business groups from other areas in China, industrial and commercial businessmen doing business away from home formed groups bonded by the notion of "fellow countrymen." However, unlike business groups from other areas, these fellow-countrymen groups did not isolate themselves; instead, they incessantly united businessmen from other areas of the same province to grow their strength. The Ningbo Business Group first united their close neighbours, the Shaoxing businessmen of great repute for their money-shop business, to form the Ningbo-Shaoxing business group, and proceeded from there to further unite businessmen from the east of the Qiantang river to form the Zhedong (east Zhejiang province) business group, and finally united businessmen from the west of the Qiantang river to form the Zhejiang business group. Even the Jiangsu business group, Anhui business group, Jiangxi business group, and so on, were united under the flag of the great Ningbo Business Group. Of course, the organisation of such an extended business group gradually took shape via personal relations and the market leadership of the Ningbo Business Group. Along with the growing influence and strength of the Ningbo Business Group, other business groups earnestly wanted to establish relationships with it, and the Ningbo Business Group also wanted to avail itself of the opportunity to incorporate people from outside its fellowship into its personal relationship network. Thus, the business group agglomeration centred around the Ningbo Business Group took form and gradually held sway over the Shanghai market. It not only dominated economic organisations such as most money shops and textile factories, but controlled most social organisations like the Shanghai General Chamber of Commerce, the Shanghai Bankers Guild, and the Shanghai Money Shops Guild.[27] The second aspect of the autonomous governance mechanism of the Ningbo Business Group manifested in the accord between the organisations of fellow countrymen and the guild organisations. The Shanghai of pre-liberation modern times was a business metropolis of relatively high autonomy where the political influence of the central authority had little sway. Thanks to the combination of the Ningbo Business Group's autonomous governance resources and spontaneous market mechanisms, the strength of the Ningbo Business Group grew and expanded with Shanghai as its main base. Its power expanded exponentially when the Ningbo Business Group absorbed trade guilds with powerful fellow-countrymen organisations that forcefully promoted self-discipline in trade. Take, for instance, the Siming Council incorporated by Ningbo people in Shanghai and the Shanghai General Chamber of Commerce, the biggest guild organisation in pre-liberation modern China. In 1904, the Shanghai Business Conference Council controlled by Ningbo people was renamed the Shanghai General Business Conference, which was further renamed the Shanghai General Chamber of Commerce in June 1912. However, such changes hardly affected the internal personnel arrangement and organisational structure; the leadership was forever firmly in the hands of Ningbo businessmen. In the nine director elections of the Shanghai General Chamber of Commerce from 1912 to 1929, except for the fifth and ninth elections, Ningbo businessmen swept the elections and were elected chairmen. No wonder French scholar Marie-Claire Bergere noted jokingly that "it seems that the Shanghai General Chamber of Commerce can only count as a branch of the Siming Council."[28] Another example involves the Shanghai money-shop guild controlled by the Ningbo Business Group. The principle through which the money-shop guild resolved disputes was that

> the principles of law officially published and regularly invoked in public litigations involving financial matters by relatively independent tribunals in the International Settlement. Once the lawful rights and interests of a local bank member is violated by an organization outside the Shanghai area and such could not be resolved through negotiation, the guild often resorts to a multilateral punishment mechanism to notify all its members and demand discontinuation of all transactions with said organization.[29]

The Shanghai money-shop guild controlled by Ningbo businessmen on one hand constantly formalised and justified the rules they stipulated, and, on the other, mobilised the powerful force of "fellow countrymen" to maintain industry credit and the member interests of the Ningbo Business Group.

The fourth is the innovation mechanism of keeping pace with the times. Compared with mechanical adhering to fixed rules of the Anhui merchants and Shanxi merchants, the Ningbo Business Group could incessantly innovate and upgrade itself in accordance with a changed situation, which enabled it to play the unique role of a mediator between foreign businessmen and Chinese businessmen. The mechanism not only enhanced the overall strength of the business group but also expanded its credit network in its industrial and commercial activities.

To follow is an illustration of this mechanism taking the money-shop business of the Ningbo Business Group as an example. Through the development of the money-shop business of the Ningbo Business Group, we can roughly get a glimpse of the generation and operation mechanism of the Ningbo Business Group.

The money-shop business was one of the principal operations of the Ningbo Business Group in pre-liberation modern times. Though classified as an old-style financial institution in Shanghai at the time, the traditional money shops could not be replaced by new-style financial institutions immediately. Quite the contrary, the new-style banks still had to count on money shops for business development. For instance, without the support of the highly developed credit of the Ningbo money shops, new-style banks would have encountered many more obstacles in their development in China. The account transfer system initiated by Ningbo exchange shops not only indicated its eminent credit but also promoted the modernisation of the operation mode of traditional money shops.[30] When the Ningbo Business Group shifted its focus from Ningbo to Shanghai, the account transfer system gradually evolved into the transfer system universally adopted by Shanghai financial institutions. By way of institutional innovation such as the account transfer system, Ningbo money shops could quickly assimilate the new banking business in the face of the competition brought in by new financial institutions such as the new banks.

Some scholars noted that, at the end of the 19th century and the beginning of the 20th century, new-style banks faced difficulties in two aspects of developing their business. The first is that, along with the rapid growth of import-export turnover, the appropriate financial-turnover speed had to quicken accordingly. Due to the fact that foreign banks did not by themselves have the business information to carry out financial transactions between Chinese and foreign businessmen, they needed the cooperation and assistance of the native financial industry. The second reason is that well-capitalised banks had taken in huge amounts of capital at low interest rates; such capital needed an outlet, and therefore these banks needed partners. Meanwhile, the traditional money-shop industry was versed in the business practices and customs of native businesses, and their business procedures were simpler and more convenient. At the same time, the import-export business to which the money shops rendered service was constrained by insufficient capital resulting from their rapid growth. Hence, the Zhejiang money-shop business and banks, Chinese and foreign, entered a situation where they forged cooperation and mutual support in business.[31] From the perspective of the mechanisms of a specific credit operation, the Ningbo money shops played an important intermediary role in Sino foreign trade in pre-liberation modern times. In doing business with Chinese businessmen, foreign businessmen were hindered by the language barrier. Moreover, some foreign trades involved a tremendous amount of capital at a time when domestic businessmen, especially those medium and small businessmen in China, were either short on capital and could not advance funds to complete such transactions or could not win the trust of foreign businessmen due to the lack of a modern mortgage security system; both problems rendered foreign trades unattainable. By way of the native financial organisation, the money shops, the Ningbo Business Group provided domestic and foreign businessmen with two-way credit guarantees. The money shops on the one hand maintained long-term loan relationships with the small and medium domestic businesses and knew their situations inside-out, which reduced the credit risk due to information symmetry. All of this enabled money shops to provide credit guarantees to domestic small and medium businesses. The latter then produced the bill of exchange issued by the money shop in place of cash; this solved the problem of fund shortages faced by small and medium businesses. On the other hand, foreign businessmen were also willing to accept such bills of exchange issued by Ningbo money shops. They would then cash the bill from the money shop after delivery of goods. The reason that the bills issued by the Ningbo money shops were accepted is that, in addition to the fact that most compradors in Shanghai were Ningbo people and these compradors had more cooperation with foreign businessmen on the plane of interpersonal relationships generating the trust of the latter, there is another important reason. The most famous trade organisations in Shanghai – the Shanghai Money Shop Guild and the Shanghai General Chamber of Commerce – were both under the control of Ningbo businessmen. What is more, Ningbo people also had a firm background in the powerful fellow-countrymen society in Shanghai, which collectively endowed Ningbo businessmen with adequate credit capability in the eyes of foreign businessmen. Hence, by way of the money shops, Ningbo businessmen bridged trade exchanges between foreign businessmen and Chinese businessmen. The credit guarantees and intermediary functions displayed in the foreign-trade exchanges by Ningbo money shops certainly kept pace with the changing times of the Ningbo Business Group. Exactly as remarked by some scholars, in the operation activities of industry and commerce, the traditional money shops operated by the Ningbo Business Group coexisted with the modern banking industry without conflict. Traditional organisations such as hometown associations and councils, and fellowship unions set up in industrial and commercial enterprises, existed side by side with modern-style trade guilds and chambers of commerce, creating a situation where the immigrant spirit of settling down where one lives and the expectation of ultimately returning home highlighted each other.[32]

2.4.3 The Internal Logic of the Inheritance of China's Traditional Credit

Traditional Chinese credit is by nature a kind of folk social credit based on the native situation; it has high compatibility with the folk economy. In the southeast coastal areas such as Guangdong, Fujian, Jiangsu, and Zhejiang, areas of contemporary China, the economic developments there are mainly thanks to the growth of the private economy. However, the growth and sound development of this private economy are primarily due to folk credit. As the lubricant of economic activities, folk credit decreases transaction costs and promotes the union of private enterprises. This kind of credit has continued to date for its high compatibility with the social and cultural traditions of China. Therefore, examining the internal logic of the historical inheritance of traditional credit has both practical value and offers insight into scientific principles. This thesis summarises the internal logic of the historical inheritance of traditional credit as follows.

Firstly, the mutual penetration between traditional credit and business activities. Chinese society has traditionally been rooted in agricultural civilisation. The institutional policy of emphasising agriculture over commerce has led to commercial activities often arising from the necessity to produce in agricultural conditions where there was a huge population but limited tillable land available. Be it the traditional Anhui merchants, the Shanxi merchants, or the Ningbo merchants of the pre-liberation modern period, it is clear that none of their prosperity was attributable to the pressure for survival. Compared with immobile agricultural activities, commercial activities require outward migration from native lands, a tendency in conflict with agricultural culture which emphasises blood relationships and geographical relationships. Therefore, such activities encounter the problem of overcoming risks. Chinese merchants came up with the solution of uniting and developing businessmen from the same geographical area. The guild halls of the Anhui merchants and Shanxi merchants and the fellow-countrymen association of the Ningbo merchants all made the practice of uniting fellow-countrymen businessmen and thus played an important role in maintaining credit for said business groups.

Secondly, blood relationships, fellowship, and so on, became a core factor in naturally bonding business groups. Emphasis on blood relationships and geographical relationships has been a feature shared by business groups in traditional Chinese society in their outward expansion. Among the traditional business groups, the Anhui merchants were high in their clan consciousness. Anhui merchants doing business away from home usually improved their clan consciousness among business groups by building clan memorial halls, amending clan pedigrees, and regularly throwing clan-gathering activities. The Shanxi merchants and Ningbo merchants paid special attention to countrymen fellowship. In risk-laden business activities, such clan consciousness and the concept of fellowship gradually developed into an identification mark for distinguishing insiders and outsiders; for instance, an Anhui merchant could be identified through consulting clan pedigrees, whereas a Ningbo merchant could be distinguished through the unique dialect he spoke. This kind of identification mark further reinforced the network of insiders, while barring outsiders from entering the network. In conclusion, traditional credit featured rich local colour and was a locally based network of credit.

Thirdly, the employment guarantee system of the businessmen groups. Traditional Anhui merchants, Shanxi merchants, and Ningbo merchants of the pre-liberation modern period, in their outward expansion of business networks, usually achieved this objective through their distinctive apprentice system. Apprentices were usually selected from one's village or one's clan and had to be vouched for by persons of some reputation and financial strength. This institution was not only an effective way of expanding business networks; it was also an extremely effective way of guaranteeing credit. The apprentice initiation system of transmission, assistance, and guidance easily led to a situation in which businessmen of fellow villagers and members of the same clan clustered in a certain trade. Absent external mandatory institutional arrangement, Chinese businessmen groups continually expanded their business by way of this model.

Fourthly, internal informal credit maintenance mechanism. As a relatively closed relationship network, the informal force spawned from inside the business group exerted forceful constraints on its members. Anyone violating or refusing to comply with the rules of the circle faced collective exclusion from members of the circle and could hardly survive. There was, allegedly, such a practice in circulation among Anhui merchants: Anyone failing to repay his debts due to business failure would be exempted from all the debts he owed so long as he signed a receipt before his creditor claiming that he would quit his business activities forever. This seemingly insignificant punishment was actually a grave one to those who did business away from home. All credit transaction activities including business exchange, borrowing and lending, and business on credit were conducted within the circle. If nobody wanted your business, that was the end of your business. Therefore, as a network of acquaintances, there came into being an informal but effective external force for credit maintenance. Inside a closed network of relationships were embedded not just business activities but also an interpersonal network. In present-day China, people from the same area usually concentrate on one area and do the same business, gradually forming a monopoly because it is hard for outsiders to intrude into the business.

Fifthly, folk society autonomous governance is the social structural condition for the inheritance of traditional credit. Due to factors like information asymmetry and high direct governance cost, it is actually very difficult for the central government to exercise direct governance in local society and grassroots society. Exactly as pointed out by some scholars, the governance of traditional Chinese society is a typical, two-layered governance model of "separate governance at the central government level and the local government level." In other words, the central government is responsible for "governing the officials" and the local government for "governing the people."[33] The duties of "governing the people" that the local government are in charge of mainly include taxes, taxes in kind, and services. Thus, the public affairs of local society and grassroots society are mostly self-governed by the locality. As regards order maintenance in business activities, these duties naturally belong to affairs of minor significance of the folk society, which are usually resolved by autonomous organisations such as the guild, the merchants' council, and so on. However, this does not mean that this mode of business operation in China always works fine. There are still dilemmas in the operation of the autonomous governance of China's traditional credit. A business dispute will always invoke the administrative intervention of the local government. The implied motivation could be that the local government covets the tremendous wealth concentrated in the hands of the merchant or that the unchecked growth of such would constitute a threat to the local government. Therefore, this government intervention shows that the "merchant" is subject to "government" regulation.

As a form of social credit taking root in folk society and getting deeply ingrained in the native socio-historical tradition, the traditional credit of China carried with it great historical inertia. It did not break up during the rapid transformation of Chinese society in modern times. Quite the contrary: As an informal social rule in folk society, it displayed great advantages by reducing transaction costs and promoting economic cooperation. Given the fact that formal rules were lacking or remained imperfect, this kind of credit showed great tenacity because it played the role of "functional substitute." Under the present environment of China's social credit building, we tend to employ the modern social credit system and institutions originated in the mature Western market economy; however, in terms of social credit governance, many places have inherited the methods and modes of traditional credit.

Notes

1 Cheng Yanjun, Du Haiying, On the Basic Characteristics and Causes of China's Ancient Contract Law System, *Journal of Inner Mongolia University* 2007(2), pp.38-43.
2 Ibid.
3 Chun Yang, *Study on Civil Dispute Mediation Mechanism of Late Qing Dynasty Rural Community*, Peking University Press, 2009, pp. 38–56.
4 See Liu Chongri, Zuo Yunhe, Preliminary Investigation of Broker and Brokerage, appeared in Collected Papers on Studies of Capitalism in Embryo of the Ming and Qing Dynasties, compiled by Ming and Qing Dynasties Research Office of the History Department of Nanjing University, Shanghai People's Publishing House, 2001, p. 199; Zhuang Weimin, *Evolution of Intermediary and Transactional System in Pre-liberation Modern Times*, Zhong Hua Book Company, 2012, p. 133.
5 Tian Tao, *Millennium of Covenant*, Law Press, 2012, p. 54.
6 Emile Durkheim, *Professional Ethics and Civic Morals*, translated by Qu Dong, Fu Degen, Shanghai People's Press, 2001, p. 66.
7 Fei Tsiao Tung, From the Soil: The Foundations of Chinese Society, p. 10.
8 Zhai Xuewei, *The Chinese Notions of Face*. Peking University Press, 2010, p. 124.
9 Chun Yang, *Study on Civil Dispute Mediation Mechanism of Late Qing Dynasty Rural Community*, pp. 232–235.

10 Li Xuelan, *Customary Law of Chinese Merchant Groups*, China Social Sciences Press, 2010, p. 72.
11 Zhang Weiying, Deng Feng, Information, Incentive and Collateral Liability – Legal and Economic Interpretation of the Collateral Penalty, Neighbourhood Administrative System in Ancient China, *Social Sciences in China* 2003(3).
12 Yang Liansheng, *The Meanings of "Report," "Vouch for," "Wrap" in Chinese*, Guizhou People's Press, 2009, pp. 15–16.
13 Li Zhuhuan, The Phenomenon of Intermediary in China's Traditional Civil Contract. Chinese Journal of Law: 1997(6).
14 Ibid.
15 Huang Zongzhi, *Laws, Society and Culture of the Qing Dynasty: Expressions and Practices of the Civil Law*, Shanghai Bookstore Publishing House, 2007, pp. 44–45.
16 E. A. Hoebel, *The Law of the Primitive Man – A Study in Comparative Legal Dynamics*, China Social Sciences Press, 1993, p. 29.
17 Zhang Zhengming et al. compiled, *Study on China's Shangxi Merchants*. People's Publishing House, 2006, p. 75.
18 Zhang Haipeng, Wang Tingyuan compil, *Anthology of Materials of Anhui Merchants in the Ming and Qing Dynasties*, Huangshan Publishing House, 1985, p. 258.
19 Ibid.
20 See Shi Hui. *The Generative Mechanism and Application Method of Shanxi Merchant's Credit System*. Postgraduate degree paper. Shanxi University, 2006, p. 13.
21 Zhengming et al., *Study on China's Shangxi Merchants*, p. 11.
22 Zhang Shouguang, *History of Ningbo Business Group*. Ningbo Publishing House, 2012, p. 142.
23 Compiled by Dou Jiliang, *Study on Fellow Countrymen Organizations*. Zhengzhong Bookstore, 1943, p. 22.
24 Lin Shujian, *The Ningbo Merchants*, Fujian People's Publishing House, 1998, p. 120.
25 Li Jian, *Ningbo People in Shanghai*, Shanghai People's Publishing House, 2000, p. 96.
26 Bao Jie et al compiled, *On Pre-liberation Ningbo Business Group*, Ningbo Publishing House, 1996, pp. 26–50.
27 Shouguang, *History of Ningbo Business Group*, pp. 38–39.
28 Wang Yuxian, *Six Hundred Years of China's Business Groups*, CITIC Publishing House, 2011, p. 241.
29 Ma Debin, Traditional Chinese Law and Commerce: an Institutional Perspective of the "Great Divergence." Liu Qiugen, Ma Debin compiled. Tradition and Evolution of China's Industry and Commerce, Financial Industry – Symposium of International Academic Seminar on China's Industry and Commerce, Financial History from the 10th to 20th Century, Hebei University Press, 2008, p. 18.
30 Cited from Chen Quanya, *A Cross Section View of China's Native Commercial Banks: Ningbo Money Shops*, Zhejiang University Press, 2010, p. 65.
31 Lv Jiansuo, *A Comparative Study of Credit Systems between Zhejiang Money Shops and Shanxi Exchange Shops*, China Social Sciences Press, 2013, p. 81.
32 Shouguang, *History of Ningbo Business Group*, p. 378.
33 Cao Zhenghan, China's Two-Layered Governance System and Its Stabilizing Mechanism, *Sociological Research* 2011(1).

References

Bao, J. (1996). *On pre-liberation Ningbo business group*. Ningbo Publishing House.

Cao, Z. (2011). China's two-layered governance system and its stabilizing mechanism. *Sociological Research*, *1*, 1–40+243. https://doi.org/10.19934/j.cnki.shxyj.2011.01.001

Chen, Q. (2010). *A cross section view of China's native commercial banks: Ningbo money shops*. Zhejiang University Press.
Cheng, Y., & Du, H. (2007). On the basic characteristics and causes of China's ancient contract law system. *Journal of Inner Mongolia University*, *2*, 38–43. https://doi.org/10.13484/j.cnki.ndxbzsb.2007.02.009
Chun, Y. (2009). *Study on civil dispute mediation mechanism of late Qing Dynasty rural community*. Peking University Press.
Dou, J. (1943). *Study on fellow countrymen organizations*. Zhengzhong Bookstore.
Durkheim, E. (2001). *Professional ethics and civic morals* (D. Qu & D. Fu, Trans.). Shanghai People's Press.
Fei, T. (1998). *From the soil: The foundations of Chinese society*. Peking University Press.
Hoebel, E. A. (1993). *The law of the primitive man: A study in comparative legal dynamics*. Trans. China Social Sciences Press.
Huang, Z. (2007). *Laws, society and culture of the Qing Dynasty: Expressions and practices of the civil law*. Shanghai Bookstore Publishing House.
Li, J. (2000). *Ningbo people in Shanghai*. Shanghai People's Publishing House.
Li, X. (2010). *Customary law of Chinese merchant groups*. China Social Sciences Press.
Li, Z. (1997). The phenomenon of intermediary in China's traditional civil contract. *Chinese Journal of Law*, *6*, 136–141.
Lin, S. (1998). *The Ningbo merchants*. Fujian People's Publishing House.
Liu, C., & Zuo, Y. (1981). Preliminary investigation of broker and brokerage, appeared in collected papers on studies of capitalism in Embryo of the Ming and Qing Dynasties, compiled by Ming and Qing Dynasties Research Office of the History Department of Nanjing University, Shanghai People's Publishing House.
Lv, J. (2013). *A comparative study of credit systems between Zhejiang money shops and Shanxi exchange shops*. China Social Sciences Press.
Ma, D. (2008). Traditional Chinese law and commerce: An institutional perspective of the 'great divergence'. In L. Qiugen (Ed.), *Ma Debin compiled. Tradition and evolution of China's industry and commerce, financial industry –symposium of international academic seminar on China's industry and commerce, financial history from the 10th to 20th century*. pp. 3–23. Hebei University Press. ,
Shi, H. (2006). *The generative mechanism and application method of Shanxi merchant's credit system*. (Postgraduate degree paper, Shanxi University). https://kns.cnki.net/KCMS/detail/detail.aspx?dbname=CMFD0506&filename=2006101863.nh
Tian, T. (2012). *Millennium of covenant*. Law Press.
Wang, Y. (2011). *Six hundred years of China's business groups*. CITIC Publishing House.
Yang, L. (2009). *The meanings of "report," "vouch for," "wrap" in Chinese*. Guizhou People's Press.
Zhai, X. (2010). *The Chinese notions of face*. Peking University Press.
Zhang, H., & Wang, T. (1985). *Anthology of materials of Anhui merchants in the Ming and Qing Dynasties*. Huangshan Publishing House.
Zhang, S. (2012). *History of Ningbo business group*. Ningbo Publishing House.
Zhang, W., & Deng, F. (2003). Information, incentive and collateral liability: Legal and economic interpretation of the collateral penalty, neighbourhood administrative system in ancient China. *Social Sciences in China*, *3*, 99–112+207.
Zhang, Z. (2006). *Study on China's Shangxi merchants*. People's Publishing House.
Zhuang, W. (2012). *Evolution of intermediary and transactional system in pre-liberation modern times*. Zhong Hua Book Company.

3 The Status Quo of China's Social Credit

In order to verify the overall assumption proposed in Chapter 1 – namely, that in China the degree of homogeneity exceeds that of heterogeneity – we attempt below to describe the phenomenon via empirical research, focusing on: (1) the current state of China's social credit; (2) the cognition of the differentiation and purity of the various aspects and levels of society (mainly including the government, market, and symbols) by the Chinese people; (3) the effect on society of benefit-pursuit activity in marketisation; and (4) the state of social-capital operation.

In this section, we first describe the various dimensions and aspects of China's social credit by analysing data obtained from a questionnaire survey. This survey inspects varying types of behaviours of social credit from three aspects, including politics–government credit, society–market credit, and individual–interpersonal credit. Then an overarching comparison and investigation shall be conducted on these different aspects.

3.1 Survey Design

3.1.1 Survey Methods

A structured questionnaire shall be employed in the survey. The reason for the adoption of a rigorous, large-scale structured questionnaire is mainly based on the following considerations: Firstly, understanding contemporary Chinese social credit involves the three main systems of social credit, namely, personal credit, market credit, and government credit, covering fields including medical services, science and technology, education, the judiciary, and administration. More importantly, due to the imbalance of economic development between the different parts of China, especially differences between the cities, we hope that we may arrive at a relatively comprehensive understanding of the basic situation of China's social credit through a nationwide sampling survey. Secondly, in order to effect this objective, the basic characteristics of China's social credit may only be arrived at through pooling the credit data of the different parts of China.

What merits explanation is that we have come to the understanding that utilising the same questionnaire across China in our investigation of China's social credit will in fact lead to ignoring the city-countryside differences; that is to say, there are marked differences between existence and development in the countryside and

DOI: 10.4324/9781003375579-5

that in the city. These differences included, for instance, modes of living, interaction and consumption, as well as government-led governance. As such, the study designed two sets of different questionnaires, with some questions appearing in both questionnaires, and some in one or the other; then a comparison is run on data collection and analysis. Moreover, there are other situations to be investigated separately.

3.1.2 Notes on the Determination of Main Research Variables

3.1.2.1 Type Classification of Social Credit

Firstly, for those parts of Chinese society that emphasise government dominance, government credit assumes a core place and plays a decisive, orientational role in the social credit system. However, political ideas and the reasonableness of political systems closely related to governmental credit also play an important role in the building of the social credit system. Of course, the concept of government credit obviously could not include more abstract entities such as political ideas and political systems.

Secondly, market credit came into being along with the implementation of the reform and opening policy, which centred "upon establishing the market economy." As the most important and essential part of the social credit system, market credit covers the absolute majority of the content of social credit, that is to say, it is both directly related to the everyday life of average people, and it is the most important extension of government credit in socio-public domains. The domains in which it operates not only include the market and consumption, but also extends to public spaces of greater range such as abstract sign systems, expert systems, and even charity. Therefore, the credit situation of these socio-public domains and the credit of the market domain jointly constitute the most important content of the social credit system.

Finally, personal credit in the economic sense is studied more from the perspective of economics or finance, and such is viewed as the ability of the individual to acquire commodities, services, or capital on the basis of personal payment or a commitment to repayment. In fact, personal credit should firstly be reduced to a set of basic moral principles that refer to beliefs and behaviours regarding integrity and promise-keeping in socio-economic activities. Therefore, personal credit not only includes the credit performance of the individual in economic activities but is also manifest in basic views on personal integrity in everyday intercourse. In addition to personal credit, credit on the micro-level also includes interpersonal credit situations.

Based on the foregoing discussion and analysis, the authors divide social credit into three major categories: politics (government credit, society), market credit, and individual credit (interpersonal credit). Research on these three aspects of credit may help us understand and grasp the current situation of China's social credit in a comprehensive way.

3.1.2.2 Measurement and Determination of Social Credit Variables

The measurement and determination of the social credit situation elaborated in this chapter mainly reflect the objective appraisal of the general public on the social credit situation of the various social realms in contemporary China.

POLITICS–GOVERNMENT CREDIT

"Politics–government credit" refers to political ideas, the rationality of the political system, and the integrity and promise-keeping of political entities in their activities. It manifests itself through the people's trust in the government and the political system, i.e., the state of the government or political system and the beliefs or faith of people's expectations. They involve both the macro- or organisational aspects – for instance, the confidence of the people in the performance of a certain political institution, organisation, or government – and they also include micro- or personal aspects – for instance, the public rating of government officials, or officials. What is reflected thereby is the potential operational costs of government as well its relationship with the people – for instance, whether such relationships are consistent, harmonious, suspicious, or conflicting.

The present research will investigate government–political credit primarily from three perspectives: institutional credit, performance credit, and personnel credit.

Institutional credit mainly refers to people's credibility in government agencies, law-enforcement institutions, and party organisations at all levels. The institutions specifically include "the central government, the provincial government, the prefectural and municipal governments, the district and county-level governments, the grass-root sub-district offices, the court, the military, public security, and party organisations at various levels." Performance credit refers to the degree of satisfaction of the people in the implementation of various policies closely related to people's everyday life. It examines the public-satisfaction rating of the key functions or institutions of the government in areas that include market supervision, employment, education, and social security. Indicators actually adopted include ten aspects such as "food supervision, earthquake and disaster relief, environmental protection, compulsory education, charity, the judicial system, the household registration system, the pension system, the medical insurance system, and the social-relief system," which covers practically all functions of government at various levels. Personnel credit refers to the satisfaction rating of the administrative staff as a whole. In this study, we will take the state public servant as a whole in our discussion of public-servant credit in the general sense of the term. It contains two dimensions: Firstly, administrative character, which specifically refers to the service consciousness of the public servant, i.e., whether they are dedicated to serving the people, display integrity, and safeguard the public interest; secondly, administrative capability, that is, whether public servants are capable of handling administrative affairs and manifest such in the execution of their duties.

SOCIETY–MARKET CREDIT

Whether politics–government credit takes root in the public political domain may be defined as a reflection of the abstract and general assessment of specific institutions, organisations, and social groups by the general public. The credit originating in the domain of society–market credit reflects the fact that the general public obtains both a greater and more intimate understanding of their personal interests.

We mainly investigate from three vantage points that rate the credit situation of public domains of society and the market: symbol and expert system credit, charity credit, and consumer credit. Symbol and expert system credit reflects the public rating of the abstract credit system, which holds considerable sway in the domain of public life. This credit of the abstract system mainly manifests itself through symbol credit and expert system credit. "Symbol credit" refers to the credit rating of symbol information (such as educational background, diplomas, qualification certificates, industrial standards, protocols, etc.), whereas "expert system credit" refers to the commitment expectation of the expert from a special area or of their knowledge, capability, and professional ethics. In addition, charity credit has manifested as one of the most prominent problems in the public domain in recent years and has gained widespread attention from the public. The authors study the charity credit of citizens in the following ways: (1) knowledge about charity organisations, (2) state of participation in charity activities (the foregoing two criteria are the basic prerequisites for the generation of charity credit), and (3) the charity credit situation of citizens, including trust in charity organisations, attitudes toward celebrity charity, trust in the means of donation, trust in the effect of charity activities, and so forth.

Market credit is generated when market entities honour their commitments and perform their obligations in market transactions. Market credit includes bank credit, corporate credit, and consumer credit. The fact that bank credit and corporate credit are in keener need of objective indicators (for instance, bad loans, non-performing loans in bank loans, enterprises dodging debt, scrapping debt, refusing to honour contracts, fiscal fraud, cooking the books, counterfeit or substandard products in market activities, and information fraud) has led to the need for the survey. Generally, such objective indicators cannot be obtained through a questionnaire survey; therefore, this study limits itself to an investigation of the consumer credit that arises through market activities. Specifically, it includes the public's cognitive rating of four phenomena: product quality, post-sales service, branding, and advertisements. It also involves the strategy choices of citizens settling civil disputes arising from consumption.

INDIVIDUAL–INTERPERSONAL CREDIT

According to the framework we set up in the foregoing chapter, personal credit is obviously the foundation of the whole social credit system. For the government and the people, only when the idea of personal integrity has been established in the whole of society can there be a solid foundation for corporate credit and government credit. Personal credit is not limited to the economic and financial realms; it also concerns socio-political life, cultural background, history, and culture. This study involves two levels of personal credit. The first level concerns the set of assumptions held by individuals regarding the goodness or evilness of human nature and the way these assumptions affect behaviour and social interaction. It is a personal attitude; we call it "personal credit" in the specific sense. The second level of personal credit involves the degree of trust or dependence on a special individual (for instance, a family member, a stranger) with whom one associates in interpersonal communication; we call it "interpersonal credit," which is also commonly known as "trust."

The value judgements of personal credit are founded on the cultural setup of the society in which one resides and include assumptions about human nature and views on personal gain and loss. Therefore, we will gauge these value judgements through an investigation of the relevant common phrases widespread in society. Interpersonal credit usually measures the subjective distance between a person and his counterpart in communication: for instance, a family member, friend, country fellow, or colleague. It also includes those outsiders and strangers who reside beyond the immediate blood relationships, genetic relationships, and geographic relationships. However, bearing a close relationship of interest with the people.

3.1.2.3 Sampling Design and Implementation of Survey

SURVEY SUBJECTS

The survey subjects in this study are adults residing in the China mainland, 18 years old or above, including regular residents of the countryside and the city.

SAMPLING PLAN

To better represent the overall situation of the country in the results, this study has taken full consideration of the differences in the sampling areas (including factors like geography, urban-country designations, levels of economic development, and so on) before settling on the six areas of Nanjing, Tianjin, Chongqing, Shenzhen, Lanzhou, and Yinchuan. The sampling area covers east China, north China, southwest China, and northwest China, respectively (given the difficulty of accessing resident homes and the fees attached, we have not considered megacities like Beijing and Shanghai). We ran the sampling method to determine which communities from the cities above we'd survey. The survey was then conducted on all the chosen urban and countryside samples. Meanwhile, in order to more effectively compare whether there were differences in social credit between areas of differing degrees of marketisation and modernisation, religion, and ethnicity, we specifically sampled the peripheral rural areas of Shenzhen and Yinchuan of the Ningxia Hui Autonomous Region. For instance, a city is divided into three levels: the district–sub-district–neighbourhood community. Thus, sampling was conducted in the 3-2-1 manner, that is, three administrative districts were sampled from each city, two sub-districts from each district, and one neighbourhood community from each sub-district, resulting in six communities altogether. The neighbourhood communities were selected based on simple random sampling. Rural areas were also sampled at three levels in the 2-2-1 manner. The three levels: county–town–village. Two administrative counties were sampled from the rural areas, two towns from each county, and one village from each town, with four natural villages sampled in total. Each village was also selected through a simple random sampling. Altogether 5,500 questionnaires were distributed through the survey, of which 3,300 questionnaires were conducted in the city and 2,200 questionnaires in the rural area. Altogether, 5,296 effective questionnaires were recovered, with a recovery rate amounting to 96.3%. Of these, 3,138 city questionnaires were recovered and 2,158 rural questionnaires, accounting for 59.3% and 40.7% of the total sample, respectively.

Due to the limitations of a data collection method for an indoor survey, we need to consider the implications of "no response" to the survey. In other words, in the actual survey process, there is a possibility that the survey will not be successful, e.g., the address is unoccupied, the household does not cooperate in the survey (refusal) or the respondent does not have the actual capacity to fill in the questionnaire. In such cases, and when we need to ensure a certain sample size, the problem of alternative samples is involved. In this case, we have adopted a supplementary sampling treatment scheme. When the sample size failed to satisfy the survey requirements, new samples would be drawn according to established sampling solutions, the specific procedures of which are as follows: Regarding a non-responsive residence on the first visit, a re-visit after one hour would be conducted; if there was still no response, a third visit would be conducted half a day later; a household visit would also be conducted on the third day, if necessary. All households with three non-responses would be considered "no response" samples. Meanwhile, in-house households sampled in which the adults were unable to fill out the questionnaires due to illness or other force majeure were also considered "no response." In response to the situation, we adopted "supplementary sampling," that is, we resampled according to established sampling plans, making supplementary samples and continuing the process until the responses reached the predetermined sample size.

SURVEY IMPLEMENTATION

The present study adopts in-house self-filling questionnaires as the data collection method. The survey is implemented in two stages. First, a pilot survey is conducted. In the pilot survey, a small-size sample is drawn from the sample subjects to collect data according to the same sampling method, so as to test the data collection instrument (namely, the questionnaire), and to evaluate the quality of the survey. Therefore, the pilot survey plays a key role in a large-scale, in-house survey. For this purpose, prior to the rollout of the formal survey, the present study in October 2011 conducted a pilot survey in accordance with the multiple-section sampling method set out in the foregoing paragraphs. The present study handed out 400 questionnaires in all, 200 for the city and 200 for the countryside. After the pilot survey, we ran a pre-analysis of the data collected and made adjustments to the original questionnaire design according to feedback on the survey process and the survey findings. The results took their final form in the official version of the Survey Questionnaire on China's Social Credit System.

The official survey was conducted between November 2011 and January 2012. In-house self-filling questionnaires were employed; that is, the interviewer decided on the interviewee after entering the resident's house according to sampling requirements and asked the interviewee to fill out the questionnaire on his own. And the interviewer explained and illustrated the survey. The advantage of this method was that the difficulties of the questionnaire could be instantly resolved, and, on the other hand, a maximal recovery rate could be guaranteed. However, there remained the biggest obstacle to an in-house survey – "gaining entrance" – that is, the interviewer had to access the resident's house and get the interviewee to fill out the questionnaire. Therefore, to improve the response rate to an in-house survey, the survey was usually conducted on weekends in the city and at noon or in the s in rural areas so as to diminish the occurrence of no responses.

METHODS OF DATA PROCESSING AND ANALYSIS

Data collected in this study were analysed in SPSS 17.0 for Windows. All questionnaire items to be rated on the social credit situation were graded on a Likert Scale of 5. The analysis methods on the returned results mainly include frequency analysis, crosstabs, hypothesis testing, etc. In order to get more intuitive results, the scale of 5 was converted to a percentage system. In conducting crosstabs analysis, the chi-square test was employed between nominal measurements and nominal measurements and between nominal measurements and ordinal measurements. tau-b and Gamma tests were employed on the crosstabs analysis between ordinal measurements and ordinal measurements.

3.1.3 Social Demographic Situation of the Interviewees

The social demographics of the interviewees in the study are presented in Tables 3.1–3.10.

Table 3.1 Distribution of interviewees in city and countryside

City or rural area	*Frequency*	*Percentage*	*Effective percentage*	*Cumulative percentage*
City	3,138	59.3	59.3	59.3
Rural	2,158	40.7	40.7	100.0
Sum total	5,296	100.0	100.0	

Table 3.2 Geographical distribution of interviewees

City or rural area	*Frequency*	*Percentage*	*Effective percentage*	*Cumulative percentage*
Tianjin	1,065	20.1	20.1	20.1
Nanjing	1,063	20.1	20.1	40.2
Lanzhou	1,060	20.0	20.0	60.2
Chong-qing	1,086	20.5	20.5	80.7
Shen-zhen	594	11.2	11.2	91.9
Ningxia	428	8.1	8.1	100.0
Sum total	5,296	100.0	100.0	

Table 3.3 Age distribution of interviewees

Age (years)	*Frequency*	*Percentage*	*Effective percentage*	*Cumulative percentage*
18–20	227	4.3	4.3	4.3
21–24	509	9.6	9.7	14.0
25–29	684	12.9	13.0	26.9
30–34	649	12.3	12.3	39.3
35–39	604	11.4	11.5	50.7
40–44	651	12.3	12.4	63.1
45–49	601	11.3	11.4	74.5
50–54	415	7.8	7.9	82.3
55–59	379	7.2	7.2	89.5
60–64	278	5.2	5.3	94.8
65 and older	274	5.2	5.2	100.0
Sum total	5,271	99.5	100.0	
System missing	25	.5		
Sum total	5,296	100.0		

Table 3.4 Gender distribution of interviewees

Gender	*Frequency*	*Percentage*	*Effective percentage*	*Cumulative percentage*
Male	2,543	48.0	48.2	48.2
Female	2,733	51.6	51.8	100.0
Effective	5,276	99.6	100.0	
Missing	20	.4		
Sum total	5,296	100.0		

Table 3.5 Marriage status distribution of interviewees

Marriage status	*Frequency*	*Percentage*	*Effective percentage*	*Cumulative percentage*
Married	4,209	79.5	79.7	79.7
Unmarried	942	17.8	17.8	97.5
Widow, widower, or divorced	131	2.5	2.5	100.0
Sum total	5,282	99.7	100.0	
System missing	14	.3		
Sum total	5,296	100.0		

Table 3.6 Ethnicity distribution of interviewees

	Ethnicity	*Frequency*	*Percentage*	*Effective percentage*	*Cumulative percentage*
Effective	Han	4,747	89.6	89.8	89.8
	Minority ethnicity	537	10.1	10.2	100.0
	Sum total	5,284	99.8	100.0	
missing	system	12	.2		
Sum total		5,296	100.0		

Table 3.7 Religious distribution of interviewees

	Religious faith	*Frequency*	*Percentage*	*Effective percentage*	*Cumulative percentage*
Effective	Non-religious	4,086	77.2	77.4	77.4
	Religious	1,195	22.6	22.6	100.0
	Sum total	5,281	99.7	100.0	
	System	15	.3		
	Sum total	5,296	100.0		

Table 3.8 Distribution in city and countryside of interviewees

	Level of education	*Frequency*	*Percentage*	*Effective percentage*	*Cumulative percentage*
Effective missing	Primary school and below	783	14.8	14.8	14.8
	Junior middle school	1,464	27.6	27.7	42.5
	Senior middle school	1,331	25.1	25.2	67.6
	Two-year degree	734	13.9	13.9	81.5
	Four-year degree and above	978	18.5	18.5	100.0
	Sum total	5,290	99.9	100.0	
	System	6	.1		
	Sum total	5,296	100.0		

Table 3.9 Income distribution of interviewees

	Annual income (yuan)	*Frequency*	*Percentage*	*Effective percentage*	*Cumulative percentage*
Effective missing	Below 2,000	154	2.9	3.3	3.3
	2,001–4,000	138	2.6	3.0	6.3
	4,001–6,000	187	3.5	4.0	10.3
	6,001–8,000	122	2.3	2.6	13.0
	8,001–10,000	641	12.1	13.8	26.8
	10,001–15,000	453	8.6	9.8	36.6
	15,001–20000	805	15.2	17.4	53.9
	20,001–50,000	1383	26.1	29.8	83.8
	50,001–100,000	522	9.9	11.3	95.0
	100,001–150,000	119	2.2	2.6	97.6
	150,001–200,000	68	1.3	1.5	99.1
	Over 200,001	44	.8	.9	100.0
	Sum total	4636	87.5	100.0	
	System	660	12.5		
Sum total		5296	100.0		

Table 3.10 Political status distribution of interviewees

	Political status	*Frequency*	*Percentage*	*Effective percentage*	*Cumulative percentage*
Effective	CCP member	926	17.5	17.6	17.6
missing	Communist Youth League member	588	11.1	11.1	28.7
	Unaffiliated mass	3,685	69.6	69.8	98.5
	Others	77	1.5	1.5	100.0
	Sum total	5,276	99.6	100.0	
	system	20	.4		
Sum total		5,296	100.0		

3.2 Basic Forms of China's Social Credit

In the foregoing chapters, we have proposed an overall assumption in research regarding the homogeneity of the contemporary Chinese social structure and its operation. Due to the fact that homogeneity cannot be attained uniformly in various fields, we would, by way of the survey data collected, demonstrate the argument from the various aspects of the four parts, namely, politics–government credit, society–market credit, individual–interpersonal credit, and the state of social participation. In this way, we will carry out a discussion of this assumption about the homogeneity of Chinese society.

3.2.1 Politics–Government Credit

First, let's examine the aspect of performance credit. On the whole, the interviewees all rated the ten items we set regarding credit of government performance relatively low. Indeed, even the highest-rated item, "earthquake and calamity relief" (rated 76.87), failed to attain a good grade in the credit rating. The rest of the grades are mostly somewhere around the pass mark, with the lowest score – "food supervision" – only achieving a 48.45 (see Figure 3.1). Specifically, the higher the education level of the interviewee, the lower the performance credit scores on the various items. In terms of political status, the politically unaffiliated give higher performance credit scores than League members, non-CCP members, and CCP members, in descending order, and that score is almost ten points higher than the lowest scoring group – the CCP member group. In terms of the differences between the city and the rural area, city-dweller interviewees score much lower than their countryside counterparts, with scores generally below the pass mark (see Tables 3.1, 3.2, and 3.3). In addition, there was also a multitude of "non-committal" attitudes recorded in the performance credit rating; for instance, 25.6% and 28.9% of interviewees endorsed the option for "charity cause" and "environmental protection" (see Table 3.11). To understand this ambiguous attitude in the cultural context of China, we must first understand the suspicion of performance credit in that context.

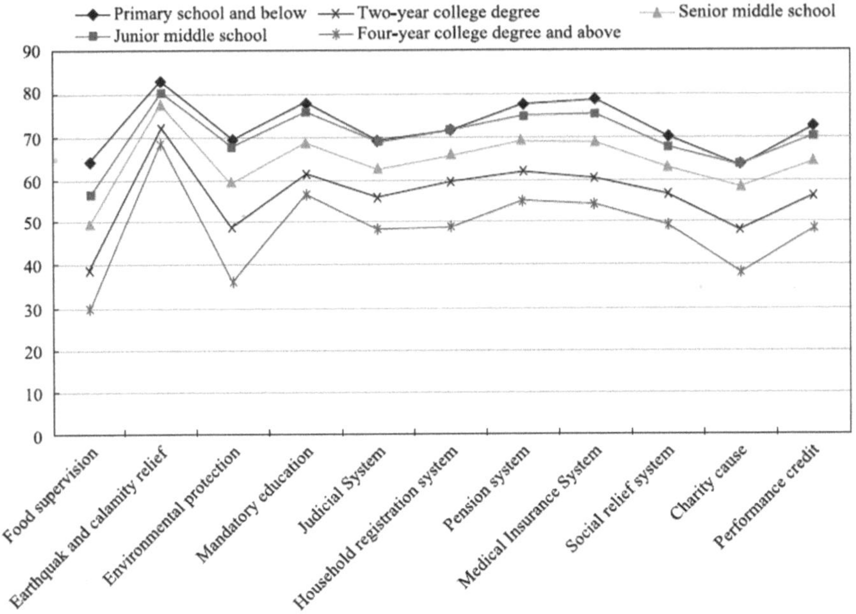

Figure 3.1 Performance credit of interviewees of different levels of education

Next, let's examine the ratings of credit performance by employees of institutions and agencies. Generally speaking, interviewees' credit ratings on the various institutions and agencies are all basically around the low marks of pass and roughly pass, with average scores standing at 70.74 (see Figure 3.4).

Specifically, from the perspective of education, the higher the education an interviewee receives, or the higher educational background an interviewee has, the lower the trust he has in governmental agencies. In terms of political status, the politically unaffiliated rate the performance credit of governmental agencies higher than CCP members, League members, and non-CCP party members. In terms of the differences between the city and the rural area, city-dwelling interviewees score much lower than their countryside counterparts (see Figures 3.5, 3.6, 3.7).

Generally speaking, credit ratings by interviewees who are government employees (public functionaries) are universally very low, all ratings are below pass marks, with the highest-rated item barely a pass (66.37) (see Figure 3.8). The lowest scoring areas were three statements, namely, "most government officials are honest and dutiful," "most government officials are dedicated to the public interest," and "most government officials can execute their duties in accordance with the law." The combined percentage of effective attitudes held by interviewees of "distrust" and "neutral/cannot explain" on these three items comprise 53.2%, 51.5%, and 58.1% (see Table 3.12). This all indicates a serious attitude of scepticism on the part of the interviewees towards the administrative integrity

Table 3.11 Effective percentage of performance credit

Government performance	*Unsatisfactory*			*Neutral*	*Satisfactory*		
	Very unsatisfactory	*Relatively unsatisfactory*	*Sum of the two*	*Cannot explain*	*Pretty satisfactory*	*Very satisfactory*	*Sum of the two*
Food supervision	18.0%	23.4%	41.3%	16.0%	32.3%	10.4%	42.7%
Earthquake and calamity relief	1.9%	4.2%	6.1%	10.8%	50.8%	32.3%	83.1%
Environmental protection	10.0%	18.9%	28.9%	17.3%	39.2%	14.6%	53.8%
Mandatory education	5.2%	10.2%	15.4%	13.0%	47.8%	23.8%	71.6%
Judicial system	5.8%	10.6%	16.4%	28.2%	41.5%	13.9%	55.4%
Household registration system	5.4%	10.2%	15.6%	23.3%	44.0%	17.1%	61.1%
Pension system	5.0%	10.3%	15.3%	16.0%	44.7%	24.1%	68.8%
Medical insurance system	5.1%	11.1%	16.2%	14.8%	44.4%	24.6%	69.0%
Social relief system	6.3%	12.8%	19.1%	26.1%	37.4%	17.4%	54.8%
Charity cause	9.1%	16.5%	25.6%	29.2%	32.8%	12.4%	45.2%

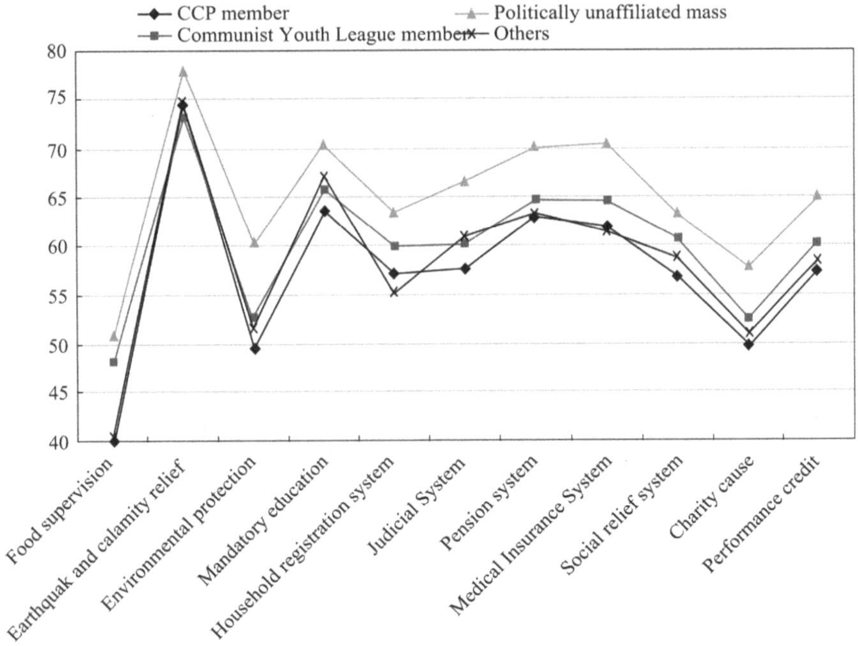

Figure 3.2 Performance credit of interviewees of different political status

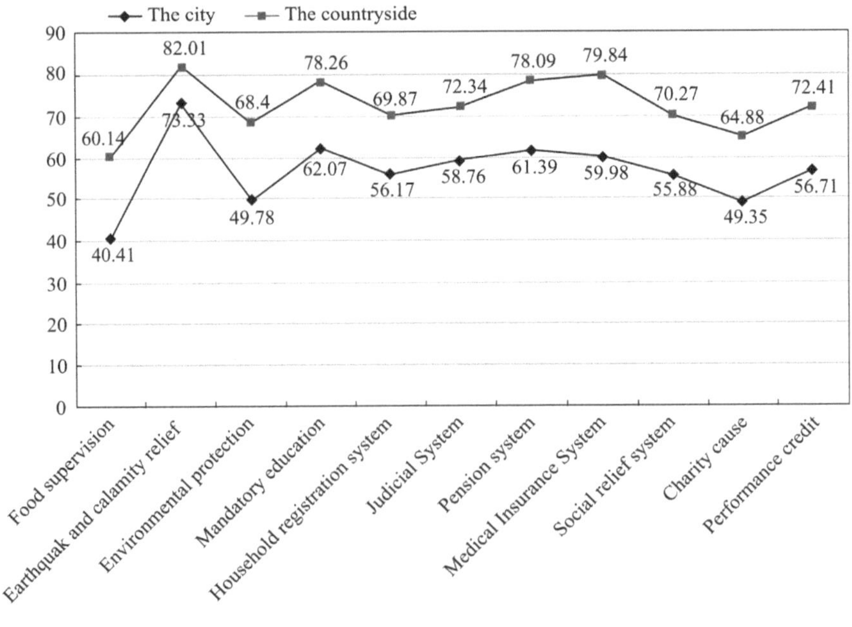

Figure 3.3 Performance credit of interviewees between the city and the countryside

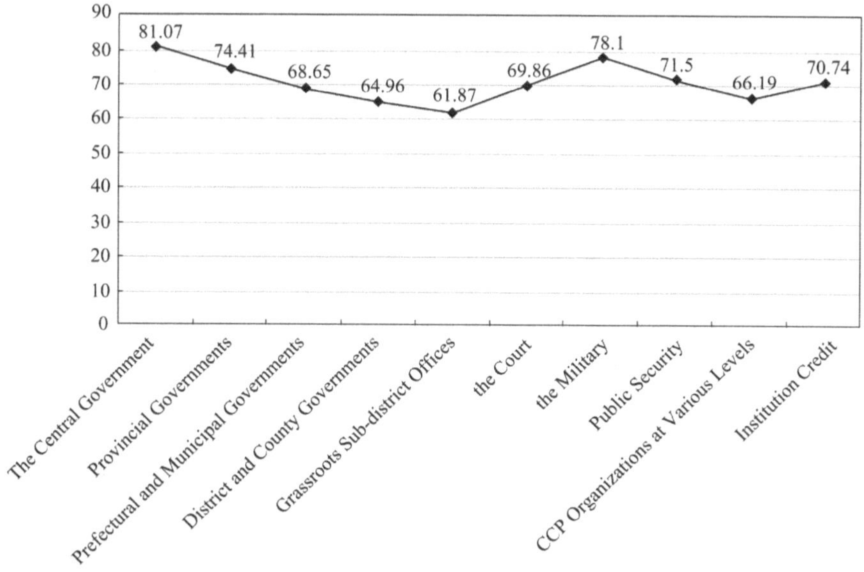

Figure 3.4 Average values of institution credit (%)

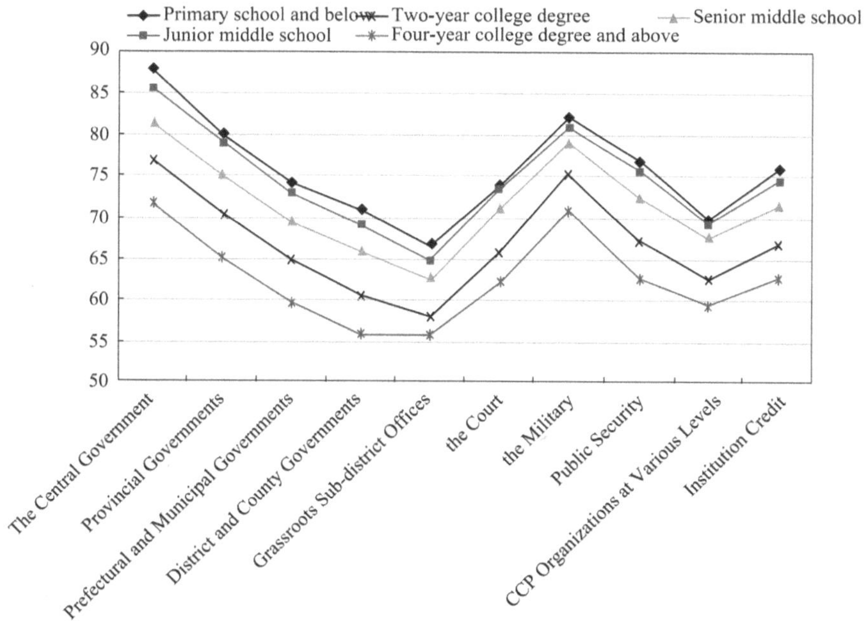

Figure 3.5 Trust in government agencies by interviewees of different levels of education

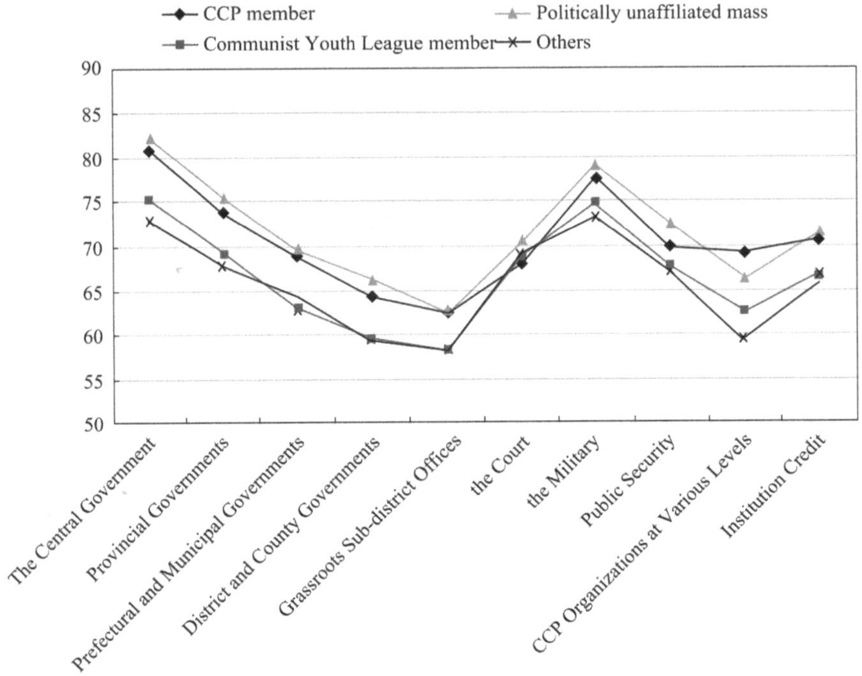

Figure 3.6 Trust in government agencies by interviewees with different political status

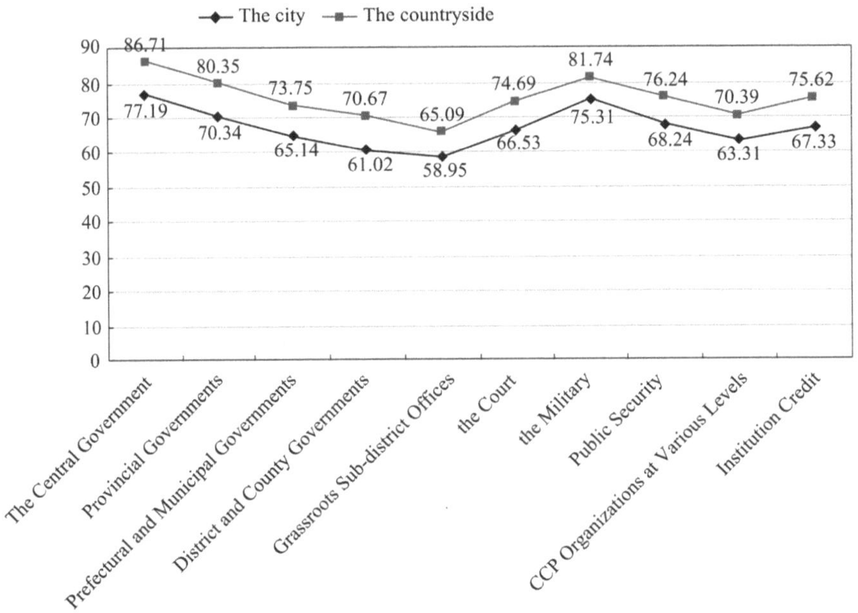

Figure 3.7 Trust in government agencies by urban and rural dwellers

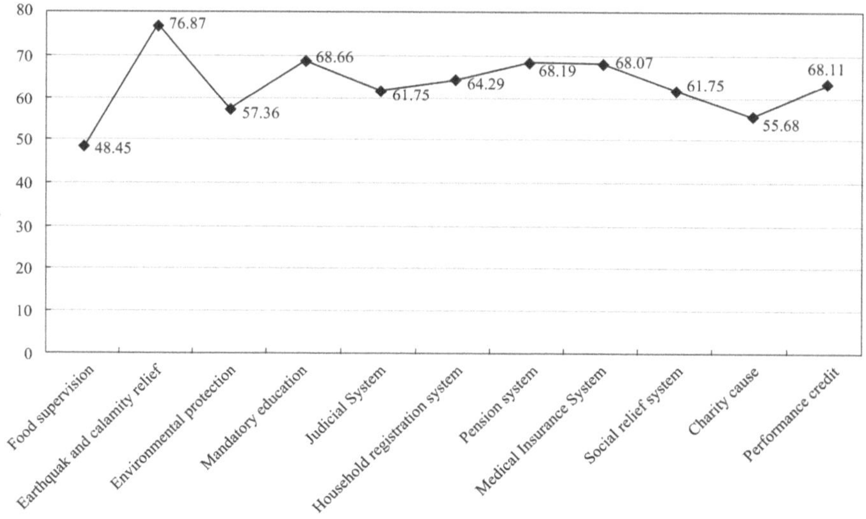

Figure 3.8 Effective percentage of personnel credit

and competence of civil servants. Specifically, judging from the perspective of political status, the level of trust that CCP members have in administrative staff still stands the lowest among the politically unaffiliated masses, the Communist League members, and the non-CCP party members. From the perspective of differences between urban and rural residents, the overall rating of urban residents shows that they have slightly less trust in public functionaries than their rural counterparts.

Here is what these facts prove: First, the political-government credit composed of institutional credit, performance credit, and personnel credit are of relatively low overall rating, of which the personnel credit stands the lowest, and with the average of the three items below the pass mark (58%) (see Table 3.13). Therefore, the overall political-government credit presents a crisis of substantial scale. Furthermore, this universally low rating on the political-government credit indicates to some degree that there is a lack of purity and distinction in the establishment of these institutional organisations; that is to say, the agencies, systems and regulations, norms, and personnel of the government have not been effectively "instituted," which makes it hard for the people to feel them dependable and thus to be assured. Still, compared with average people, the higher the education one has, the higher the political status one has, and the more urbanised one is, the more one becomes distrustful of governments of various natures, of policy performance, and of administrative personnel, which reflects the co-efficiency among educational background, the degree of development of an area, and the degree of trust.

b.) Let's first examine symbol and expert credit. On the whole, the interviewees returned an overall passing grade on symbol credit, with an average score of 62.75,

Table 3.12 Effective percentage of personnel credit

Personnel Credit	*Distrust*			*Neutral*	*Trust*		
	Disagree strongly	*Disagree a little*	*Sum of the two*	*Cannot explain*	*Agree a little*	*Agree strongly*	*Sum of the two*
Most government officials are honest and dutiful	5.5%	20.1%	25.6%	27.6%	28.3%	18.5%	46.8%
Most government officials are public-interest-minded	10.0%	16.3%	26.3%	25.2%	35.6%	12.9%	48.5%
Most government officials can execute their duties in accordance with the law	4.2%	16.9%	21.2%	36.9%	28.8%	13.1%	41.9%
Most government officials do not only care about their own achievements	3.3%	10.0%	13.3%	26.5%	38.5%	21.8%	60.3%

Table 3.13 Overall situation of China's social credit

	N	*Average value*	*Standard deviation*
Political-government credit	5,220	58.0488	13.53349
Socio-market credit	5,217	55.6657	12.81455
Personal–interpersonal credit	5,204	65.5006	10.06024

	Personnel credit	Most government officials are public-interest-minded	Most government officials are honest and dutiful	Most government officials can execute their duties in accordance with the law	Most government officials do not only care about their own achievements
Average value	59.65	56.26	58.56	57.39	66.37

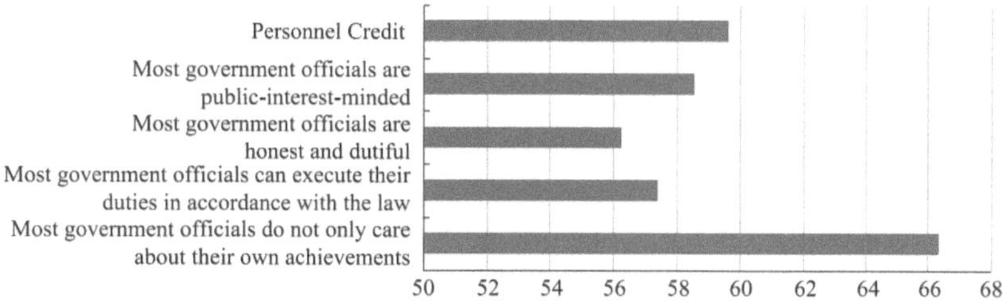

Figure 3.9 Mean value of personnel credit (percentage)

with the symbol credit under the educational production category standing only at 53.41 (see Table 3.14). The overall rating on the expert credit stands slightly above the "passing grade." Specifically, in terms of differences between the city and the countryside, city dwellers show more distrust in the symbol and expert system than their rural counterparts; in terms of educational background, interviewees of various backgrounds rated such evidential reflecting personal capabilities as diplomas and certificates below a pass mark, with interviewees of intermediate educational backgrounds (junior high school, senior high school, and two-year college degree) returning the lowest scores (see Table 3.15). In terms of political status, be it CCP members, League members, or the politically unaffiliated masses, all rated pretty low the credit of such symbols under educational production as diplomas and certificates, with League members returning the lowest score, which stands at a meagre 49.91 (see Table 3.16). In addition, up to 23% of interviewees returned a response of "cannot explain" on the credit of such symbols under educational production as diplomas and certificates, whereas interviewee responses to the credit situation of expert systems, including college teachers, lawyers, and technical specialists, reach

Table 3.14 Overall situation of symbol credit

Trust of symbol	*Disagree strongly*	*Disagree a little*	*Cannot explain*	*Agree a little*	*Agree strongly*	*Average score*
Symbol credit of the educational production category	11.1%	20.6%	22.3%	35.4%	10.6%	53.41
Symbol credit of socio-consumption category	2.8%	7.1%	15.1%	48.7%	26.2%	72.08

Table 3.15 Symbol credit by groups of different educational backgrounds

Trust of symbol	*Primary school and below*	*Junior high school*	*Senior high school*	*Two-year college degree*	*Four-year college degree and above*
Symbol credit of the educational production category	56.90	53.62	50.16	51.05	56.46
Symbol credit of socio-consumption category	71.67	72.67	72.13	71.27	71.97

Table 3.16 Symbol credit by groups of different political status

Trust of symbol	*CCP member*	*League member*	*Politically unaffiliated*
Symbol credit of the educational production category	54.95	49.91	53.68
Symbol credit of socio-consumption category	72.16	71.45	72.15

25%, 31.8%, and 27.1%, respectively. These ratings clearly demonstrate the lack of authority of the symbol and expert systems.

All in all, the credit situation of the symbol and expert systems indicates that in contemporary Chinese society these systems fail to sufficiently and effectively manifest the superiority of the symbol distinctiveness in the heterogeneous nature of society. Holding qualification certificates or diplomas has no practical effect on assessing whether a person is professionally capable, and the existence of contracts and certificates might not be the final deciding factor in guaranteeing interests. In addition, experts and specialists in relevant fields that embody professionalism and a heterogeneous social nature have failed to establish professional standards and a fine image; indeed, in a few critical fields and industries, people seem to have the impression that specialists are not as good as average people.

Next, let's focus our attention on product characteristics (quality, service, brand, and advertisements). Firstly, there is the aspect of product quality. Trust in product quality by interviewees gets a 60.98 score, which is still within the "basically pass" level. Meanwhile, 21.4% of interviewees had the equivocating attitude of "cannot explain." Specifically, from the differences between the city and the countryside, the rural dweller rates the credit of product quality higher than his urban counterpart; from the perspective of vocation, workers and college students rate the credit of product quality higher than clerks and businesspeople. From the perspective of educational background, the higher the education one receives, the lower one rates the credit of product quality (see Figures 3.8, 3.9, 3.10).

Secondly, there is product service. The interviewees rated product service credit at a mere 53 points, a score below the pass mark, and selected "cannot explain" for 24.8% of the whole (see Table 3.17).

Thirdly, brand credit is rated relatively good, with an average score of 67; however, in this category, 17.2% of people still indicate "cannot explain" (Table 3.18).

Fourthly, there is advertisement credit. This aspect gets the lowest rating among the four foregoing items, with an average score of 43, and with the credit

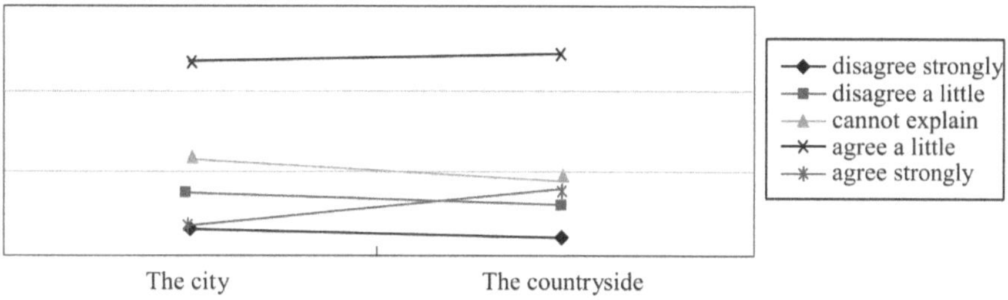

Figure 3.10 Crosstabs analysis of product quality credit between the city and the countryside

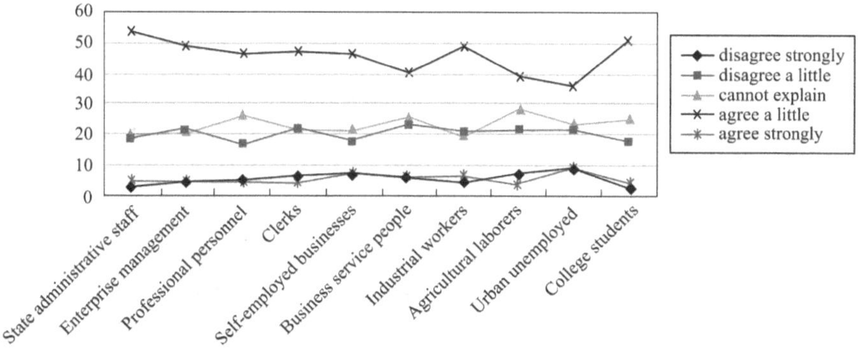

Figure 3.11 Crosstabs analysis between vocation and product quality credit

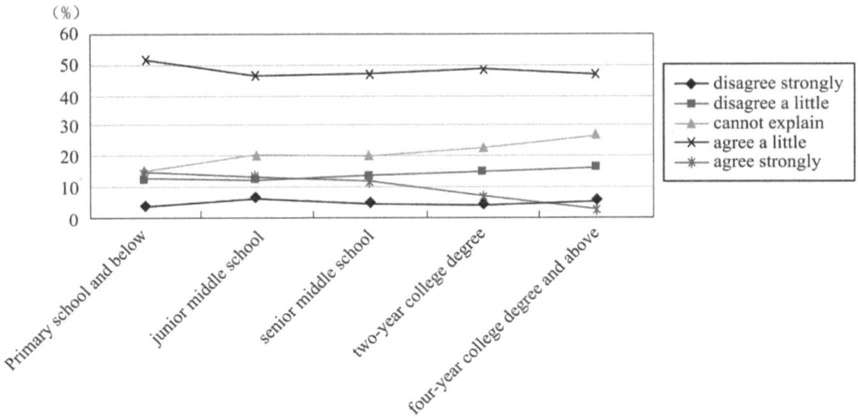

Figure 3.12 Crosstabs analysis between education level and product quality credit

Table 3.17 Overall situation of product service credit

	Disagree strongly	*Disagree a little*	*Cannot explain*	*Agree a little*	*Agree strongly*	*Total*
Number of interviewees	337	1,271	1,312	2,039	333	5,292
(%)	6.4	24.0	24.8	38.5	6.3	100

Table 3.18 Overall brand credit situation

	Disagree strongly	*Disagree a little*	*Cannot explain*	*Agree a little*	*Agree strongly*	*Total*
Number of interviewees	258	568	911	2,504	1,046	5,287
(%)	4.9	10.7	17.2	47.4	19.8	100

of advertisements featuring celebrities standing at a mere 38 points. Interviewees with the attitude "cannot explain" account for the largest share, a whopping 28.7% (see Table 3.19). What merits note is that the higher the educational background of the interviewee, the less trustful he will be of celebrity advertisements.

Lastly, let's examine the issue of charity credit. First, the interviewees rate the overall charity credit at 54 points, of which governmental charity organisation credit is 55.36 and private charity organisation credit is 54.38. Interestingly, there is an immensely large number of interviewees who have chosen "cannot explain" on these two items, accounting for up to 34.2% and 33.2%, respectively (see Table 3.20).

Table 3.19 Overall credit situation of advertisements

	Disagree strongly	*Disagree a little*	*Cannot explain*	*Agree a little*	*Agree strongly*	*Total*
Number of interviewees	695	1,686	1,517	1,227	167	5,292
(%)	13.1	31.9	28.7	23.2	3.2	100

Table 3.20 Basic situation of charity organisation credit

	Disagree strongly	*Disagree a little*	*Cannot explain*	*Agree a little*	*Agree strongly*	*Average score*
Government charity organisation	6.9	17.4	34.2	30.4	11.1	55.36
Private charity organisation	6.9	19.9	33.2	28.8	11.2	54.38

Table 3.21 Credit of different modes of donation

	Organised by the company to which one is affiliated	*Making voluntary donations through government charity organisations*	*Making voluntary donations through private charity organisations*	*Directly delivering donations to the recipient*	*Others*
Number of interviewees	767	478	220	1,587	85
%	24.5	15.2	7.0	50.6	2.7

Second, from the credit of the different modes of donation, only 15.2% and 7.0% of interviewees are "making voluntary donations through government charity organisations" and "making voluntary donations through private charity organisations," respectively; whereas the two items of "making donations through the company to which one is affiliated" and "directly delivering donations to the recipient" account for up to 24.5% and 50.6%, respectively (see Table 3.21), which fully manifests the organising capability of the government. What merits special note is that the higher the educational background, the more one is inclined to deliver donations directly to the recipient.

Third, in terms of the processes and results of charity operations, the interviewees have also returned very low credit scores for both phenomena.

All in all, social-charity causes have yet to become an independently operating field of high credit in Chinese society today. Charity programmes are, to a substantial degree, promoted by the government.

Table 3.22 Credit situation of the process and result of charity operation

	Disagree strongly	*Disagree a little*	*Cannot explain*	*Agree a little*	*Agree strongly*
I believe that the operations of all charity organisations are open and transparent (%)	15.2	25.3	32.4	19.5	7.6
I believe that the donated money or articles will be delivered into the hands of recipients as stated (%)	10.7	22.8	30.5	26.1	9.9

3.2.2 Personal–Interpersonal Credit

First, let's examine the plane of personal credit. Generally, interviewees' assumptions about human nature are complicated; there are both theories of original goodness and altruistic inclination and theories of evil human nature and egoistic inclination. However, relatively speaking, the attitudinal preferences of "protecting those on one's own side" and "guarding against those not on one's own side" stand out more prominently (see Table 3.23).

Regarding city and countryside, the rural residents have returned a score of a mere 48 points on "egoistic inclination," whereas their urban counterparts returned an 80-point score (see Figure 3.13), reflecting the altruistic nature of traditional society and the egoistic nature of modern society. From the of educational background, it could be seen that educational background and egoistic inclination stand in a relationship of positive correlation; namely, the higher the education one receives, the more one identifies with the theory of original evil human nature and the more he is prone to display egoistic conduct or inclinations in actual or possible scenarios. This inclination is manifested more conspicuously in the group of interviewees with two years of college education and above (see Figure 3.14). That is to say, education, especially higher education, lowers one's expectations regarding the kindness of human nature instead of raising such expectations.

Furthermore, the egoistic and altruistic dualistic assumption of human nature reflects changes brought about by the changing social values of modern people. Comparatively, the more one is exposed to urban life and modern education, the more practical his suspicion of credit will seem and the less trustful he will be of the theory of the original goodness of human nature.

Next, let's examine the issue of interpersonal credit. We examined the degree of recognition of different social relations among urban and rural residents by scoring the trust they placed in different relationships (variable assignment 1 = distrust strongly, 2 = distrust a little, 3 = neither trust nor distrust, 4 = trust a little, 5 = trust strongly); please see Tables 3.24 and 3.25). Generally, whether urban or rural, all interviewees displayed structural traits of a "differential pattern" featuring an obvious distinction between who is inside one's own circle and who is outside. Many

Table 3.23 Result of factor analysis of personal credit

Item	*Egoistic*	*Belief in original goodness*	*Altruistic inclination*	*Belief in original evil*
If a major social incident takes place, I will protect my family from harm at all costs, then I may consider other people	.818			
The vigilance of guarding against possible wrongdoing by others cannot be dispensed with	.811			
One cannot break his promise even if he can benefit from such a deed	.809			
Most people in society are honest and reliable		.730		
Most people would happily help others		.659		
Good-heartedness often meets with recompense		.607		
All within the four seas are brothers		.587		
Helping others leads to no reward			.778	
Nevertheless, when I see people who need help, I will do my best to help			.748	
I am willing to sacrifice myself and strive for the welfare of others			.741	
People place their personal interests before the interests of others				.782
Men are born selfish				.703
Nowadays, going back on one's words for personal interests is understandable				.596
In society, nobody genuinely cares about others				.491
Eigenvalues	2.413	1.960	1.8431	1.802
Deviation value (%)	17.236	14.003	13.167	12.872

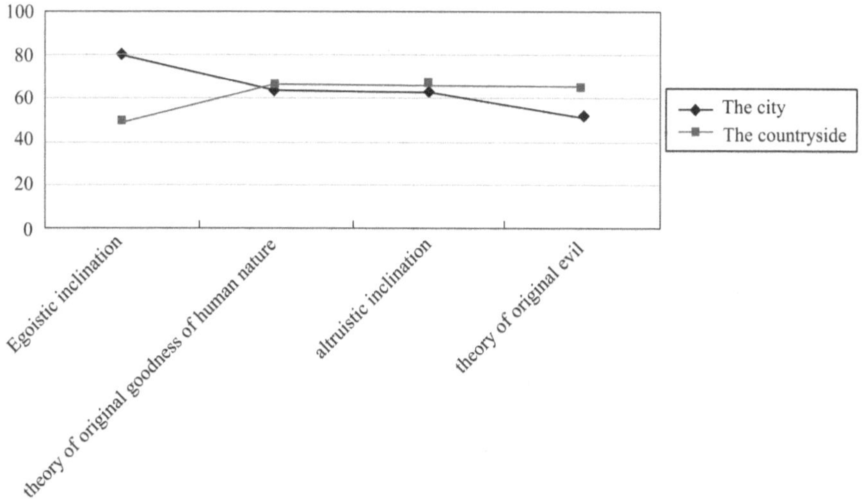

Figure 3.13 Differences of credit between the city and the countryside

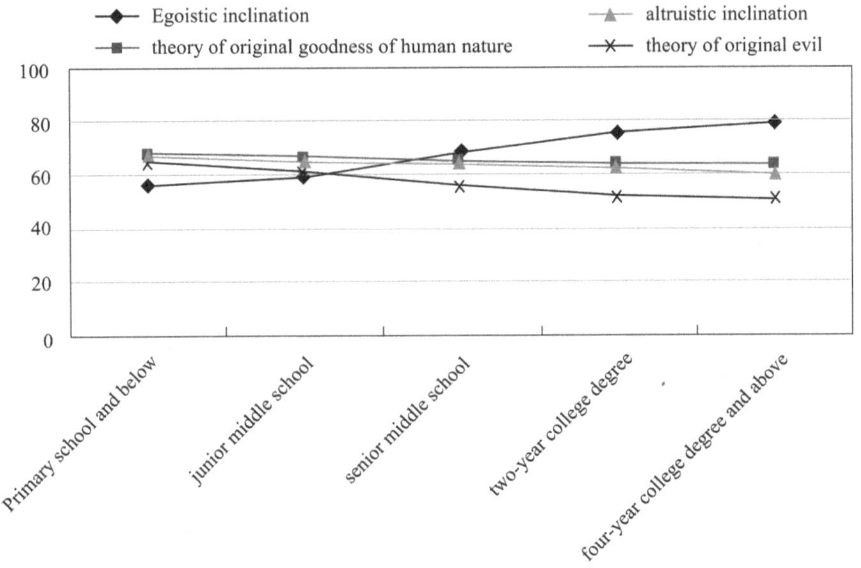

Figure 3.14 Influences of differences of education background on personal credit

Table 3.24 Description of variables of level of trust in social relationships (city samples)

	Number of cases	*Average value*	*Standard deviation*
Core family members	3,136	4.72	.545
Immediate family	3,137	4.55	.609
Close friends	3,134	4.06	.681
Other relations	3,130	3.86	.754
Colleagues	3,132	3.36	.746
Average friends	3,133	3.35	.719
Superiors	3,135	3.30	.826
Neighbours	3,133	3.29	.711
Average acquaintances	3,136	3.12	.704
Hometown fellows	3,131	3.07	.714
Producers	3,133	2.72	.848
Vendors	3,132	2.68	.848
Net friends	3,134	2.30	.867
Strangers	3,135	1.93	.901

scholars have proved this point with research data, and it got large-scale substantiation in the present research.[1] Specifically, on one hand, family-oriented social relationships and relation-oriented social relationships are crucial among both urban residents and rural residents. That is to say, relationship networks with blood relationships and marriage relationships at the core complemented and expanded geographic relationships, contingent relationships, and business relationships and

Table 3.25 Description of variables of level of trust in social relationships (rural questionnaire)

	Number of cases	*Average value*	*Standard deviation*
Core family	2,157	4.66	.664
Immediate family	2,158	4.59	.656
Relations of blood relationship	2,155	4.14	.816
Close friends	2,155	3.87	.840
Relations without blood relationship	2,152	3.67	.939
Neighbours	2,156	3.47	.898
Extended family	2,152	3.45	.943
Average friends	2,157	3.27	.904
Village cadres	2,154	3.14	1.032
Business proprietors	2,152	2.98	.935
Producers	2,156	2.73	.913
Vendors	2,152	2.63	.910
Strangers	2,158	1.76	.881

remain the centre of Chinese life. On the other hand, the importance of extra-family relationships such as professionalism, heterogeneity, level of organisation and institutionalisation diminished substantially, for instance, the level of trust of urban residents in producers, vendors, and net friends is below 3 for all; the level of trust of rural residents in business proprietors, producers, and vendors is, similarly, below 3, leaning to the distrust side on the scale. However, strangers, who symbolise the heterogeneity of modern society, are placed directly in the group of the untrustworthy (with scores from both categories below 2, which is roughly between "distrust a little" and "distrust strongly"). In addition, regarding educational background, an increase in years of education strengthens trust in kith and kin but also weakens trust in strangers. What's more, political status also increases trust in kith and kin and strengthens distrust in strangers or outsiders.

The above data is sufficient to demonstrate that, regardless of place of residence and educational background, family relationships (in the broad sense) remain the core and basis of social trust, whereas social relationships outside the family stand in a secondary position and within the suspicious circle. In a deeper sense, it predicts the difficulty of social differentiation, division of labour, organisation, and institutional establishment. What it reflects is the underlying "circle" characteristics of society, instead of professionalism; it is a reflection of the phenomenon of the distinction between the inside and the outside of the circle, instead of the differences within and among organisations.

3.2.3 The Situation of Social Participation

In the "situation of social-organisation participation," variable assignment 1 = no participation, 2 = average member, 3 = active member, and 4 = core member;

and in the "situation of social participation," variable assignment 1 = never participates, 2 = participates occasionally, 3 = participates sometimes, 4 = participates frequently. Social participation mainly takes place in the city (see Tables 3.26 and 3.27). Generally speaking, there is little social-organisation participation among urban and rural residents; their social participation mainly concentrates in the social groups extended from such relationships as college graduation, geographical relationships, and business relationships (for instance, fellow-students associations, fellow-countrymen associations, and so forth), as well as various QQ groups and internet forums associated with the various internet platforms. There is extremely low participation in social organisations outside the family, for instance, in public-charity organisations, industry associations, academic organisations, folk art groups, and religious groups.

Now let's turn to the participation situation of social activities (see Tables 3.28 and 3.29). Similarly, we have chosen some relatively universal social activities

Table 3.26 Situation description of social-organisation participation (city samples)

	Number of cases	*Average value*	*Standard deviation*
Fellow-students association	3,131	1.77	.842
Various QQ groups	3,128	1.58	.726
Fellow-countrymen association	3,132	1.34	.656
Trade union	3,133	1.34	.608
Internet forum	3,129	1.31	.559
Public-charity organisation	3,134	1.24	.536
Industry association	3,134	1.19	.510
Academic groups	3,131	1.14	.456
Folk art groups	3,131	1.14	.437
Veteran groups	3,117	1.13	.451
Community-property owner committee	3,130	1.12	.414
Religious groups	3,133	1.08	.338

Table 3.27 Situation description of social-organisation participation (countryside samples)

	Number of cases	*Average value*	*Standard deviation*
People's congress at various levels	2,156	1.04	.245
Science and technology associations	2,156	1.05	.290
Senior-citizens association	2,157	1.06	.305
Veteran association	2,156	1.10	.386
Propaganda team	2,155	1.11	.396
Internet forum	2,155	1.12	.392
Public-charity organisation	2,156	1.18	.461
Religious groups	2,156	1.21	.479
Various QQ groups	2,156	1.23	.526
Village committee	2,156	1.34	.606

Table 3.28 Situation description of social-activity participation (city samples)

	Number of cases	*Average value*	*Standard deviation*
Associations with kith and kin	3,135	3.12	.876
Fellow-students' parties and activities	3,135	2.49	1.035
Everyday-interest activities, yango dance, poker, chess, etc.	3,131	2.16	1.018
Recreational and sports activities organised by the organisation to which one is affiliated	3,130	2.03	1.038
Participation of one's own accord in various charity-donation activities	3,131	1.99	.906
Participation in voluntary public-service activities (e.g., caring for the elderly, etc.)	3,129	1.83	.900
Various political elections (e.g., electing congress representatives)	3,131	1.73	.982
Participating in online discussion of popular social issues (for instance, on microblogs, in forums, etc.)	3,132	1.53	.831
Election activity of community-property proprietor committee	3,134	1.52	.853
Participating in various voluntary blood-donation activities (including organ donation)	3,134	1.46	.758
Various democratic appraisal activities of CCP works	3,128	1.45	.823
Recreational and sports activities organised by community-neighbourhood committee	3,134	1.44	.757
Contributing comments and suggestions to government departments (including offer suggestions and feedback on government websites)	3,134	1.30	.653
Spontaneous exchange activities between fellow religious followers	3,132	1.24	.604
Religious activities organised by temples or churches	3,132	1.23	.591

from urban and rural everyday life for measurement. The overall results are also similar to the situation of social-organisation participation, that is, urban and rural residents generally participate very little in the various social activities, and their limited participation mainly concentrates in the circles of blood relations, geographical relations, and business relations. Specifically, the highest level of participation or the activities most frequently participated in are mainly associations and parties with kith and kin. For instance, urban residents score 3.12 on associations with kith and kin, while rural residents score higher on the two items of "visiting relations during the Spring Festival and holidays" and "everyday associations with kith and kin." Here the scores are 3.48 and 3.28, respectively, which translates to extreme frequency. The items that follow the leaders are still activities that take place inside the relation circles and acquaintance society. In the city, such activities include fellow-student parties, everyday hobby activities, and recreational and sports activities organised by the organisation to which one is affiliated; in rural areas, these activities include rural market day and temple fairs. However, what

Table 3.29 Situation description of social-activity participation (countryside samples)

	Number of cases	*Average value*	*Standard deviation*
Participation in various voluntary blood-donation activities	2,154	1.32	.702
Burning incense and praying in temples	2,150	1.42	.775
Church activities of Christianity, Islamism	2,149	1.45	.936
Various science and technology popularisation, skill-training classes	2,152	1.48	.818
Various hygiene and healthcare activities, female reproduction classes	2,149	1.51	.852
Various policy, law popularisation activities	2,150	1.61	.912
Mahjong, poker, gambling, etc.	2,147	1.72	.927
Various recreational and sports activities	2,152	1.73	.966
Democratic appraisal activities of village cadre	2,151	1.81	1.056
Villager representative congress	2,155	1.86	1.039
Voluntary participation in public-service activities	2,148	1.90	.980
Public-service activities, including environmental protection	2,154	1.92	.985
Voluntary participation in various charity-donation activities	2,151	1.97	.921
Rural market, temple fair	2,154	2.05	1.041
Election activities of village-level grassroots organisations	2,153	2.11	1.100
Everyday association with kith and kin	2,158	3.28	.860
Visiting relations during Spring Festival and holidays	2,155	3.48	.784

merits attention is that in the countryside the survey somewhat reflects that rural residents participate in grassroots election activities.

The foregoing data reflects the participation situation of Chinese in social groups and social activities, which demonstrates to a considerable extent that Chinese literally "could not care less" about social groups and public affairs beyond the family boundary. In other words, to a considerable extent, these organisations and groups outside the acquaintance relationship lack the social function and significance they claim to possess. The implication is that "the structure of homogeneous society is that of a network, whereas the structure of heterogeneous society is that of an organization … Homogeneous society sets store by relationship, and heterogeneous society lays emphasis on social capital."[2]

3.3 Discussion of Homogeneous Society

In examining mechanical union and organic solidarity, Durkheim viewed mechanical solidarity as an entity composed of people of collective consciousness. Differences in other aspects of society matter little; the point is that people are organised through common belief and feeling. Whereas organic solidarity is based on the social division of labour, vocational ethics and legal person corporation constitute the basis for social integration. Comparatively speaking, mechanical solidarity focuses on how a collective consciousness formed out of common belief, morality, and customs punish and reject misconduct. The homogeneous society under discussion refers to the homogeneity originating from the basis of a defined social division of labour and professionalism; this homogeneous connotation makes areas where heterogeneity is required homogeneous. Based thereon, the connotation of mechanical solidarity fails to notice two characteristics of a homogeneous society: The first is the homogenisation trend within the various social planes and aspects; that is, there is no obvious distinction between any social organisation that can be divided from the whole and any other organisations. If there is any distinction to be made, such may better be manifested in scale or complexity of said organisation, instead of the aspect of divisional boundaries between different social organisations, which further leads to the conclusion that a particular characteristic of a certain aspect of the society may be, to a considerable degree, typical of the entire society and may reflect the characteristics of the society of a certain stage in the whole. The second is the trend to seek transitional zones between the boundaries of social planes and aspects, a trend that defies definition. A transitional zone is a gradient, continuous, and flexible part of society that leaves room for manoeuvre and spawns a plethora of folk wisdom: For instance, chance-taking, expedience, and string-pulling, etc. In such an environment, the focus of society and of market operation lies not in systems, but in the expediency of means: for instance, grey zone, formalism, face-keeping efforts, separation of name and essence, and so forth. They collectively constitute a sort of "energy" of social operation.

Of course, motives of opportunism and free-riding appear in societies of all kinds. However, different social forms entail different directions of development. For instance, similarly, behaviours of pillaging and free-riding also lurk in heterogeneous society; however, in order to prevent and check such behaviours and uphold the normal operation of society, a heterogeneous society will mete out heavy fines and punishments for any irregularities by resorting to the law, institutions, social groups, and codes of ethics. While homogeneous society shows more tolerance and empathy, the mentality that "the law cannot be enforced when everyone is an offender" tends to encourage such behaviours. For instance, in the political realm, the various institutions, laws, and regulations are usually enacted out of good original intentions and the design of such are well executed; however, in actual operation, especially when punishment measures are to be meted out and enforced, then such factors as relationship, favour, and face must often be taken into consideration. The wrongdoer is usually, in the name of "curing the patient of the illness" and out of a hope for the benign nature of humanity, dealt with leniently and even let go after paying some insignificant fines. In the economic realm, this will spawn the aforementioned phenomenon where copycat products, common products, and products of renowned brands compete on the same shelf, where sometimes it is difficult to tell the genuine from the counterfeit, the superior from the inferior; hence, there comes the phenomenon where the inferior product drives out the superior. For instance, if people find that a certain big-name mobile phone is good, the rich will buy genuine goods, the average people will buy "smuggled products" (sold outside the mainland), while the poor, who cannot afford genuine goods, will choose exquisite imitations and copycat versions. Compared to city dwellers, rural residents who earn less will often pursue fake products or exquisite imitations that replicate genuine goods in appearance; meanwhile, these fakeries are themselves "bases" of some small workshops in the locality. There, they contend with genuine products and even with famous-brand products, which highlights the advantages that they possess: for instance, low prices and passable quality. On one hand, in the cultural field, there appear to exist highly exacting forms of ranking that may compare people and items down to the point of several decimal places; on the other hand, this field is awash with certificates, such that all students enrolled in colleges can almost rest assured of being able to graduate. The value of degree diplomas and qualification certificates are dwindling by the day, especially when accompanied by the phenomena of fake diplomas, fake certificate, fake education backgrounds, and fake identification certificates. The direct result is that there are college graduates everywhere and the number of postgraduates is increasing by and by; however, the number of people with true knowledge and ability does not match with the growing number of college graduates. Today, people ridicule college students for "idling for a diploma."

The spread of homogeneity leads to a social consensus among the people. That is to say, if a sympathetic society views everything as permissible, then it would emulate the practice, and the underlying logic would be "if he can, why can't I?" Ultimately, all institutions and norms, industry standards, and realm boundaries would be superficial and remain in form only, whereas the "law of the jungle" would become the essence and operation principle of society, and mechanisms of relationship, favour, and face would become the unwritten law of society. However, in a heterogeneous society, being intolerant and unsympathetic are the prerequisite for setting up boundaries. Only in this way can society guarantee the quality and grade of the various social organisations, thus guaranteeing the credit of society by establishing corresponding technologies, specialities, vocations, and industrial standards as well as supporting institutions and laws. The order of a society with a social division of labour can only be guaranteed by establishing boundaries between institutions.

Therefore, if a society is highly developed in social homogeneity, does that mean that the act of establishing the quality or grade of social organisations has lost its significance? For instance, if a certificate cannot prove the work performance of a person or a social organisation or the quality of a brand, doesn't that mean that certificates have lost their significance? In fact, this is a misunderstanding of the homogeneous society. Social homogeneity does not equal the homogeneity of the individual. From any perspective, as biological entities, individuals cannot be homogeneous. Individual differences, including physique, appearance, gender, health, status, competence, experience, background, technique, knowledge, profession, work, etc., will never disappear. The so-called homogeneity or heterogeneity of society can only exist on the social plane, so the problem is, whether a society based on a certain form is motivated by the heterogeneity of the individual and establishes accordingly its unit distinction and purity, or whether it ignores individual heterogeneity and forges a living trend that is extremely similar in terms of the grand social direction and grand goal. For instance, typically, a heterogeneous society and a civil society are similar. In such a society, different organisations, associations, clubs, etc. are set up. The rules of membership are used to differentiate insider and outsider, and the articles of incorporation are imposed on insiders. If a society does not factor in the heterogeneity of the individual but appeals to the individual with the foregoing grand goal and grand direction, then a sort of "high probability values" might take form in said society. Such high probability values, on the one hand, will lure all social strata to rush to a trend resembling a great mass fervour in a particular period without regard to their respective characteristics: for instance, the craze for starting a business, the craze for going abroad, the craze for diplomas, the craze for buying houses, the craze for speculating in stocks, the craze for buying cars, and so on. On the other hand, the situation also compels society to cater completely to the prevailing taste of the people and stimulates many to dream of overnight riches, which places the good and the bad in the same environments. "Coexistence" does not mean that inferior quality can beat superior quality and even less that the superior will drive the inferior from the market; it means that society lacks a set of mechanisms to cull the substandard, the bad, the irregular, the fake from the market. The situation is simply left to the discretion of the people, a situation in which prosperity and crisis coexist in the same playground. Here the privileged class requires a "special supply" to maintain their quality of life.

Hence, people might wonder why Chinese society cannot be heterogenised. Can't relevant standards, institutions, and laws be enacted and enforced? Perhaps we should consider it this way: Regardless of the form of society, so long as it has enacted and enforced such rules and regulations, social credit *will* be guaranteed, correct? These questions touch on the deepest core of the issues operating in society. The answer to the former is, if the law of the jungle is to prevail, then society will move toward homogenisation, which features a negative function. And the answer to the latter is, regarding social form, a homogeneous society has a network structure, whereas a heterogeneous society has an organisational structure. A society with a network structure emphasises that all barriers can be penetrated through relationships. A society with an organisational structure values qualifications, demarcations, and relevant laws and regulations. In order to safeguard differences, such a society will try all means possible to place public affairs under the supervision of insiders of a group or the public in general. It follows that homogeneous society emphasises relationships, and heterogeneous society emphasises social capital. The focus of relationships lies in breaking ground for favour and face to be set in motion. The focus of social capital lies in the institutional relationship between the individual and the social group so as to promote information dissemination and trust establishment. Therefore, in a society where relationships such as favour and face are employed to operate society, people may overstep institutions in order to cope with possible troubles arising from the distinction and purity a society should naturally possess. While social capital organises the social structure through the participation of the individual in the organisation, or through an organisation linking to another organisation, a relationship of shared responsibility or shared benefit is entered into by involving the social organisation in the process. In other words, in a homogeneous society, entering into a relationship alone would beget strength, whereas in a heterogeneous society, strength comes from getting organised. Therefore, the operation of relationship best fits a homogeneous society, whereas the operation of social capital suits a heterogeneous society.

In conclusion, homogeneity has found its way into all aspects of Chinese society, which makes it difficult to distinguish purity, the distinctiveness of social norms, and organisation quality. This is different from the operation of social capital, which is also the empirical basis for the distinction between "relationship" and social capital.

Notes

1 See Li Weimin, Liang Yucheng, Special Trust and Universal Trust: Structure and Characteristics of Chinese Trust, *Sociological Research* 2002(3); Wang Shaoguang, Liu Xinwang, Basis of Trust: A Rational Explanation, *Socialogical Research* 2002(3); Lin Juren, *Reconstruction of Social Trust and Social Capital*, Shandong People's Publishing House, 2007; Wang Yijie, Zhou Fuxian, Differential Pattern of Urban Residents' Trust. *Tianfu New Idea* 2009(20); Zou Yuchun, Ao Dan, Li Jiandong, Trust Pattern and the Effect of Social Capital of Chinese Urban Residents – Illustrated with Guangzhou, *Social Sciences in China* 2012(5) etc.

2 Xuewei, The Social Cause of Credit Crisis.

References

Li, W., & Liang, Y. (2002). Special trust and universal trust: Structure and characteristics of Chinese trust. *Sociological Research*, *3*, 11–22. https://doi.org/10.19934/j.cnki.shxyj.2002.03.002

Lin, J. (2007). *Reconstruction of social trust and social capital*. Shandong People's Publishing House.

Wang, S., & Liu, X. (2002). Basis of trust: A rational explanation. *Socialogical Research*, *3*, 23–39. https://doi.org/10.19934/j.cnki.shxyj.2002.03.003

Wang, Y., & Zhou, F. (2009). Differential pattern of urban residents' trust. *Tianfu New Idea*, *2*, 102–105+133.

Zhai, X. (2014). The social cause of credit crisis. *Jiangsu Social Science*, *1*, 85–96. https://doi.org/10.13858/j.cnki.cn32-1312/c.2014.01.030

Zou, Y., Ao, D., & Li, J. (2012). Trust pattern and the effect of social capital of Chinese urban residents: Illustrated with Guangzhou. *Social Sciences in China*, *5*, 131–148+207.

4 Humanity and Morality

The phenomena and issues arising from China's social credit are by no means abrupt or accidental. They have deep-level, structural, and traditional origins, which require theoretical examination. Credit is often manifested in the form of social interaction, while interaction is based on information acquisition. What buttresses the truthfulness of information is morality and ethics, and the latter in turn becomes the bottom line of society. The mode of construction of a society is usually premised on the assumption of human nature by its culture, while different assumptions of human nature lead to different directions of institutional design. Therefore, in order to investigate the root causes of the Chinese social credit crisis, we must start by examining the unchanging assumption about human nature that has been handed down to date in China's culture.

4.1 "Credit" Assumption on Human Nature

All societies are formed so that people can "trust" each other, otherwise, society itself would fall apart. As to why there must be "credit" in human society, we would first make such a conjecture: Suppose an individual is "omnipotent and omniscient" as, for instance, God or a god might be. The question is, does he need society and credit for his life? The answer is "no," because such an individual has the capability to acquire all information and accomplish all tasks by himself; conversely, if an individual is absolutely "ignorant and impotent" like, for instance, a baby, an infant, the infirm, the disabled, etc., does he then need trust? The answer is "absolutely," because such a person cannot exist for a moment without help from others. By comparing the two extremes, we can see that the evolution of human civilisation, or the growth of a baby, is a process of growing from being absolutely dependent on others to depending on others as little as possible. This is the force that drives cultural acquisition and technological innovation. The same is true of society; improving knowledge and skills is the basic requirement that any culture places on its members. Of course, humanity has so far substantially improved its knowledge of the self and skills; however, despite all these achievements, so long as the individual still cannot be omnipotent and omniscient, he will still fall back on the strength of the collective to fend off the elements, the aggression of alien races, and the internal conflicts of society.

DOI: 10.4324/9781003375579-6

In sociology, the cooperative relationships among humans can be collectively referred to as "social exchange." According to the theory of social resources, the content that people exchange with each other is variegated. Generally speaking, there can be six categories: Goods, information, money, services, status, and emotions. But all exchanges must be premised on trust, regardless of the category of exchange, as any dishonest conduct will either result in the disintegration of the social cooperation or even the social group itself or lead to a situation where exchanges are carried on with increased cost and the accompaniment of potential risks. On this issue, individuals engaging in social exchange must possess two basic elements: Rationality (the ability to judge and choose) and morality (conscience, integrity). Then, the next question is, what is the relationship between rationality and morality? We believe that the most important reason for a person to possess rationality is for information acquisition. If the truthfulness of the information in circulation in a society cannot be determined, then rationality and judgement will see radical deviation. Hence, it follows that rationality is the trait of the individual, while information belongs to both the individual and the social realms. The fidelity of information requires not only the institution of personal morality but also of social ethics. Therefore, either morality or ethics is presumed to be the bottom line of society. This point ultimately relates to assumptions regarding human nature.

The implication of the so-called human-nature assumption means that man has so far failed to get down to his own nature and has no effective means to verify a deeper understanding of that nature. Therefore, any exploration of human nature could only be carried out via a certain specific social phenomenon and characteristic that gets at assumptions about human nature. Of course, the construction of society may also start from an assumption of human nature. Now, if human nature can only be assumed, it seems we are unable to prove the correctness of that assumption; however, in making these inquiries, we may discover the modes of operation and the cultural characteristics of society, regarding, for instance, religions or beliefs. Indeed, assumptions about human nature in Western societies are typically discussed in the context of religion. The West entrusts its bottom line of ethics and morality to religion, which embodies the deductive relationship they wanted to establish between man and god. Whereas in the context of Chinese cultural tradition, human nature has never been a religious issue (of course, the introduction of Buddhism into China had brought similar concepts to the Chinese people and had a profound effect on Chinese culture) but an issue in the relationship between heaven and man. In other words, conjecture about the origination of morality and the persistence thereof by native Chinese thinkers comes from the analogical extension of the relationship between heaven and man. With the development of this thinking, Chinese culture became more and more inclined to perceive a "union of heaven and man," and the assumption regarding human nature finally rested on the internality of man. The examination of human nature in the context of Chinese culture is meant to discover the transcendence of man's internality; that is, it attempts to demonstrate whether human nature is "good" or "bad" by resorting to the natural inclination of man.

Concerning intellectual exploration in this field, there are differences between the Confucianist school and the Taoist school. Comparatively, the Taoist view on human nature returns to primitive simplicity. The Taoist holds that so-called morality is the product of the evil nature of humanity. This line of thought first originates in the notion that "the ways of Taos are conditioned by the Self-so" (Ch. 25, Tao Te Ching), which means that the ways of man do not lie ultimately in man himself, but in nature. Nature seeks nothing, desires nothing. If the ways of nature are to be followed, man should also cease to seek. Therefore, the Taoist establishes a "natural" standard outside the social culture – "Tao" – as the ultimate standard in demonstrating natural humanity. Man and Tao equal a high degree of integration between human nature, with nature becoming the ultimate standard of the human-nature assumption advanced by the Taoists. The root cause of human society's relish for morality lies in its loss of Tao. However, due to the fact that the Taoists conducted the deduction in the reverse direction, it negated the function of morality on the speculative plane; thus, morality is considered not only unhelpful in maintaining the social order but unable to diminish human desire, strife, and greed. Therefore, no matter how profound the critique of the social system was by Lao Zi, so long as the desires of most people linger, morality and rite must stay; and the latter becomes the focus of consideration for the Confucianist.

In the opinion of Confucius, setting up a system of rites is necessary. However, the biggest issue of the system of rites lies in that it only regulates people's behaviour but does nothing for people's minds. Therefore, it is necessary to introduce a constraint on the mind on top of the system of rites. Only by doing so would people conduct themselves in accordance with the requirements of the rites of their own accord instead of merely trying to avoid punishment or to maximise expediency and gains. To target this point, Confucius advanced two important concepts, one being "benevolence," the other "the virtuous man (gentleman)." "Benevolence" corresponds to "rite": One manifests the internal traits and the other the external traits, which shows that institutions and norms should be buttressed by morality. "Virtuous man" refers to he who practices benevolence, or a man of benevolent personality. It stands in contrast to the "mean man," illustrating that the virtuous man conducts himself on the principle of righteousness, whereas the mean man conducts himself on the principle of gains. It may thus be said that the main topic that concerns the Confucian is expounding the implication of benevolence and the demonstration of why man possesses benevolence. The Analects of Confucius starts with a simple proposition: The reason man has benevolence originates with his parents and siblings; if a man wants to perform filial and brethren duties, then he should start by practising benevolence. The one important characteristic of benevolence is that it is something that everyone is capable of to the extent that the virtue of the Sage is actually attainable by everyone ("Everyone can be Yao and Shun, the Great Sages"). This statement implies that though the mean man harbours the intent for private gains, he still has the opportunity to attain gentleman-hood (virtuousness) through cultivation of the person. In addition, in realising this goal, the closer the relationship between the people, the more easily the goal is achieved. If a person can practice benevolence in relationships, he can extend the practice by analogy; hence, comes the saying "extend my filial piety to elders beyond my family, and treat other youngsters kindly as though they were your own" (Mencius – King Hui of Liang). And extending the practice by way of analogy, benevolence would be brought about for the entire empire. If the virtue of the mean man is weighed against that of the virtuous man, then the most prominent characteristic of the mean man is that he acts for personal gain. If a person is to place personal gains in the first place, he will not think of others or care for others. Having demonstrated the Confucian thought this far, radical anxiety arises: Is there any means to prove that there exists such a natural love in human nature, at least in intimate relationships? Confucius made few remarks on the topic. Therefore, the absolute foundation for "benevolence" is intimate interpersonal relationships (the first of which are family blood relationships). Discovering the natural basis of this hierarchical love is the solution to this absolute radical anxiety.

When the anxiety of Confucius was handed down to Mencius and became the question he had to face, what Mencius attempted to prove was the natural existence of love in human nature. The resulting proposal was Mencius' assumption regarding human nature, the idea that all men have "compassion for others." Indeed, he held that all men are born with "four feelings":

> The feeling of commiseration is the principle of benevolence. The feeling of shame or dislike is the principle of righteousness. The feeling of modesty or complaisance is the principle of propriety. The feeling of approving or disapproving is the principle of knowledge.
>
> (The Works of Mencius – Part I Gongsun Chou)

They constitute the basis for human relationships.

The reason the Confucianists laid such emphasis on the human-nature assumption is that they were living in a society of ruined rite and propriety, of social upheavals, so they were not only thinkers but also social reformists. Their thoughts implicitly contain their intent to find the crux for restoring social order, and that crux finally rests on the issue of human nature. In the times of Mencius, there had been heated debates on the issue of human nature, and a slew of hypotheses regarding human nature had sprouted. It may be said that the discussion of human nature we come across today has popped up at almost all times in history. This notion of human nature may concern nothing about good or evil, but instead physiology (instinct); it may ultimately be that human nature is evil, or that it can be good or evil, and so on. And the Confucianist thought that grew from Mencius's amendment became an adamant exponent of the idea of human nature as originally good, which set the keynote for future Confucianist thought. When Confucianist thought finally prevailed in China, the idea that "men are born benevolent" ultimately became the fundamental assumption of traditional culture.

Ancient Chinese sages who had assumed the benevolent nature of humanity held that man is born with a kind heart. However, this heart could be tainted after birth, and the purpose of moral inculcation was to remove one of these traits and restore him to his original nature, that is, to rectify his mind by cultivating his person. So, what could be done to rectify people's hearts? Mencius believed that man could return to his original nature through cultivation of the person because man has integrity in his character. The reason that integrity is naturally inherent in people is due to the endowments of heaven. The operation of heaven begets integrity, and integrity manifests itself in the person if man is to conduct himself in accordance with the way of heaven. In the opinion of the Confucianist, heaven has a way of itself; however, this way manifests itself by way of man. To fully bring out his virtue, a man has to attain a perfection of virtue, that is, the virtue of heaven or "virtue worthy of heaven and earth."

From this discussion of the assumptions regarding human nature by the Confucianists, we find that the focus of the thought system rests on moral education, inculcation, and even moralisation. Of course, there are also anomalies within the Confucianist school, including the possibility that some Confucianist scholars hold views not in line with traditional Confucianist thought in these matters. For instance, Xunzi insisted on "the theory of the original evil of human nature." To put forward a theory of the original evil nature of human beings inside the Confucian thought system, two logical problems had to be solved. One was the relationship between heaven and man, and the other was the relationship between what was instinct (nature) and what was acquired (falsehood). The two problems figured prominently in the Confucianist and Mencian thought systems and have been demonstrated sufficiently. Regarding the former, Xunzi believed that heaven had nothing to do with man, for heaven had its own law of operation, while man had his own rule of conduct. If the affairs of man equal the affairs of heaven, then why were there differences between the universal peace of the Yu (prior to the first Dynasty in China's history – the Xia Dynasty) and the great social upheaval of the Jie of the Xia Dynasty? Could we claim that heaven had undergone changes? Further still, the changes of the stars, sunshine, rainfall, and dews would not undergo any change due to the prayers or non-prayers of the people (see Xunzi – On Heaven). Regarding the latter, Xunzi held that there were the drives of mitigating hunger and of repelling cold, jealousy, and sensual desires in human nature. If free rein were given to them, there would be grabbing, and if compliance were thus afforded, the sense of propriety, justice, integrity, and honour would vanish (see Xunzi – On the Nature of Original Evil). Actually, if the demonstration of human nature started from the original evil of humanity, then such a demonstration would in fact claim from the very start that everyone was a mean man. It followed that the reason a society required the establishment of hierarchy, rites, and institutions lay in the fact that they could guide, inculcate, and restrain the evil in human nature. Xunzi's views influenced Hanfeizi and thus gave birth to Legalist thought in China. Hanfeizi extracted the assumption regarding human nature by Xunzi as follows: There is the pursuit of private gains in human nature, and, facing such a nature, to conduct proper governance, a country must "remove benevolence and righteousness, intelligence and scheme, and discipline them with the law" (Hanfeizi – On Dispelling Doubt). Having demonstrated this far, the Legalists had almost gone to the opposite side of the Confucianists, thus playing an important role in the unification of China in the Qin Dynasty; however, the transience of the

Qin regime afforded the ensuing rulers of the Han Dynasty the opportunity to reinstall Confucianist thought.

4.2 Comparison of the Assumption Regarding Human Nature between East and West

The foregoing discussions demonstrate that the construction of Chinese society in the realm of thought swung between morality and institution. Although Chinese society had never lacked institutional regulations, people were more inclined to achieve social harmony through moral inculcation.

When we examine the West's moral assumptions regarding human nature, we can see the role of religion. The basic train of thought running through Western Christian culture is that man was created by the hand of an omnipotent and omniscient God. Man was then tempted by Satan and sinned; hence, he could only get back to the side of God through redemption. Of course, the exiled man had to endure tests. Whether he became "chosen" or continued to fall depended on how he behaved in his lifetime. Generally, the introduction of the concept of "redemption" into Christianity resulted in a situation in which salvation required the office of a transcendental god. This teleological mode of thinking was one of externalisation. The externalised object was formless; that is to say, though people embodied the existence of God by way of churches, doctrines, priests, holy images, rites, and so on, such externalised core objects were after all nothing more than imaginary. Because they were imaginary, they had to find their way back into the human mind; that is, man must have a godly mentality. This mentality in an individual impels him to perform good deeds out of his consciousness of his original sin. In short, the kindness of the Westerner originates in an internal mentality that is brought forth by external guidance.

Unlike Western thought, Chinese thought emphasises the concept of "heaven," which, as an objective entity (albeit one that lacks the significance of God), could have widespread punitive effects on the people (via the concept of retribution). The effect worked perfectly well in folk belief. However, this effect had been dissolved by Confucianist thought. In the structure of Confucianist thought, the "benevolence and righteousness" held high by Mencius, as inherited from Confucius, linked the conscience of the people with heaven. The good in human nature derived from the integrity of the ways of heaven. The relationship between "heaven" and "man" was not one of retribution, but one of impact and communication. In this way, heaven was at the bottom of the human mind in the sense that people commonly referred to through sayings like "heaven bequeaths virtue to me" and the "conscience of heaven and earth." Theoretically, such an arrangement was both sacred and sublime; however, it left no room for the private desires and personal gains of the people. Whoever found a place for such desires would be deemed a mean man, but a man could transform himself into a virtuous man (a gentleman) by cultivating his person. Hence, the practical life and the realm of attainment were detached. Apart from the sages and the great Confucianist scholars, most people could only practice duplicity, a mismatch between word and conduct, name and essence. Meanwhile, Legalists advanced the opposite thought, regulating people's conduct through stringent punishments. This situation could not properly express the true intent of the people either.

As there was no monotheistic belief tradition in traditional Chinese culture, the discussion of human nature was from the start about the internality of man. We believe that without the imaginary covenants of externality the requirements for self-discipline would be much higher for man. The ancient sages of China guided us in this direction, imposing a great challenge for future Chinese. The point is that examining the history of China's thoughts, including its assumptions about human nature, seems nice. This pleasantness is another reason Confucianist thought has always been held high; however, discussion confined to the realm of thought may lead easily to a situation in which the harsh social reality is ignored. For instance, many adamant proponents of the former view tend to believe that they must return to Confucianist thought for panacea whenever social problems arise, and they unjustifiably claim that contemporary views are not as good as those of the ancients because morality is spiralling, the times are experiencing moral degeneration, and so forth. Through such theorisation, they want to demonstrate that the contemporary world has failed to act according to the principles of Confucianist thought; otherwise, society would not have been reduced to its present sorry state. However, in fact, there exists a giant gap between Confucianist thought and social reality. As we stated above, the Confucianist proposed the following assumption in its exposition of the credit issue through its ideal rule of virtue: If everyone is of integrity, then the interaction of the individuals would beget trust, and the credit of the entire country would operate properly, which is an exact replica of the lofty ideal of "cultivating the person, regulating the family properly, governing the state rightly, and bringing peace to the empire." In this mode of inference, the logical starting point is obviously personal morality; hence, it is believed that so long as the issue of personal morality is solved, all other ensuing problems will be solved. This hypothesis is logically sound; however, logical soundness does not mean that it will work in social reality, as it is difficult for everyone to be honest in practical life.

Although the ultimate purpose of both Chinese "introspection" and Western "religious beliefs" is to attain self-discipline, compared with the resorting to externality (god or deity) of Western "religious beliefs," Chinese "introspection" totally depends on self-discipline, which is more challenging, more uncertain, and more difficult to attain. The character of benevolence Confucianists pursued can also be explained as the collective pursuit of "benevolence, righteousness, rite, intelligence, integrity." Here "integrity" means "to be honest and dependable" in conducting oneself. So, on what precondition can this character be attained? Though we have no answer to this question, it could only be a question of scale when returning to the sociological perspective to discuss the issue: The smaller the scale of a society – for instance, between two persons, or within a family, or among people of close relationship such as a friend group – the greater the possibility that this character will manifest itself. But with the increase of social scale, the smaller the possibility this character will be manifest. As a result, it follows that two conditions must be in place when a society attempts to regulate its order with the rule of virtue: (a) everyone must be honest and (b) the society must be of very small scale. When it comes to China, neither of the two conditions applies. The end result is that what Confucianists had constructed, in the final analysis, is an ideal form of society rather than an effective form of governance for a real, modern society. However hard the Chinese work at it, the ideal state of universal peace, harmony, and prosperity will not materialise.

What's more, Confucianist thought is not perfect in itself; its inherent inconsistency has been open to question since ancient times. For instance, the benevolence the Confucianists pursued was originally meant to maintain consistency among different rites. However, there is a core issue of internal logic in Confucianist thought that is unsolved: The "filial piety" and "virtue" it sets store by often come into conflict. That is to say, on the one hand, the Confucianist wanted to demonstrate the top priority of the principle of "respecting the elders" ("loving relatives being the supreme principle"), and, on the other hand, he also emphasised personal cultivation as the basis for benevolence. This quickly led to a paradox, that is, with what character should one treat his parents and other relatives? If this problem is not fixed, then implementing the principle of "Do unto others as you would do unto yourself" leads to a greater problem. Actually, this problem was raised by the Duke of She in the Confucian Analects.

> The Duke of She informed Confucius, saying, "Among us here there are those who may be styled upright in their conduct. If their fathers have stolen a sheep, they will bear witness to the fact." Confucius said, "Among us, in our part of the country, those who are upright are different from this. The father conceals the misconduct of the son, and the son conceals the misconduct of the father. Uprightness is to be found in this."
>
> (The Confucian Analects – Zilu)

It seems that Confucianism may justify itself logically. What it tries to express is that if the son denounces the father, it would be the biggest unvirtuous deed. Therefore, there should be kindness in human nature, and kindness manifests itself in the form of filial piety, in the form of the care administered to the father by the son. However, if we are to return to the moral ground preached by the Confucianists, then the principle of conducting oneself is gone. If, in the words of Confucius, "uprightness" is found in kindness, then "uprightness" is actually a pretext; "uprightness" cannot always subsume "kindness," so one cannot always be upright and kind. To put it in a graver tone, if kindness is treated with uprightness, the consequence is the elimination of kindness with truthfulness retained; however, if uprightness is treated with kindness, the consequence is un-uprightness, or even the elimination of truthfulness. Confucianist doctrine pins its hopes on the individual being honest, upright, and abiding; however, it also hopes that the "benevolence" it advocates incorporates tender love, fraternity, and compassion. The Confucianist aspires to have it both ways; however, these internal contradictions have long plagued the Chinese people. The immediate consequence is that, on one hand, people agree with the statement that "denouncing your close family for the sake of uprightness" is an act of justice; on the other, people also subscribe to the principle of "concealing the crime of your close relations." Hence, it may be seen that the human-nature assumption pursued by down-to-earth Chinese is a mixture of good and evil, while the "hierarchy" embodied in benevolence becomes the optimal solution to resolve the foregoing contradiction. Virtually all Chinese agree to apply the virtues of kindness, trustfulness, and integrity to relationships without vouching for applying the same to strangers. In other words, indifference and selfishness between strangers do not negate the morality of the Confucianist; it all depends on how far the interpersonal relationship goes.

In conclusion, on the issue of the human-nature assumption, Confucianist thought is not as consistent in its ideas as those of "original sin" are in Western Christianity. The Confucianist thought system has internal limitations and contradictions as well as major disagreements with other schools of thought, including the Taoist and the Legalist. In addition, the characteristics of human nature in the real world differ considerably from those described in ancient texts. In the long run, this problem has to some degree contributed to the formation of the situation-dependent characteristics of the Chinese mentally and behaviourally. In other words, under the façade of superficial formal harmony, the Chinese have, in essence, been coping with different practical issues by using many sets of standards to suit different social scenarios and social requirements.

5 Institution and Trust

Morality, public opinion, networks, and the norms formed on the interpersonal level can sustain credit in a small-scale society; however, these things cannot be counted on exclusively in a large-scale society or in a modern society with elaborate social division of labour. Western sociological theory holds that trust and risk are closely related in modern society, and the institution of a trust system may help prevent risks.[1] Luhmann noted, "Due to the inevitability of risk, the form it takes will be decisive … The system can relatively easily assume the complexity of risk inherent in trust."[2] Giddens too believed that risk and trust are interwoven; however, the types of risk can be institutionalised.[3] Institutionalisation may be the basic characteristic of the establishment of modern credit, so the establishment thereof cannot be taken for granted. How institutions are designed and run involves a culture's assumptions about human nature and is also sustained by social credit. If the establishment of a certain institution does not take into consideration the basis of popular trust, the operation of such an institution must rely heavily on control instead of credit. Because this point seems hard to put across, this chapter shall be devoted to an examination of the issue.

5.1 The Relationship between Institution and Trust and Transformation Thereof

In order to understand the relationship between institution and trust, let's take domestic traffic rules for illustration: Smooth traffic depends on most drivers' understanding and abiding by the rules stipulated by the specific area. Therefore, if you are driving on a road, even if you have absolutely no knowledge of the driver of the vehicle driving towards you, so long as you keep to the correct side of the road while driving in accordance with traffic rules, you will not be worried about being hit. The reason for this certainty is that you know for sure that the traffic law provides that all drivers must drive on a particular side of the road; otherwise, there will be either stringent punishment or a crash and casualties. The function of institutions is that people are encouraged or punished through their subscription to the stipulations. Institutions may confine people's behaviour within a certain boundary so as to attain certainty from social uncertainty, and thus they compel people to form some expectation of the pending actions.[4] The instance of traffic rules illustrates, on the one hand, that punishment in traffic situations can be expected and is

DOI: 10.4324/9781003375579-7

not to be toyed with; on the other hand, it illustrates that the institution guarantees mutual trust between drivers. From this angle, it follows that the institution itself can ensure mutual social trust, reduce uncertainties in social exchange, and enhance the stability of social operations. However, there is a grander trust embodied in "every trust includes an element of trust in the constraining mechanism itself."[5] However complex and however perfect an institution may be, the prerequisite for its performance still depends on people's trust in the institution itself. Giddens has a similar argument. He believed that the characteristics of the modern institution are closely related to the trust mechanism of abstract systems (especially the trust in the expert system) and is, to a substantial degree, constructed out of trust from abstract systems.[6] For example, when we are driving, we are able to do so not because we trust another driver but because we believe that most drivers will abide by the rule of keeping to the correct side of the road while driving. To run this argument further, we trust that the traffic rules will create definite traffic effects. If the precondition of trust in an institution is lost, the principal control effected by the institution would not be to punish dishonest behaviours but to cope with the absence of credit in the environment. Concerning this point, let's review a story about Shang Yang, the famous Chinese legalist:

Shang Yang failed to obtain an important position in his native country, so he went to the Kingdom of Qin in an attempt to find employment for his talent. He presented his reformist statements to King Xiaogong of Qin and won the approval of the monarch. However, his reforms met with fierce opposition among the nobles of Qin. As King Xiaogong had freshly ascended to the throne and was worried about the instability of the political situation, he had to postpone the reforms.

Two years later, when King Xiaogong found the time ripe for reformation, he appointed Shang Yang the prime minister and decreed that Shang Yang would be fully in charge of the reform affairs.

Having drafted the reforming laws, Shang Yang was concerned that his laws were not being observed by the people. Therefore, he had a pole ten metres tall raised at the South Gate of the capital and decreed that "anyone carrying this pole to the North Gate will be awarded 10 taels of copper coins." In no time, a crowd clustered around the South Gate. The crowd noted, "it's a pole of no considerable weight for anyone; how could moving it carry a ten-tael copper award? Aren't these officials playing a prank on us?" They stood there conversing and conjecturing; nobody moved.

Shang Yang knew that the people still did not take his decree seriously, so he raised the award to 50 taels of coppers. To his surprise, the higher the award, the fewer people dared to try. All thought the newly installed prime minister mad. While people were in wild conjecture on the matter, a man stepped forward, saying, "Let's try." With these words, he lifted the pole and carried it to the North Gate. Having seen the deed done, Shang Yang awarded 50 taels of coppers on the spot.

When this story got out, it took the country by storm. The people of the Qin Kingdom remarked universally, "the Law of Shang Yang means business." After this event, Shang Yang promulgated his newly drafted reform laws, with clearly demarcated stipulations on punishment and award in the new law. Since the Shang Yang Reform, the Qin Kingdom saw substantial growth in national strength, which laid the foundation for its future cause of unifying the six kingdoms. This anecdote explains the allusion of "standing a pole at the south gate" and is also the origin of the Chinese idiom "to build up credit by moving a pole." By the Song Dynasty, Wang Anshi, the famous reformist statesman and literary giant, commended the noble spirit embodied in the resolution to carry out reformation and the dedication to one's promises, saying,

> Integrity is the principle of employing the people from old,
> A word said weighs heavier than a million gold.
> Shang Yang is not to be rubbished by men of today,
> He could enforce his decrees without delay.

The moral of the story is clear, that is, if the efficacy of an institution is to be fully brought out, the first thing is to make people have faith in it. This is the lesson the story intends to communicate to us. Having read so far, we can't help but ask: If trust in the institution is successfully formed, will the people still get the award the first ones got when they vied with each other to implement the institution for purposes of gain? For instance, if there is an institution that sets an award for courageous acts, will courageous acts really be rewarded? The very question demonstrates that efficacy is dwindling. A deeper issue is that behind the institution are the social assumptions of its members. The assumptions based on human nature guide the direction of institutional design. For instance, in a traditional or relatively simple society, familiarity is the precondition for the most direct and effective credit. In a familiar environment, all share a common world outlook, so a common mode of interaction can be expected by all. Hence, Fei Hsiao-tung said, "In rural society, trust derives from familiarity." This kind of trust has very solid foundations, for it is rooted in customary norms. Even today, Western merchants often remark that trustworthiness is an innate quality of the Chinese.[7] Similarly, Luhmann also noted,

> In interpersonal communication, only a portion of this familiarity is said, while the rest is presumed as the basis of understanding. Moral assessment is self-evident from the perspectives of kindness and correctness. As to questions of "who" is experiencing, or what is the subject of the meaning construction, the sincere, familiar being itself has no motive to pursue.[8]

Furthermore, even if we have encountered problems like immorality or differences of identity, they have already lost the significance of difference in a world of perfect consensus and will neither induce serious doubt nor generate uncertainty. In such a society,

> We are totally inseparable from our community, because we have absolutely no self in it, and the society exists and operates within us ... when the collective

> consciousness overlaps all our consciousness and communes with us in all aspects, then the union derived from similarity has developed to its perfection.[9]

However, when people get familiar with each other is established as a public assumption of a society; in that case, people of such a society still employ the network of familiarity to settle the issue of unfamiliar people even if there are people unfamiliar in interactions. In other words, it is still sufficient for such a society to cope with the situation of unfamiliar people by extending social networks via interpersonal trust. However, with the development of society, the expansion of social divisions of labour, the deepening of specialisation and the intensification of differentiation as well as the growth of the scope of social interaction, interpersonal trust fails to cope with the indirect, inter-community, inter-organisational interaction among strangers. At that point, trust has ascended to the status of a social system, whereas trust on the personal level has also upgraded to the level of social-system trust. Fei Hsiao-tung had a straightforward remark on this:

> Modern society is composed of strangers. We do not know each other's pasts. When we talk, we must explain things clearly. Even then, we fear that oral agreements are not binding: therefore, we draw up written contracts to which we sign our names. Laws arise in just this fashion … Modern society composed of strangers cannot use the customs of a rural society to cope with the trust issue.[10]

Luhmann made a still more academic and reasoned argument. He believed that

> When a social order turns more complex and versatile, generally speaking, it tends to lose the natural ground justifying its character and the natural familiarity known to all, because it can only be conjectured or reviewed in fragments via everyday experience. However, it is this complexity of social order that creates greater need for cooperation, and in turn, creates need that determines the future; that is to say, the need for trust is now getting increasingly turned away from familiarity. Under these environments, familiarity and trust must seek to form a new mutually reinforcing relationship. This type of relationship is no longer built on an adjacent world of immediate experience, guaranteed by tradition. Guarantees of such a relationship can by no means be provided by keeping strangers, enemies, and unfamiliar people out of some sort of bounds. It follows that trust derived from familiarity is limited to an interpersonal relationship, and along with the advent of modernity, no endeavors on the plane of interpersonal relationship can acclimate such a society. If future uncertainty, insecurity, and unpredictable events are to be tolerated, the society would need a systemic trust. It includes adventure as a conscious activity, the discarding of some possibly deep-level information, and a consistent control of results.[11]

In this way, human society would "naturally" evolve to the stage of "trust of institution." At this time, the institution, the organisation, and the role in which the individual exists have gradually replaced the important role of experience and familiarity in the domain of trust. People usually begin to think about the importance and reliability of the former to their personal interests. Exactly as Giddens remarked, "symbolic sign" and "expert system" are both included in the development of modern social systems and faith is expressed in the trust of institutions.[12] That is to say, when interpersonal trust retreats to the secondary position and

> people think about whether a system is favourable to themselves, they usually rely on the specific content of the system; that is to say, when interpersonal trust retreats to a secondary position, people tend to base their considerations on the specific content of the institution in weighing whether an institution is favorable to themselves. However, when they judge whether an institution can be effectively implemented, they consider organisations related to the institution, and such organisations are composed of people. In other words, an institution is implemented by specific social roles such as policeman, doctor, teacher. Therefore, trust in an institution entails trust in the institutional rules, the organisation, and the roles implementing such an institution.[13]

Trust in an institution includes both a consensus and a covenant within a culture towards the institution (at least the collective sanction and observance by the group of social members addressed by the institution). It also includes the trust of certain individuals in the process, mechanisms, and efficacy of the institution's implementation. The former implies social values regarding institutional design, whereas the latter implies an expectation or a judgement regarding an institution's implementation. The practical effects of institutional operation will readjust these expectations and judgements of the institution according to the effects returned. When the internal effectiveness of punishment and reward of an institution declines, it indicates the failure of such an institution, and it will lose the trust of the people within and around it.

5.2 Matching Cultural Presupposition with Institutional Design

We may also discover that, at the macro-level, as a cultural rule, trust may be viewed as an overall property of society, which entails an obligation to conform to norms and has a powerful binding force on both parties to a trust relationship.[14] Furthermore, the environment, the operation of a society, as well as the practical issues it faces have a great bearing on the type of trust system to be instituted. For instance, the trust system of a rural civilisation differs from that of an industrial civilisation; that of a planned economy differs from that of a market economy; the blueprint for social development of a Confucianist differs radically from that of a republican. Behind these conspicuous practical forms lie important questions, such as, why are a series of systems instituted this way rather than that way? These questions concern the humanity assumption underlying a society (or organisation).

Past discussions regarding cultural type and the humanity assumption come mostly from philosophy, economics, political study, ethics, anthropology, and even literature. The discipline that directly connects the humanity assumption and the trust system is primarily management, perhaps because management lays more emphasis on how the assumptions of a cultural philosophy relate to a system. This method of examination further benefits from some research findings from economics, psychology, sociopsychology, and management. For instance, when the "assumption of economic man" is adopted and transformed by scholars of classical management theories, including those of Frederick W. Taylor, there comes into existence a set of scientific management modes, which include task management, incentive systems, and supervision systems. Sociopsychologist G. E. Myao founded the study of management in sociopsychology for proposing the "hypothesis of social man" in the Hawthorne Experiment, which led to the study of teamwork, collective honour, interpersonal communication, and so forth by the management circle. Further, in the field of psychology, the leading researcher Abraham H. Maslow set the "self-realization of man" as the supreme need in his hierarchy of needs theory, prompting management scholars to assume it as an assumption about humanity, all of which resulted in the appearance of the humanistic management model. The management models arising from the humanity assumptions of economic man and the self-realising man were summarised as the X theory and the Y theory by Douglas M. McGregor.[15] Along with the American management researchers' study of the Japanese enterprise management model, they further advanced the Z theory to manifest the possibility of a pluralistic humanity behind the management models.[16] In the repeated changes of the humanity assumption, we can clearly see the lockstep movement between humanity and institutional arrangement. It follows that so long as we want to make any institutional arrangements, it will necessarily involve the issue of the humanity assumption.

So, specifically, how does the humanity assumption in Western society and culture relate to the institution, the operation, and the guarantee of social trust? First, we may inspect the significance of the "hypothesis of economic man" on institutional trust. For instance, Olson held that, in addition to people engaged in the private economic sector, participants in public activities are also constrained by institutional trust; and both have the inclination to maximally amplify their interests, the so-called public interest (collective interest).[17] It follows that the existence of an organisation or community is meant to promote the interest of its members. That is to say, if any collective action is to be made possible, it is necessary to make all members of the specific group or organisation realise that the interest obtained from collective action outweighs that obtained from individual action.[18] This necessity requires that certain effective incentive measures be established and certain punitive measures to curb any "freeriding" behaviour. Only in this way can a basis for the long-term existence of trust in an institution be formed.[19] Actually, proceeding from this hypothesis of economic man, Douglas C. North noted bluntly that

> the crux of system operation lies in that foul-play entails cost, and there is also a varying degree of gravity of punishment … the primary function of

an institution in a society is to establish a stabilising mechanism by which people may interact in order to reduce uncertainty.[20]

Sociologist James Coleman made a slight modification to the economic man hypothesis by implementing a relatively general rational-choice theory of the individual as the precondition for discussing the issue of social trust. In this way, he tried to analyse the trust relationship between the client, the trustee, and the intermediary from the integrated macro and micro theoretical perspective he himself set up, channelling the discussion of interpersonal trust towards the importance of the role, the community, and the related punishment measures of the institution-related agent.[21] Meanwhile, in the realm of politics, democratic politics is regarded as the "institutionalised distrust" of power and power-holders by many Western researchers.[22] A certain distrust is critical to a viable democratic order.[23] In other words, democracy needs to prove the rationality and credibility of all powers; these powers are in essence viewed as doubtful.[24] Therefore, extra monitoring mechanisms and measures of checks and balances are required to guarantee the reliability of a democracy. It could thus be said that, economically, sociologically, and politically, institutional trust in Western society is grounded in a universal, presupposed distrust in institutions and a guarantee of preventative and monitoring measures. The style of design of this institution necessarily relates to its humanity hypothesis and the problems this suggests. The rational "economic man" theory will doubtlessly push the "man is selfish" argument that arises from the "hypothesis of the evil nature of humanity" out of the topmost position in Western culture's hierarchy of humanity assumptions. When this assumption is carried out in practice, a set of complicated institutions and corresponding punishment measures are created, which realistically guarantee the effectiveness of institutional trust. Following this logic, we may understand all the set of cultural assumptions about human nature and the institutional arrangements for trust in Western societies.

Now let's examine some institutional arrangement issues in Chinese society. In the discussion of the preceding chapter, we can see that, in his review of the humanity assumption, the traditional Chinese thinker aims to find the internal transcendence of man, that is, he is trying to demonstrate the good or evil nature of man. When Confucianist thought prevails in Chinese history, the argument "man is kind by nature" ultimately becomes the basic statement on the human nature of traditional Chinese culture. The kind nature of man and the expectation of his morality are employed in combination in practice, with the original purpose being to encourage people to have self-discipline in action. However, our research data indicates that these are not the current assumptions and expectations of China. The Chinese manifest distrust in practical life; absent external institutional constraints, the people would, as a rule, manifest no self-discipline. The following examples make this point all the more clear:

When we live away from home in a hotel, there is always a waiting period for the hotel attendant to check the room when we step up to the reception desk to check out. This step shows the hotel has no faith in the report by the guest on what he has consumed or has taken away; it must be verified by the room attendant prior to his release.

There are usually pretty firm rails to keep the lines of people in order in the ticket booths of China's railway stations and long-distance bus terminals, even though such measures cannot completely ensure ticket purchase. Consequently, ticket-inspection personnel are installed at almost every exit to inspect whether there are freeriding passengers, slowing the flow of the multitudes of passengers eager to get out. In order to find the assumed freeriding passenger, all passengers must pass the inspection before leaving.

There are many hawkers vending tourist maps in the bus and railway stations of Chinese cities as well as at their docks. Conversely, there are few tourist maps available at the airports, bus and railway stations, and docks for people to take for free.

If one is to conduct business with government departments, he will have to pass the gate guards and the reception booth. He needs to register, call for an appointment, or even arrange for someone from inside the department to take him in. Anyone who tries to enter straightforwardly shall be forced out as a disrupter of order.

What is more, the reimbursement processes of the various agencies in China are each unique in their own way. Consider the stipulations on project funding for academic research at a university or research institution. The use of project funds is subject to strict provisions. For instance, the joint signature of three persons (the college or institution leader, a library employee, a handler) is required to buy a book in accordance with these provisions, and at least two official seals (college or department seal, library seal) are to be affixed to the paperwork; only then will such an expense be reimbursed from the project funds. What is most incredible is that if a section member has taken a flight on a business trip, he will have to bring back the boarding pass to prove that he has really taken the flight.

The aforementioned cases may seem insignificant, but all these regulations and institutions reveal one important piece of information, i.e., that the institutions were established on the basis of distrust: "I don't trust you" is the orientation of institution design. Hence, when institutions are established according to such a credo, credit must be proved through various links, resulting in an extremely complex, tedious, and bureaucratic set of tasks that greatly increase the human cost. For instance, under the reimbursement regime, from the financial staff to the company providing consumption articles to the consumer, all are required to furnish evidential materials to prove their honesty. Obviously, the more popular these instances are, the more they reveal that the Chinese doubt the idea that humanity is kind or moral. In other words, in Chinese society, with its Confucian roots, hardly anyone would deny that human nature is kind, but this society also demonstrates through its institutional design that such an assumption cannot be accepted. The institution tries to effect a goal of zero-tolerance; that is, so long as there is one bad guy in a group, all members of the group must be placed under examination so that this one bad guy will not go unpunished. This example indicates how the costs will escalate.

However, do such institutions actually work? What effect does an institution established on such an assumption bring about? What we have seen are irregularities (which should be viewed as malicious acts) of ever-increasing scale, which have even developed into various "industries." Indeed, the more the institution tries to prevent people from going beyond bounds, the more people rack their brains to find ways of going beyond bounds. In cities across China, we are flooded with enquiries asking whether we need an invoice; this happens through the posters and graffiti for fake certificates in bus and railway stations and on the docks as well as through mobile phone text messages and even private e-mail messages. Fake invoices and fake certificates are customised for the various processes of various financial and verification regimes. Similar phenomena may also be found in China's many fake, copycat, and inferior products, as well as in its many instances of copyright plagiarism and piracy, all of which render China an obvious place of fake and inferior products and of piracy and copyright infringement.

Over the past ten years, the integrity crisis has had a far-reaching and wide-ranging impact on China. The government, judiciary, enterprise, stock exchange, education, literature and art, media, medicine, and academia are all involved. The government has introduced new institutions, hoping to contain the problems of dishonesty by various crack-down measures; however, any such crack-down could provide only temporary relief, given that the credit crisis has not been foundationally solved. However, technological innovation has rendered some original institutions insignificant. For instance, the Chinese go online to buy tickets when they go on a journey; this makes the iron railings in front of the ticket windows pointless. However, in other areas where there is no similar technological advance, credit issues remain. Credit treatment in China often falls into a weird cycle: The government incessantly demands that pertinent departments step up supervision, while the people ceaselessly cook up new methods to evade such supervision. On the one hand, China aims to effect a rule of law where there is leniency, yet it lets no criminal go; on the other hand, the fact remains "that the cheater often outwits the chaser." In this game of cat and mouse, there is no final winner, just a society that pays a tremendous price.

There exists an inverse relationship between the strictures of an institution and the operations of trust: The more numerous the institutional regulations and provisions a society introduces, and the more such regimes proliferate in general, the less trust exists within that society, making external controls even more necessary. On the other hand, the more people are honest and trust each other, the less institutional regulation needs to be invoked. This can be likened to the state of security windows in a city: The more widespread security windows are, to some extent, the worse the public security the city faces, and the more burglaries there are. On the opposite side of the continuum, the better the folk custom, the fewer burglaries, and the more likely the people there will be honest. From the orientation in which current social institutions are designed, people will have to prove themselves good people through repeated verifications when taking a vehicle, drawing cash, visiting the doctor, shopping, gaining admission through a janitor, checking in to a hotel, obtaining authorisations, in reimbursement procedures, etc.

Regarding the relationship between institutions and trust, we have so far gained another understanding: There is a preventative principle of institutional design that holds that evil will necessarily occur. In terms of preventing human nature from developing into evil, the institution might not be able to change the human mind, but it could prevent people from engaging in evil conduct. There is another institutional design principle that holds that most people are good, and such an institution is established on the trust of the people, which manifests faith in human kindness. However, what if someone really does evil? This issue could not be fixed due to the lack of rigour of the institution or the inherent inadequacy in its design. Such institutions could do nothing but watch helplessly as it is exploited. However, its supportive measures could apply punishment after the commitment of irregularities. For instance, an institution has a stringent fiscal policy that presumes distrust in people. If a person passes the review of the institution, it indicates that there is no financial issue with this person, even though such a person may really be in financial trouble. The possibility of such a situation is due to the pursuit of so-called "preparing the account" or "no apparent issue with the account." The stipulations of another institution's fiscal policy may be easier, under which many expenses are not allowed (assuming trust in people). However, if misappropriation or illegality occurs, such will be punished after the fact; that is, punishment shall be carried out through methods of tracking down or surprise inspection, sampling inspection, and so on. Once a person is proven to be engaging in irregularity, he would be punished with the most stringent measures. We may conclude that the orientation of institutional design falls in the former category; however, when there is a scenario where punishment of the latter category is required, Chinese culture will fall back to the philosophy of treating people with kindness and punishing the wrongdoer lightly.

5.3 Returning to Tradition in the Paradox of Institutional Operation

Having analysed so far, some might ask: Don't Western cultures also emphasise that it is in the nature of man to avoid suffering and harm? Isn't human nature held to be selfish, i.e., don't men pursue the maximisation of their personal interests? Actually, through analysis of Western institutions, we arrived at the conclusion that at least their institutional design is kindness-oriented (this is also the reason why some overseas Chinese can exploit their institutions and capitalise to their advantage). To prevent people from engaging in evil conduct, the only resort is stringent punishment after the fact. This kindness-oriented design philosophy originates in the assumption that human desire may be salvaged even though it is by nature evil. Actually, in *The Protestant Ethic and the Spirit of Capitalism*, Max Weber makes a similar point. Weber holds that one can manifest the glory of God only through the property that one acquires through hard work, frugal living, and lawful business conduct in the secular world.[25] This point also suggests that the industry and frugality of Westerners are externally guided.

However, the "hypothesis of the good nature of humanity" in Chinese culture leads to a discrepancy between concepts and behaviour. The Chinese sing high-sounding tunes on the moral plane while at the same time guarding strictly in practical operation, which leads to a situation wherein the people have to constantly switch between values, institutions, implementation, and punishment. Hence, compared with Western institutional arrangements, we find that Chinese institutional design falls into a paradox of hypothesising the kindness of human nature on the value plane while holding men (and especially strangers) as not to be trusted.

In fact, the shift between good and bad manifested under the institutional arrangement based on these dual assumptions of human nature will lead to a situation wherein people lose confidence in the effect of institutional implementation; some will even start to doubt the effectiveness of the institution itself, which will lead to the prevalence of substanceless formalism, or movement-style correction, in turn seriously harming an institutional arrangement that aims at conscientious conformation by the people.

We may discover signs of this phenomenon by availing ourselves of the data gleaned from the present survey.[26] For instance, from the perspective of the attitude towards trust in institutional enforcement agencies, the public shows a typical differential mode of "strongly favourable to the central government and pertinent departments thereof and less favourable to the local government and pertinent departments thereof" in terms of the degree of trust. Public trust in immediate enforcement agencies is much lower than that of more abstract or remote central agencies, with the gap standing at nearly 30%. Compared with the trust in various levels of governmental agencies, the degree of trust in various levels of party organisation is lower. From the perspective of public trust in institutional enforcement officials, the interviewees rate the credit situation of administrative personnel quite poorly. Less than 20% of the public gives a rating of "strongly agree" when evaluating the administrative character and administrative competence of most officials. The public particularly questions the corruption and graft of officials. In addition, the public generally rates the effectiveness of institutions as quite low. Among all the ratings of policy institutions, only five items show 60% of interviewees rating them as satisfactory, including earthquake and disaster relief, mandatory education, socialised old-age services, medical security, and the household registration system. On the other hand, public ratings of institutions closely related to people's well-being, like food-safety supervision and charity, had less than 50% rated satisfactory.

We also found in our survey that rural dwellers rated social credit higher than city dwellers. The main reason underlying this phenomenon is that the rural area keeps the characteristics of the rural society; there, the familiarity and immobility in space make it possible to maintain the reputation punishment mechanism of the individual. The practical effect far exceeds the constraining mechanism based on jurisprudence or covenant, as in everyday interaction people would prefer relationship trust to institutional trust. In the city, the social network and the moral constraint typical of the rural society seem to have disappeared, but in practice, most people still rely on the trust established through familiarity and relationships such as classmates, colleagues, comrades in arms, teacher-student, and fellow countryman. These relationships are especially important on occasions of critical importance in life, such as choosing a kindergarten, entering a key primary or middle school, as well as seeing the doctor for critical illness.

Therefore, as we emphasised at the beginning of this book that when Chinese people are unable to trust and confirm the credibility of various social institutions in real life, their psychosocial path dependence will "instinctively" return to the family relatives they have always valued and their extended network of relationships to seek refuge, in other words, to use the limited familiarity and experience of their original acquaintance network to obtain a basis and guarantee of trust and to overcome the credit anxiety caused by the uncertain modern social environments. We may also extend this view to the macro society. For instance, over the past ten years, China's urban population of migrant workers has numbered about 100 million. However, further examination reveals that large proportions of these migrant workers have replicated and extended their original village fellow relationships in their city life even though they have migrated to the city in pursuit of a job. There is a vivid description of this phenomenon in Henan province, namely, "pulling the vines": Pulling one vine may end up getting up to dozens of vines.[27] Social movement effected via means of relationship chains means migrant workers are not lone actors in their outbound work. However, this mode of life makes it impossible for them to survive in a new place. They are insulated from the local residents, and it is hard for them to forge trust with the locals. Therefore, they can only migrate to a city in a group of country fellows – and can only enter the same factory if they are to maintain mutual help. Even if they do not work in the same city or factory, their direction of migration will still follow the acquaintance network to prepare them for the next job. In this way, floating villages have formed on the peripheries of metropolises, clustered into settlements (e.g., Zhejiang village). There is also the phenomenon of fellow countrymen engaging in the same trade or commercial division. This phenomenon takes place not only at home; it even has its derivatives overseas (for instance, Wenzhou merchants in Paris).[28] Of course, in actual life, the likeness of "relationship" can be found almost everywhere, be it job hunting, seeing the doctor, going to school, doing business, or even solving trivial matters of life. To summarise, Chinese people today still use relationships to strengthen their trust in each other in the face of increased social mobility and uncertainty in all aspects of society.

5.4 Endemic Morality and External Guidance

Generally speaking, the outlook on humanity expressed by the residents surveyed in this empirical study shows an equivocal attitude of "both good and bad." Upon further factor analysis, we found that, when it came to morality and mental consciousness, the interviewees were inclined to place the hypothesis of good human nature before the hypothesis of evil human nature. That is to say, most Chinese tend to consider others as kind and hence trustworthy. This coincides with the overall assumption of traditional Chinese thinking and morality regarding the hypothesis of the good nature of humanity. However, the complexity lies in that when we descend into the realm of concrete behaviour in real life and get away from an abstract outlook on human nature, this positive outlook on human nature wavers. Specifically, Chinese in real life tend to place self-interest before actions benefiting others. That is to say, when it comes to specific action volition and action judgement, most Chinese tend towards the hypothesis that others are not trustworthy and should be guarded against. This means that, although people tend to place the idea of a good human nature before that of an evil human nature, in practice, people reverse the order of the two. Be it an average everyday event or major social event, when an event occurs, the first thing people do is to weigh the matter in a way mixing both good and evil aspects, thinking that "you may not harm others; however, you must also guard against the possible harm others may inflict on you," and prioritise private interest. What is more complex is that the private interest not only includes the individual self, but also the relationship network linked to the self, which produces a clearly demarcated situation of the insider and the outsider.

In China, the biggest issue in traditional Confucianist thought on the humanity assumption is the absence of that external guiding mechanism (including a punishment mechanism). Such an absence will inevitably lead Chinese people to reorient their focus to the examination of "conscience." Extremists would attribute this phenomenon to the inferior national nature of the Chinese. However, in fact, such an attribution takes a detour from reality and experience and reverts to the original place of the assumption of humanity. It could be seen that such an attribution is futile, for it does not offer a real answer; what it offers is only unhinged rhetoric. In other words, what does "inferior national nature" even mean? Is it innate or cultural? Our answer to the question is that any measures aiming to right the mind of the people without external guidance are as futile as milking the bull, because this practice of pinning hope on the awakening of conscience presumes the good nature of humanity, while its scope of effect hardly extends to strangers.

The humanity assumption on which the contemporary Chinese credit system is based may be said to be a hybrid of Confucianist, legalist, socialist, and Western legal ideas. The original intent was to draw from the merits of each, but the result is an illogical hodgepodge. This has led to a situation in which people are clueless when problems arise, while the government can find no effective solution other than to be a firefighter. The absence of an external guide that we have pointed out above refers to the problem of how a person should conduct good deeds in contemporary society if his internal morality or cultivation has failed to regulate his personal conduct. The other path to good, via the so-called external guide, refers to the fact that man could achieve goodness through faith. For instance, among the Chinese people (excluding, of course, orthodox Confucianists), there was a strong belief in retribution. Even today, there is still a saying among Chinese: You've got to pay it back, sooner or later.

We might ask, why, after all this history, has the good nature of humanity preached by the Confucianists only become a problem today? Doesn't that demonstrate that Confucianist ideas have worked well in maintaining the credit of the Chinese? We hold that this previous history of credit success did not originate in the forceful cultivation powers of the Confucianists, but arose instead from the communities in which people lived, which in turn points to the acquaintance society. The trust network coincides with the manipulation of public ethical opinion to a high degree. The coincidence of the "rule of virtue" ideology preached by the Confucianist with the actual structure of China's rural society aims not only at reconstructing the individual mind through moralisation but also at maintaining a relationship network that works as a social control that makes it difficult to generate internal trust. In other words, even if the norms of Confucianist thought are not effective, genetic relationships could generate basic interpersonal trust among people, making it easier to feel an affinity with Confucianist thought. Meanwhile, due to the characteristics of the relationship network, the traditional institution of collective liability guaranteed the feasibility of credit at the national or regional level.

From a traditional society to a planned economic society, the social-control mechanism of credit followed similar characteristics and a continuous texture. In both, it was situated in a relatively closed, immobile hometown community or unit community, forming an effective control mechanism over the people residing there. It did so whether it emphasised relationship, including reciprocal favours and public opinion, or whether it relied on the unit system, including the life-employment system and the archiving system. Either way, an effective control mechanism was formed, which rendered the credit issue implicit and hidden from view. Even if problems occurred, they would be regional and isolated, fixed under the categories of morality and irregularity, which did not require much mediation from the law. If the state implemented some sort of ideology or morality education in support of such an institution, it would similarly reinforce the superstructure of the social structure.

However, when China shifted to a market economy, the constraining force of the rural community almost completely disintegrated. People who migrated to industrial civilisation and urban life did not need the moralisation of Confucianist thought. The reason underlying this changed situation was that the acquaintance society vanished, and the interpersonal network was gone. Residents lived in neighbourhoods where they did not know their neighbours, with diversified businesses that rendered the original unit system ineffective. Together, these factors predicted that morality and public opinion would cease to have the kind of constraining power they had in a small-scale society. Of course, some would argue that the issue also involved education. Indeed, this understanding was not wrong in itself. However, external guidance had to be acquired from education, for simple slogans, which could not touch the soul of the people, would not do. If those preaching such slogans failed to have their souls touched, then all such slogans were nothing but an empty formalism that would not affect the operation of Chinese society. In our survey, we have indeed found that education, especially higher education, not only does not have a moralising effect but also lowers the individual's expectation of the good nature of humanity, thus reducing that individual's altruistic behaviour in real life. Analysis reveals that those who have received higher education understand the untruthfulness of sloganeering.

Comparatively speaking, the external guidance of traditional Western culture emphasises that the source of morality originates in the call of God instead of the mind of the individual. Ruth Benedict refers to this as "shame culture." Benedict writes that

> Real shame culture relies on foreign coercive force to conduct good deeds, while real guilt culture relies on the internal reaction out of a sense of guilt. Shame is a reaction to other's criticism. A person feels ashamed for being publicly ridiculed, discriminated against, or scorned. Regardless of type, the sense of shame is an effective coercive force. However, the sense of shame requires the presence of others, at least that the presence of others must be felt, while the sense of guilt does not work this way. In some nations, the connotation of reputation refers to living according to the ideal in one's mind. Here, even if the misconduct is not exposed, the person would still feel guilty, and such sense of guilt would be relieved upon confession.[29]

The "connotation of reputation" refers to its external guidance. Though the Chinese have not developed their own religious doctrines and corresponding institutions in this respect, they have many similar expressions and rituals in Chinese folk beliefs. Expressions such as "there are spirits everywhere," "your conduct will incur retribution," and especially "don't disgrace your ancestors" all fall under the category of external guidance: They place a constraining force on the everyday life of the Chinese. However, such effects are not only not embodied in Confucianist thought, they also ceased to play a role in the market economy after the advent of modernisation.

Perhaps we need to scrutinise the distinction further. Does the foreign coercive force of "shame culture" in Benedict's view also denote external guidance? The crux to understanding all this is that foreign coercive force does not mean external guidance. Foreign coercive force refers to the means through which society controls the individual, whereas external guidance denotes the characteristics of belief, in other words, how social force motivates people to be good. However, the choice of external guidance or internal guidance involves whether the source of goodness of humanity is presumed to be internal or external. Obviously, in the Chinese cultural context, the human heart is presumed to be innate to the individual, whereas in the West, because humanity is presumed to be originally evil, only external guidance can drive people to goodness: God ushers man into the light. By contrast, in China, the good humanity assumption forces Confucianist theory to focus on how to maintain the goodness of human nature. As the inborn good nature of a man may grow to be bad over his lifetime, that man must maintain his goodness by constantly reminding and cautioning himself through the cultivation of his person, which renders external guidance pointless. However, if a person is evil at the bottom of his heart, what does he have to maintain? Confucianist morality cannot answer this practical question.

Notes

1 See Ulrich Beck, Anthony Giddens, and Scott Lash, *Reflexive Modernization: Politics, Tradition and Aesthetics in the Modern Social Order*, translated by Zhao Wenshu, Commercial Press, 2001; Ulrich Beck, *Risk Society: Towards a New Modernity*, trans-

lated by He Bowen, Yilin Press, 2004; Ulrich Beck, *Global Risk Society*, translated by Wu Yingzi, Nanjing University Press, 2004; Piotr Sztompak, *Trust: A Sociological Theory*, translated by Cheng Shengli, Zhonghua Book Company, 2005, pp. 38–51; Anthony Giddens, *The Consequences of Modernity*. Translated by Tian He. Nanjing: Yilin Press, 2011.

2 Luhmann. *Trust: A Simplification Mechanism of Social Complexity*, p. 40.
3 Giddens, *The Consequences of Modernity*, p. 31.
4 See L. G. Zucker, Production of Trust: Institutional Sources of Economic Structure 1840–1920. In B. M. Staw & L. L. Cummings (Eds.), *Research in Organizational Behavior* (8), pp. 53–111. JAI Press, 1986.
5 Zhang Jing, Issues of Trust. *Sociological Studies* 1997(3).
6 Giddens, *Consequences of Modernity*, p. 73.
7 Fei Hsiao-tung, *From the Soil: Foundations of the Chinese Society*, SDX Joint Publishing Company, pp. 5–6.
8 Luhmann, *Trust: A Simplification Mechanism of Social Complexity*, p. 24.
9 Emile Durkheim. The Division of Labor in Society. P. 90.
10 Fei Hsiao-tung. *From the Soil: Foundations of the Chinese Society*, p. 5.
11 Luhmann, *Trust: A Simplification Mechanism of Social Complexity*, p. 27.
12 See Giddens, *The Consequences of Modernity*, p. 19.
13 Fang Lijie. Formation Process of Trust in Institution. Sociological Studies. 2009(2).
14 Sztompak, *Trust: A Sociological Theory*, p. 33.
15 See Daniel A. Wren, *The Evolution of Management Though*, translated by Sun Yaojun et al., China Social Sciences Press, 1986; Mickle D. Boton, *Management of 100 Years*, translated by Wen Gang, China Textile Press, 2003.
16 See William Ouchi, *Theory Z: How American Business Can Meet the Japanese Challenge*, translated by Sun Yaojun et al., China Social Sciences Press, 1984.
17 Mancur Olson, *The Logic of Collective Action*, translated by Chen Yu et al., Shanghai SDX Joint Publishing Company, Shanghai People's Publishing House, 1995. "Prologue by the translator, p. 1.
18 Olson. *The Logic of Collective Action*, pp. 5–8.
19 Ibid., pp. 39–42.
20 Douglas C. North. *Institutions, Institutional Change and Economic Growth*, translated by Hang Xing, Truth & Wisdom Press, Shanghai SDX Joint Publishing Company, Shanghai People's Publishing House, 2008, p. 5, p. 7.
21 See James Coleman. *Foundations of Social Theory, vol. 1*, translated by Deng Fang, Social Sciences Academic Press, 1999, Ch1, 5, 8.
22 See Sztompak, *Trust: A Sociological Theory*, Ch 7.
23 B. Barber, *The Logic and Limits of Trust*, Rutgers University Press, 1983, p. 81.
24 S. Holmas, Tocqueville and Democracy. In D. Copp et al. (Eds.), *The Idea of Democracy*, pp. 23–63.. Cambridge University Press, 1993.
25 See Max Weber, *The Protestant Ethic and the Spirit of Capitalism*, Penguin, 2002.
26 Please refer to Chapter 3 for specific data.
27 Liang Hong, *Exodus from Liangzhuang Village – Details and Experience of China*, p. 120.
28 See Wang Chunguan, *Wenzhou People in Paris*, Jiangxi People's Publishing House, 2000.
29 Ruth Benedict, *The Chrysanthemum and the Sword*, translated by L. V. Wanhe, The Commercial Press, p. 202.

References

Barber, B. (1983). *The logic and limits of trust*. Rutgers University Press.
Beck, U. (2004a). *Global risk society* (Y. Wu, Trans.). Nanjing University Press.
Beck, U. (2004b). *Risk society: Towards a new modernity* (B. He, Trans.). Yilin Press.

Beck, U., Giddens, A., & Lash, S. (2001). *Reflexive modernization: Politics, tradition and aesthetics in the modern social order* (W. Zhao, Trans.). Commercial Press.

Benedict, R. (1990). *The chrysanthemum and the sword (expanded version)*. The Commercial Press.

Boton, M. D. (2003). *Management of 100 years* (G. Wen, Trans.). China Textile Press.

Coleman, J. (1999). *Foundations of social theory, vol. 1* (F. Deng, Trans.). Social Sciences Academic Press.

Durkheim, E. (2000). *The division of labor in society* (D. Qu, Trans.). SDX Joint Publishing Company.

Fang, L. (2009). Formation process of trust in institution. *Sociological Studies, 2*, 130–148+245. https://doi.org/10.19934/j.cnki.shxyj.2009.02.007.

Fei, T. (1998). *From the soil: The foundations of Chinese society*. PeKing University Press.

Giddens, A. (2011). *The consequences of modernity* (H. Tian, Trans.). Yilin Press.

Holmas, S. (1993). Tocqueville and democracy. In D. Copp et al. (Eds.), *The idea of democracy* (pp. 23–63). Cambridge University Press.

Liang, H. (2013). *Exodus from liangzhuang village: Details and experience of China*. Huacheng Publishing House.

Luhmann, N. (2005). *Trust: The reduction mechanism of social complexity* (T. Qu & Q. Li, Trans.). Shanghai People's Publishing House.

North, D. C. (2008). *Institutions, institutional change and economic growth* (X. Hang, Trans.). Truth & Wisdom Press, Shanghai SDX Joint Publishing Company, Shanghai People's Publishing House.

Olson, M. (1995). *The logic of collective action* (Y. Chen et al., Trans.). Shanghai SDX Joint Publishing Company, Shanghai People's Publishing House.

Ouchi, W. (1984). *Theory Z: How American Business can meet the Japanese challenge* (Y. Sun et al., Trans.). China Social Sciences Press.

Sztompak, P. (2000). *Trust: A sociological theory*. Cambridge University Press.

Sztompak, P. (2005). *Trust: A sociological theory* (S. Cheng, Trans.). Zhonghua Book Company.

Wang, C. (2000). *Wenzhou people in Paris*. Jiangxi People's Publishing House.

Weber, M. (2002). *The protestant ethic and the spirit of capitalism*. Penguin.

Wren, D. A. (1986). *The evolution of management thought* (Y. Sun et al., Trans.). China Social Sciences Press.

Zhang, J. (1997). Issues of trust. *Sociological Studies, 3*. https://doi.org/10.19934/j.cnki.shxyj.1997.03.016

Zucker, L. G. (1986). Production of trust: Institutional sources of economic structure 1840–1920. In B. M. Staw & L. L. Cummings (Eds.), *Research in organizational behavior* (pp. 53–111). JAI Press.

6 Social Credit

Relationship or Social Capital

The advent of social capital theory offers a brand-new theoretical perspective to the study of trust. This chapter is an attempt to analyse the survey data with concepts of social capital in order to reflect on the relationship characteristics repeatedly mentioned in the foregoing chapters and on social capital. Which can better explain the characteristics of China's social credit?

6.1 Connotation and Measurement of Social Capital

Ever since its appearance, the concept of "social capital" has raised widespread debates. Scholars dispute endlessly aspects of social capital, including the definition, origin, composition, function, and measurement, which has resulted in the fact that there is not a uniform theoretical framework for the subject. Still, some core connotations and structures are relatively established, and these may be employed as foundations for the present study.

6.1.1 Connotations of Social Capital

As a compositional concept, the connotation of social capital evolves from the term "capital." Mercantilism, as the historical forerunner of Western classical economics on capital theory, understood capital from the field of circulation, viewing money capital as the sole form of capital. After mercantilism, classical economics shifted its view from the field of circulation to the field of production, and capital acquired its modern sense, with its connotation expanding from money to the means of production. Adam Smith, as a representative figure of British classical economics, regarded capital as all assets that can bring forth income or profit, further classifying these assets into fixed capital and moving capital. From then on, material capital, labour, and land have been considered the three primary factors in the realisation of economic growth, thus constituting the key foundational stones in economics' theoretical edifice.

In the 1960s, with the demystification of the myths of the "rational man" and "economic man," classical economics dwindled away, and economists started to blaze new trails on the way to economic prosperity. American economists Theodore W. Schultz and Gary Becker made an in-depth analysis of and systematically expounded on the concept and nature of "human capital." Different from material

DOI: 10.4324/9781003375579-8

capital, human capital refers to the added value a labourer gains through the acquisition of knowledge, skill, and other qualities useful to the employer or company in production and exchange processes. Thus, the idea of human capital expanded the connotation of "capital." Capital was no longer just a kind of material, but any resource that could bring about a value increase. This shift in connotation provided an etymological foundation for raising the idea of social capital. By the 1970s, the function of institutional factors in economic growth was highlighted, and the institution was considered the fundamental factor in explaining sustained differences in economic growth rate. A series of institutional factors such as government, law, and hierarchical enterprise organisations effectively reduce the transaction cost of exchange activities and provide a powerful guarantee of the effective functioning of the various material factors and human factors. However, now that the institution plays such an important role in economic performance, why are there still poor countries and rich countries when so many countries have adopted the same best institutions? The clumsy response from the institutional economist has not satisfied the people. Meanwhile, as a response to human capital, the sociologist has also failed to satisfy the people; the sociologist has started to include social-relationship networks and social-interaction contexts when discussing economic development, proposing "social capital" as the basis. French sociologist Pierre Bourdieu was the first scholar to introduce this concept into the field of sociology, conducting preliminary analysis in that regard.

Bourdieu's pioneering research on social capital was based on the methodology of his relationalism, which is closely related to concepts like field, habitus, and practice. In his view, all entities in the social realm are in relationships of all sorts – objective relationships "independent of personal consciousness and volition."[1] On this precondition, Bourdieu proposed, "a field can be defined as a network or a configuration between various objectively existing relationships."[2] It is formed by connecting different social factors, while different social factors play their roles by taking up different positions in the field. Based on that, Bourdieu derived the concept of capital from the concepts of field and position. He held that capital mainly disguises itself in three basic forms: Economic capital, cultural capital, and social capital. The so-called social capital is

> a collection of actual or potential resources; these resources are inseparable from some sort of lasting hold of a network, and such a network is what everyone is familiar with and recognizes. It features institutional relationships, and relates to the identity of group members.[3]

Bourdieu put forward two core concepts to explain the connotation of social capital: Social capital is both a collection of social networks and a dynamic concept of practice.

After Bourdieu, Coleman conducted a systematic exposition of the concept of social capital. He argues that the most basic social system is composed of two parts – the agent and resources. The various resource exchanges or resource transfers conducted continuously by the agent constitute lasting social relationships, and such social relationships not only constitute the elements of social the structure but are more important as individual resources; when they exist as the latter and emphasise their productive nature, the concept of "social capital" comes on the scene. Coleman holds that

> the definition of social capital evolves from its function; it is not any stand-alone entity, but entities of a variety of forms. The entities have two characteristics in common: they are composed of a variety of factors that constitute the social structure, and they provide facility of action for the individual situated inside the structure. Like capital in other forms, social capital has a productive nature; possession of social capital dictates whether people can attain some set purposes.[4]

Consequently, Coleman further divides social capital into six different forms, namely, (1) obligations and expectations, (2) information networks existing inside a social relationship, (3) norms and effective sanctions, (4) authority relations, (5) multi-function social organisations, and (6) purposely instituted organisations. Thereafter, Coleman explores the creation, maintenance, and disappearance of social capital. He proposed that the closeness of a social network, the stability of the social structure, and ideology are the main factors affecting social capital.

The closeness of a social network will increase the mutual reliance and trust between agents inside the system, reduce their reliance on agents outside the system, and enhance the ability to substitute resources, which creates the precondition for the establishment of effective norms and in turn influences the creation of social capital. The stability of the social structure is conducive to the accumulation of social capital. Based on the above, Coleman put forward a comparatively more complete theory of social capital than Bourdieu did.

Putnam held that Coleman's work laid the foundation for the analytical framework of social capital theory; he even took the Foundation of Social Theory by Coleman as the main source of reference in his study of Italian citizen participation. In his 1993 book *Making Democracy Work*, Putnam definitively advanced his social capital theory. In his 20-year tracking study of the performance of the southern and northern Italian governments, Putnam found that explaining the differences in institutional performance through varying degrees of economic modernisation met with great limitations. On that basis, Putnam assumed that the actual actions of an institution are influenced by the social relationships in which it is embedded, so he explored the relationship between the characteristics of citizen life and institutional performance. He finally attributed the substantial performance differences between the southern and northern governments to differences in citizen participation and to the degree of trust among the people. In the last chapter of *Making Democracy Work*, Putnam pointed out that "social capital refers to the characteristics of social organisation, for instance, trust, norms, and network, which could enhance the efficiency of society through promoting cooperative activities."[5] Or, more exactly, "social capital refers to the folk participation network of the average citizen, as well as to the norms of mutual benefit and trust under such a covenant."[6]

Here, Putnam views social capital as a productive capital, a public commodity: "the outstanding stock of social capital, for instance, trust, norm, and network usually feature characteristics of self-enhancement and cumulativeness."[7] Among the three aforementioned outstanding stocks, trust propagates through the network by way of universal mutual benefit and grows from private trust to social trust. This is because mutual benefits effectively constrain opportunistic behaviour and increase the level of trust between those who have repeated mutually beneficial exchanges, while the dense social-exchange network will increase the repetition and connection of relationships, further improving the level of social trust. Conversely, social trust reinforces the norms of mutual benefits and citizen participation. Therefore, vigorously developing social capital is a shortcut to enhancing collective action, and social capital is the critical factor in making democracy work.

Although there are explorations of social capital from different disciplinary perspectives and at different levels, there is one concept which receives widespread attention in social capital theory, that is, trust. In Coleman's discussion, trust is taken as a kind of social relationship and an important form of social capital, which is centrally embodied in the two factors of obligation and expectation. That is, the degree of trust in the social environment – whether the obligation pending has been performed or the scope of obligations have been personally assumed – affects the realisation of people's obligations and expectations. Putnam takes trust as an inseparable component of social capital, which promotes spontaneous cooperation and enters into a relationship of mutual support and mutual reinforcement with other aspects of social capital, such as mutually beneficial norms and the citizen participation network, to collectively generate institutional performance. Fukuyama repeatedly emphasises that trust is a universal cultural characteristic, brought into existence by a boost from the norms and value concepts that promote cooperation, with the latter acting as a kind of social capital. However, what role do trust and the credit derived therefrom play in social capital? Does trust promote the formation of social capital or does trust itself represent a kind of social capital?

It should be mentioned that the demarcation within social capital theory between social credit and social capital makes it difficult for us to understand the relationship between them; the multi-level and multi-dimensional characteristics of social capital increase the complexity of the discussion. Hence, before dwelling on the problems of social capital utilisation, it is necessary for us to demarcate the levels and dimensions of social capital. We lowered the analytical complexity by introducing the grid lines of levels and dimensions. On one hand, this can differentiate the three levels of social capital – namely, the micro, the medium, and the macro level – or differentiate social capital into two levels from the perspective of private or public property, dividing it into individual social capital and group social capital. On the other hand, a distinction must be made between social capital existing as a social-network structure and social capital existing as the content (resembling trust and norms) of a social relationship. In other words, we should horizontally differentiate the structural dimension and the relational dimension of social capital. Under such a grid of horizontal and vertical dimensions, social capital can be specifically analysed as seen in Table 6.1.

Table 6.1 Conceptual dimensions of social capital

Configuration dimension of social capital	*Levels of social capital*	
	Individual level	*Group level*
Structural	Position of the individual in the network, individual relational ties	Network configuration, organisation form
Relational	Private trust, exchange relationship, rules of action	Social trust, social norms

Social capital at the individual level includes the place of the individual in the social network and various social ties, while at the group level, network configuration and the organisational form are emphasised. Social capital in the individual relational dimension exists between private trust (especially reciprocating trust between pairs), and voluntary cooperation is achieved through the exchange relationship between obligation and expectation. Social capital in the group-level relationship dimension manifests itself through the degree of social trust or universal trust. The reciprocal norms between pairs become formal or informal social norms because of widespread sanctions by the group.

Under such an analytical framework, the relationship between trust and social capital stands out more clearly. Firstly, the interpersonal trust growing out of the exchange relationship between obligations and expectations on the one hand creates more ways for the individual agent to acquire and use resources, and it becomes an important component of individual social capital. What is more, through the transmission of networks and norms, this interpersonal trust becomes the precondition for the generation of social trust and group social capital. In this process, the position that the individual agent holds in the social network and his choice of behaviour collectively determines the transmission of trust through the network, while the externality of these behaviours prompts the generation of norms, in turn guaranteeing the transformation of private trust into social trust. Secondly, regarding social capital at the group level, social trust, social network, and social norms collectively constitute the three elements that are inseparable from social capital; they interact, reinforce each other in a reciprocating way, collectively support social capital, and become its functional intermediary. Still, the degree of compactness, scale, and the specific form of the network at the group level and the intensity of punishment norms all affect whether the individual agent trusts, or how much he trusts, such a network, which in turn affects the scale of the individual's social-relationship network, his personal position in the network, and so forth. It can be said that both social trust and social capital fall under the category of so-called "duality": They are inseparable in actual life, and they exert a reciprocating influence in the dynamic practical processes of life, entering into a reciprocating cause-effect relationship.

6.1.2 Measurement of Social Capital

In order to quantify the relationship between social capital and social credit, it is necessary for us to operationalise the concept of social capital and transform it into a measurable index. Having examined the theoretical connotations of social capital above, it is not difficult for us to find that, as a micro-level measurement grounded in the individual, the concept of social capital should be measured at the individual level, that is, we should measure social capital in the individual configuration dimension and the relational dimension. The former refers to the position that the individual occupies and his social relation in the social network, which is to be measured through the concept of social participation; and the latter mainly refers to the degree of trust and credit between individuals, which is to be measured through the concept of interpersonal trust. Therefore, the concept of social capital contains two aspects, interpersonal trust and social participation, of which social participation is further operationalised into two aspects, namely, social-group participation and social-activity participation, which are employed to reflect the degree of involvement in social groups by the individual and the frequency of social activity, with values varying between 1 and 4. Higher scores show higher participation. By contrast, the measurement of interpersonal trust is realised through a 5-point Likert Scale, with scores ranging from 1 to 5 points – the higher the score, the higher the interpersonal trust. To follow is a specific demonstration of the measurement method and research findings of social participation and interpersonal trust.

6.1.2.1 Social Participation Variable

In the city sample, the social-participation variable is composed of 16 indices, the reliability analysis of which returns a Cronbach alpha value of 0.771, which shows that the measurement of the scale is quite reliable. Descriptive statistics of the indices of the scale-return results are shown in Table 6.2.

Among the 16 indices of social participation, the three highest-rated items in ascending order are interactional activities between friends and relations, various classmate get-together activities, and daily interest activities, with averages of 3.12, 2.49, and 2.16, respectively. This result shows that nowadays the social participation of urban dwellers is more concentrated in the domain of private activities, which include leisure activities pertaining to blood relationships or private interests, and interactional counterparts are mostly private groups such as relations and friends. Relatively speaking, the lowest-rated items are activities of some spontaneously organised and relatively formal social groups as well as other forms of activities; the participation value averages only 1.12 for spontaneously organised formal committees such as a community owners' committee, reflecting weak participation of urban dwellers in public affairs, especially when these unofficial organisations are not the focus of urban citizen's social participation. They display no desire to participate actively even in community affairs. This situation of social participation, which displays low intensity in group participation and high intensity

Table 6.2 Descriptive statistics of the social participation variable (city sample)

	Number of cases	*Average*	*Standard deviation*
Religious groups	3133	1.08	0.338
Community owners' committee	3130	1.12	0.414
Academic groups/bodies	3131	1.14	0.456
Industry association	3134	1.19	0.510
Participation in religious activities organised by temples or churches	3132	1.23	0.591
Spontaneous-exchange activities of religion followers	3132	1.24	0.604
Public-charity organisations	3134	1.24	0.536
Participating in submitting suggestions and strategies, etc. to governmental agencies	3134	1.30	0.653
Internet forum	3129	1.31	0.559
Democratic-appraisal activities concerning various CCP and government work	3128	1.45	0.823
Participating in online discussion of social hotspots (for instance, Microblog, BBS, etc.)	3132	1.53	0.831
Various QQ groups	3128	1.58	0.726
Various political-election activities (for instance, electing people's congress members)	3131	1.73	0.982
Everyday-interest activities, doing the Yangko dance, playing poker, chess, and so on)	3131	2.16	1.018
Various classmate get-together activities	3135	2.49	1.035
Interactional activities between friends and relations	3135	3.12	0.876

of social participation, is recognised by many scholars as the main characteristic of social participation in China.

Due to the crowdedness of measurement indices in social participation, we have conducted a dimension reduction treatment on them through factor analysis. Five common factors out of 16 indices of social participation have been extracted. In order to make the factors clearer, we have conducted orthogonal rotation around the factor axis via the Varimax method. After altering the space loading of factors, the result after rotation is shown in Table 6.3.

Factor analysis found five significant factors. Of these, factor 1 is closely related to participation in community owners' committees, public-charity organisations, industry associations, and academic bodies, for these types of participation all take place in relatively formal social organisations. We have categorised these types of participation as **formal-organisation participation**; the loadings of factor 2 in the three items, namely, the various QQ groups, internet forums, and online participation in social hotspots, stand at 0.805, i0.802, and 0.713, respectively. As these items collectively involve participation on the internet and in cyber society, we categorise them as **internet participation**, for the purpose of illustrating the degree of involvement of urban dwellers in internet activities. Meanwhile, the characteristics of the next three items – namely, democratic appraisal of the CCP

Table 6.3 Social participation (urban sample): factor loading after rotation[a]

	Participation in formal organisations	*Internet participation*	*Political participation*	*Religious-activity participation*	*Everyday-activity participation*	*Communalities*
Community Owners' Committees	**0.708**					0.531
Public-charity organisations	**0.699**					0.547
Industry associations	**0.697**					0.552
Academic bodies	**0.660**					0.515
Various QQ groups		**0.805**				0.684
Internet forums		**0.802**				0.699
Participating in online discussions of social hotspots		**0.713**				0.611
Democratic-appraisal activities concerning various CCP and government work			**0.857**			0.765
Various political-election activities			**0.781**			0.655
Participating in submitting suggestions and strategies, etc., to governmental agencies			**0.756**			0.680
Participation in religious activities organised by temples or churches				**0.839**		0.725
Spontaneous-exchange activities of religious followers				**0.775**		0.664
Religious bodies				**0.669**		0.597
Interactional activities between friends and relations					**0.802**	0.651
Various classmate get-together activities					**0.705**	0.629
Everyday-interest activities, playing poker, chess, and so on					**0.701**	0.507
Eigenvalue	4.029	1.768	1.727	1.310	1.176	
Cumulative common factor variance (%)	25.182	36.232	47.026	55.217	62.568	

a. Factor extraction method: principal component analysis method; rotation method; orthogonal rotation based on Varimax method

and government, various political-election activities, and participation in submitting suggestions and strategies to governmental agencies – can be explained well through factor 3, whose factor loading stands at 0.857, 0.781, and 0.756, respectively. As these three items all fall under the category of political activity, we have categorised them as **political participation.** The characteristics of factor 4 have been categorised as **participation in religious activity**, which includes participation in religious activities organised by temples or churches, spontaneous-exchange activities of religious followers, and participation in religious bodies. Lastly, interactional activities between friends and relations, classmate get-together activities, and daily interest activities are rated highest in terms of loading in factor 5. We can categorise these activities as **daily activity participation**. On factor analysis, the commonalities for all variables exceed 0.5, meaning these factors can explain over 50% variance variation of all measurement variables and could, in fact, explain all indices.

In conclusion, in the urban samples, upon factor analysis, the 16 indices of social participation have been transformed into five factors, namely, formal-organisation participation, internet participation, political participation, religious participation, and daily activity participation, in an effort to represent the actual situation of social participation for the entire society. The contribution rate of cumulative variance of the five factors reached 62.540, which indicates that the five factors could still explain a 62.54% variance variation in social-participation factors. In other words, the five factors formed after factor analysis could still reflect most characteristics of the original variables.

Similarly, we have also sorted out the variables of social participation in the rural samples. In the rural samples, the social-participation scale is composed of 16 indices, a reliability analysis of which returns a Cronbach alpha value of 0.751. This value shows that the measurement of the scale is quite reliable. Descriptive statistics of the indices of the scale return results as shown in Table 6.4.

In the samples of rural social participation, the three highest-rated items in ascending order are interactional activities, visiting relations and friends during festivals and holidays, and grassroots elections at the village level, which shows that like its urban counterpart, the social participation of rural residents also concentrates in the domain of private activities. Comparatively, the lowest-rated fields are in formal organisations, especially political bodies or political activities organised by higher-level governments. What merits attention is that rural-resident participation in grassroots elections at the village level shows higher involvement than its urban counterpart, which indicates the activeness of self-governance of contemporary villagers in the countryside.

Similarly, we have conducted a dimension reduction through factor analysis (the KMO value hit 0.789). Six significant factors in all have taken form after factor analysis (see Table 6.5), of which factor 1 is closely related with grassroots elections at the village level, democratic appraisal of village leaders, villager congresses, grassroots elections activities at the village level, various policy, law, and regulation dissemination activities. As these indices all concern political activities of the village at the grassroots level, we shall categorise them as **social-activity**

Table 6.4 Descriptive statistic of social participation variable (rural samples)

	Number of cases	*Average value*	*Variance*
People's congress at various levels	2116	1.04	0.245
Propaganda teams	2116	1.11	0.398
Internet forums	2116	1.12	0.394
Religious bodies	2116	1.20	0.478
All sorts of QQ groups	2116	1.23	0.526
Village committees	2116	1.34	0.607
Religious activities of Christianity, Islam	2116	1.47	1.038
Training classes of all sorts of popular science and skills	2116	1.49	0.944
Training classes of various hygiene and healthcare	2116	1.51	0.853
Various policy, law, and regulation dissemination activities	2116	1.60	0.911
Various cultural, sport, and recreational activities	2116	1.73	0.967
Democratic appraisal of village leaders	2116	1.81	1.055
Villager congresses	2116	1.86	1.040
Grassroots elections at the village level	2116	2.11	1.101
Everyday interaction with friends and relations	2116	3.28	0.859
Visiting relations on festivals and holidays	2116	3.50	1.132

participation. Factor 2 mainly involves various types of training classes and cultural, sport, and recreational activities, and we shall categorise them as **social-activity participation**. Factor 3, **internet participation**, shall be used to reflect the internet behaviour of rural residents. Factor 4 registers relatively higher loading in two descriptions of religious activity, and we designate them as **religious participation**. What merits attention is that factor 5, which includes three indices of people's congress at various levels, including propaganda teams and villager committees, resembles factor 1 in that it also involves political activity. However, compared with factor 1, it includes more participation in formal organisations. To better distinguish it from factor 1, we shall categorise it as **formal-organisation participation**. Factor 6 shall be categorised as **private-activity participation** as a way of referencing the urban sample.

6.1.2.2 Interpersonal Trust Variable

In the measurement of interpersonal trust from urban samples, the alpha value registers 0.841, which shows that the scale has a sound structural consistency and the measurement result of the scale is quite reliable. The data result of such a measurement reflects that there are substantial differences in urban dwellers' trust in groups of people of different natures. They display a much higher degree of trust

Table 6.5 Social participation (rural sample): factor loading after rotation[a]

	Political participation	*Social-activity participation*	*Internet participation*	*Religious participation*	*Formal-organisation participation*	*Private-activity participation*
Grassroots-election activities at the village level	**0.854**					
Democratic appraisal of village leaders	**0.839**					
People's congress at various levels	**0.827**					
Various policy, law, and regulation dissemination activities	**0.604**					
Training classes of all sorts of popular science and skills		**0.724**				
Various cultural, sports, and recreational activities		**0.710**				
Training classes of various hygiene, healthcare, and female fertility training classes		**0.687**				
Internet forums			**0.878**			
All sorts of QQ groups			**0.861**			
Religious activities of Christianity, Islam				**0.869**		
Religious bodies				**0.853**		
People's congresses at various levels					**0.763**	
Villager committees					**0.644**	
Propaganda teams					**0.643**	
Visiting relations on festivals and holidays						**0.815**
Everyday interaction with friends, relations						**0.792**
Eigenvalue	3.877	1.893	1.602	1.229	1.104	1.012
Cumulative common factor variance (%)	24.230	36.059	46.073	53.752	60.651	66.975

a. Factor extraction method: principal component analysis method; rotation method; orthogonal rotation based on the Varimax method

in their own people as opposed to outsiders. Table 6.6 shows that the average trust values register 4.77, 4.52, and 3.86 for core family members, immediate relations, and other relations, respectively, which top all interpersonal trusts. This situation indicates urban dwellers trust blood relationships or marriage relationships most, while their trust in strangers and internet pals brings up the rear among all interpersonal trusts, with average values of 1.93 and 2.3, respectively, which are literally attitudes of distrust. It could be seen, in essence, that average internet pals and strangers share similar properties in interpersonal trust. It should be acknowledged that the basic description of the state of interpersonal trust could reflect the special trust characteristics of the differential nature in Chinese interpersonal trust; those "of their own" who stand in ascribed relationships and intimate interactions are far more reliable than outsiders, and along with the weakening of interpersonal inaction and the distancing of "relationships," the degree of trust is dwindling away correspondingly.

Having conducted dimension reduction (KMO=0.838) through factor analysis, these 14 indices are transformed into four common factors, and these four common factors are categorised as **relational trust, instrumental trust, genetic relation trust, and business relation trust**. Factor 1 involves mostly everyday private interpersonal interactions outside the family; in such interactions, the degree of trust generation includes an overall appraisal of the character, volition, and behavioural conduct of the counterpart. There are not only elements of cognition, but also of affective content. It is a generalised internal reaction process. Based on that, we designate this category relational trust, which indicates that such trust is generated through contact with people outside the family, representing private relationships that include both cognition and affection. Factor 2 registers relatively higher loadings on four items, namely, trust in vendors, producers, strangers, and internet pals; we believe that these trusts are mostly without emotional commitment or private relationships. They are built on timeliness or on role-play interactional processes, and they are mostly based

Table 6.6 Descriptive statistics of interpersonal trust (urban sample)

	Number of cases	*Average value*	*Variance*
Stranger	3135	1.93	0.901
Internet pal	3134	2.30	0.867
Vendor	3132	2.68	0.848
Producer	3133	2.72	0.848
Country fellow	3131	3.07	0.714
Casual acquaintance	3136	3.12	0.704
Neighbour	3133	3.29	0.711
Organisation leader	3135	3.30	0.826
Casual friend	3133	3.35	0.719
Colleague	3132	3.36	0.746
Other relation	3130	3.86	0.754
Close friend	3133	4.06	0.681
Immediate relation	3137	4.55	0.609
Core family member	3136	4.72	0.545

on pursuit of definite material or emotional objects; we therefore categorise this as instrumental trust to indicate the rationality inhering in this type of trust as well as the one-sidedness and timeliness of interaction. We categorise factor 3 as genetic-relational trust as it registers relatively higher loadings on the trusts of three items, namely, immediate relations, core family members, and other relations. The mode of establishment of the three types of trust all involve the ascribed kinship, or, in other words, blood relationships, involving comprehensive interaction that includes emotion. Factor 4 includes trust in two items, namely, organisational leaders and colleagues, with loading standing at 0.832 and 0.786, respectively; obviously, this type of trust is established on the basis of vocation or working-environment interaction. Hence, we categorise these types of trust as business-relational trust.

Social Participation (rural sample): Factor loading after rotation

We employed a similar analysis method on the rural samples, analysing the basic situation of rural-resident interpersonal trust by way of descriptive statistics and factor analysis. From the descriptive statistic shown in Table 6.8, we can see that trust in relations is rated the highest among rural-resident interpersonal trust; however, rural residents' trust in core family members is lower than that of the urban dweller. On the other hand, their rating of trust in neighbours (3.47) is much higher than that of their urban counterparts. Meanwhile, rural residents display a stronger tendency to distrust strangers, the rating of which ranks among the lowest three items and is lower than that of their urban counterparts. In conclusion, we hold that the interpersonal trust of rural residents displays a more obvious differential characteristic.

By incorporating factor analysis (KMO = 0.810), it is not difficult to find that the differential trust of rural residents can be divided into three primary dimensions, that is, relational trust, representing everyday interaction, instrumental trust, representing timeliness and intentionality, as well as genetic-relational trust, representing blood relationships and long-term interaction. Due to the fact that the respondents are mainly left-behind groups in the villages, trust arising from vocational ties has a relatively weak bearing on them and could not be reflected in the factor analysis. This is also the difference in the analysis of interpersonal trust between rural and urban residents.

6.2 Main Characteristics of the Capital Situation of Urban and Rural Residents

In the present study, we attempt to explore two important dimensions of social capital via social capital theory – social participation and interpersonal trust – and establish the function of overall social credit. Prior to this, we would first briefly summarise the primary characteristics of the social capital situation of urban and rural residents.

Firstly, let's analyse the state of social participation of urban and rural residents. Research results indicate that the overall level of social participation of urban and rural residents remains low, with most urban and rural residents swinging around the horizontal line of "occasionally participate – never participate." The main social-interaction behaviour still takes place between "those of their own," that

Table 6.7 Interpersonal trust (urban sample): factor loading after rotation[a]

	Relational trust	*Instrumental trust*	*Genetic-relational trust*	*Business-relational trust*	*Commonalities*
Casual acquaintances	**0.787**				0.690
Average friends	**0.768**				0.681
Neighbours	**0.743**				0.620
Country fellows	**0.699**				0.609
Close friends	**0.527**				0.528
Vendors		**0.822**			0.765
Producers		**0.822**			0.781
Strangers		**0.707**			0.603
Internet pals		**0.689**			0.573
Immediate relations			**0.828**		0.703
Core family members			**0.797**		0.638
Other relations			**0.626**		0.604
Organisational leaders				**0.832**	0.780
Organisational colleagues				**0.786**	0.762
Eigenvalue	4.879	2.150	1.249	1.060	
Cumulative common factor variance %	34.850	50.206	59.130	66.703	

a. Factor extraction method: principal component analysis method; rotation method; orthogonal rotation based on the Varimax method

Table 6.8 Descriptive statistic of interpersonal trust (rural sample)

	Number of cases	*Average value*	*Variance*
Core family members	2131	4.66	0.666
Immediate relations	2131	4.60	0.656
Relations without blood relationships	2131	3.68	0.938
Extended relations	2131	3.45	0.942
Close friends	2131	3.87	0.842
Average friends	2131	3.27	0.905
Neighbours	2131	3.47	0.897
Village leaders	2131	3.14	1.031
Producers	2131	2.73	0.909
Vendors	2131	2.63	0.910
Strangers	2131	1.76	0.878

Table 6.9 Interpersonal trust (rural sample): factor loading after rotation[a]

	Relational trust	*Instrumental trust*	*Genetic-relational trust*
Extended relations	**0.773**		
Average friends	**0.764**		
Neighbours	**0.691**		
Close friends	**0.690**		
Relations without blood relationships	**0.679**		
Vendors		**0.883**	
Producers		**0.868**	
Village leaders		**0.614**	
Strangers		**0.508**	
Core family members			**0.868**
Immediate relations			**0.835**
Eigenvalue	3.956	1.714	1.118
Cumulative common factor variance (%)	35.964	51.546	61.713

is, the frequency and depth of social participation are closely related to how close the relationship is. Most social activities of urban residents still concentrate on the category of traditional family interaction, which mostly manifests itself as long-term, intimate, and private interactions. Conversely, political participation or formal-organisation participation, which displays more "citizen property," receives relatively less attention. Contrastive analysis indicates that urban residents show a higher degree of internet participation than rural residents, which is closely related to the higher degree of development of the internet and the mode of living in the city. Urban residents display more reliance on the internet, which can be inferred from their media preference and frequency of internet access.[8] They prefer participating in the discussion of social hotspots via internet platforms such as Microblog and WeChat. These "micro platforms" have gradually become important channels for social participation and public activity among Chinese urban residents. In this respect, rural residents use the internet substantially less than their urban counterparts, and a substantially smaller portion of rural residents express their volition and participation in public activity via the internet. Another difference mainly manifests itself in political participation. The results from the research data indicate that rural residents show higher levels of political participation than urban residents, in that they show a higher degree of participation in grassroots political activity. In contrast, urban residents participate in fewer grassroots political activities and hardly take part in grassroots political activities such as owners' committees and democratic appraisals. This might be attributable to differences in the mode of living between urban and rural lives. Rural residents concentrate in relatively compact clusters, the populace is less mobile, and residents are comparatively more familiar with each other, with most village affairs resolved through pooling villager wisdom and strength. By contrast, urban communities include many neighbourhoods, with the populace relatively thinly spread. They feature higher mobility and lower familiarity and seldom require collective activity to resolve community public affairs. Besides, in the era of the unit system, most urban residents relied on their "unit" to get involved in political participation; such activities were uniformly organised and arranged by the unit to which they belonged. However, along with the gradual disintegration of the unit system, most urban residents drifted away from the system, and political participation dropped sharply. As a result, they are literally outside political activity.

Secondly, let's examine the state of interpersonal trust among urban residents. Interpersonal trust is usually employed to represent a sort of expectation and belief about a specific interaction held by an individual in the interaction, who believes the other party will always perform goodwill deeds towards him- or herself. In the interpersonal trust research of the Chinese, it is considered a special trust formed and maintained on blood relationships and extended into other favour-based interactional activities through various behaviours (for instance, forging brotherly relationships, entering into nominal kindships, and so on).[9] Therefore, blood-relationship ties, intimacy, and relationships based on favour have become keywords in Chinese interpersonal trust. In actual research, our data results have also demonstrated this point. The interpersonal trust of the urban and rural residents shows obvious differential characteristics, which form types of interpersonal relationships such as the categories of blood-relational trust, relational trust, and instrumental trust. Here, what stands out most is that both the rural residents and the urban residents display strong blood-relationship trust, and their degree of trust in core family members and immediate relations is much higher than in other groups. Urban residents display a comparatively higher degree of trust in core family members. The outlier in this differential trust pattern is trust in strangers. Both the urban and rural residents display distrust in the stranger group or the timely interaction group; however, comparatively, urban residents show a little more trust in strangers than rural residents. This reflects the fact that urban residents have more timely and purposeful interactions with strangers in actual life, and person-to-person trust is established in this type of frequent interaction. Conversely, rural life retains more countryside features, and the interactional object is comparatively more familiar. Thus, they show a stronger attitude of exclusion towards strangers. From this point, we believe that for urban residents the characteristics of this differential pattern in interpersonal trust remain in practice; however, this pattern is not as strong as it is for rural residents. This point manifests itself for rural residents as a trust materialises of more pluralistic characteristics, which no longer hold a degree of intimacy as the standard for determining the degree of interpersonal trust.

6.3 Social Capital and Social Credit

As illustrated above, social capital maintains countless ties with trust. Interpersonal trust formed out of social exchange accumulates social resources for the individual that constitute the social capital of the individual. The accumulation and constant exchange of such individual social capital bring into existence the socialised network that constitutes the social capital for the entire society and that in turn becomes the institutional guarantee for social credit. Exactly for this reason, social capital has long been zealously studied by most sociological scholars, holding it as an effective means to explain individual life, social development, and political democracy. For instance, Putnam had once remarked, to energetically develop social capital is a shortcut to solving a collection action dilemma. Social capital is the critical factor that makes democracy work.[10] Fukuyama emphasised in his study that social capital can improve the operational efficiency of any group or organisation.[11] Under such a perspective, we focus on the characteristics of the relationship of Chinese society's social capital and social credit. This relationship in fact provides a soft institutional constraint for the social credit of the entire society. In other words, social capital is an invisible net of modern society; its values, norms, trust, and network constrain the mode of interactional activity of the individual and even the entire society, sustaining the credit level of the society on the interactional plane.

In what follows, we shall analyse the relationship between social capital and social credit from two perspectives. As discussed above, social capital is mainly represented by two variables, interpersonal trust and social participation; on social credit, we also focus on two main elements, that is, we focus on the universal trust and the political trust of the individual from the dual angles of "government – society" and proceed from there to determine the influence of the level of social credit and social capital on the entire society.

We need to explain the practical connotation of the two macro-level variables. Firstly, in contrast to interpersonal trust, social trust is more like a kind of cognition and basic attitude generated by the trust universally held in a society. As a general social trust, it reflects the basic level of trust in a society. In studies relating to social credit, many scholars have made a distinction between it and interpersonal trust. Weber once remarked that Chinese society lacks such universal trust.[12] However, some recent studies have considered that such a concept of universal trust has undergone some change along with the change in social structure and cultural characteristics.[13] Hence, we will take social trust as an important variable and conduct measurement using the Likert Scale. Secondly, political trust is systemic trust. It is the faith that the people operating a political system will generate results consistent with expectations.[14] The level of political trust concerns not only the legitimacy of government conduct and the institution itself but also becomes a simplification mechanism between the people and government,[15] ensuring the effective operation of the political system. There are also scholars who view this kind of trust as an indispensable factor in the operation of democracy.[16] In the present study, we used government trust in the narrow sense to reflect the degree of governmental social credit. As a narrow sense of political trust, government trust points to specific government agencies and the personnel working in them, which makes it easier for the individual to arrive at a judgement. Similarly, we also used the Likert scale in the measurement. Government trust is composed of five indices of "the central government – provincial government – prefecture and municipal government – district and county government – grassroots subdistrict office/town government," with the end results arrived at by summing up the total.

6.4 Social Capital and the Universal Concept of Trust of Urban and Rural Residents

Regarding measurement of the universal concept of trust, we have employed 10 indices and 12 indices in the urban questionnaire and rural questionnaire, respectively. After the dimension reduction operation of factor analysis, three factors are employed to represent the universal concept of trust for urban and rural residents. Table 6.10 shows the factor analysis table of the universal concept of trust for urban and rural residents.

Based on the results of factor analysis (see Tables 6.10 and 6.11), we have run an analysis on the universal trust variables of the urban and rural samples, finalising them into three significant factors. Factor 1 registers the highest loading on descriptive items, including "Most people in society are honest and reliable," "Most people are generous to help others," "If I treat others with sincerity, others will treat me with sincerity." and "People are willing to be helpful." As all these items emphasise that most people in society are kind, sincere, and reliable, that is, that most people hold a kind and honest attitude in general social interactions, we designate them as "Reliability Assessment Factor" to indicate that most people hold an attitude of reliable assessment. Common Factor 2 registers a relatively higher loading on items that include "People are all selfish," "People place personal interest above others' interests," "If you are not vigilant in society nowadays, you'll be taken advantage of" (in assigning value, we have transformed negative descriptions so they are consistent with those of positive description). As these items of description all involve judgements regarding whether people value their personal interests over those of others, we have designated them as "(non) Selfishness Assessment Factor" in order to make the reliability assessment consistent. In this factor, the higher the selfishness factor is rated, the lower the selfishness of most people is deemed. Similarly, common factor 3 is also a reverse factor. The three items of description all emphasise the importance of various interests in

Table 6.10 Universal concept of trust (urban sample): factor loading after rotation[a]

	Reliability assessment	*(Not) selfishness assessment*	*(Not) utilitarian assessment*
Most people in society are honest and reliable	0.842		
Most people are generous in helping others	0.841		
If I treat others with sincerity, others will treat me with sincerity.	0.704		
People are willing to be helpful.	0.663		
People are all selfish		0.822	
People place personal interest above others' interests		0.753	
If you are not vigilant in society nowadays, you'll be taken advantage of		0.676	
In society, nobody genuinely cares about others			0.800
Interpersonal relationships are purely ones of interest			0.765
People nowadays pursue self interest at the expense of credit; this is understandable			0.614
Eigenvalue	2.702	2.282	1.063
Cumulative common factor variance (%)	27.025	49.841	60.467

a. Factor extraction method: principal component analysis method; rotation method; orthogonal rotation based on the Varimax method

the trust relationship established through general social interaction. Based on the index content, we designate it as "(Not) utilitarian assessment factor." Similarly, the higher the factor is rated, the lower the utilitarian assessment is rated for most people, as individuals, in society. Therefore, the indices of the concept of universal trust have been divided into three factors: reliability assessment, (Not) selfishness assessment, and (Not) utilitarian assessment. This division illustrates the relationship between them and the individual social capital.

In what follows, we will analyse the relationship between social capital and universal trust through relevant coefficients, of which the eight main control variables are gender, age, marital status, educational background, vocation, annual income level, type of household registration, political status, and religious belief. Detailed analysis results are shown in Table 6.12.

In Table 6.12, we can roughly see that social participation does not have a very close connection to universal trust; the variables that affect substantial influences are formal-organisation participation, political participation, everyday (private) activity participation, and religious participation. These types of social participation generally show a positive correlation with universal trust; that is, the higher level of social participation, the higher degree of universal trust. Specifically, political participation plays a role of positive influence on the universal trust of rural and urban residents. The key area influenced by political participation is the reliability

Table 6.11 Universal concept of trust (rural sample): factor loading after rotation[a]

	Reliability assessment	*(Not) selfishness assessment*	*(Not) utilitarian assessment*
Most people in society are honest and reliable	0.759		
Most people are generous in helping others	0.758		
There are good returns for kindness	0.702		
If I treat others with sincerity, others will treat me with sincerity	0.664		
All within the four seas are brothers	0.619		
People are willing to be helpful	0.523		
People are all selfish		0.784	
If you are not vigilant in society nowadays, you'll be taken advantage of		0.734	
People place personal interest above others' interests		0.527	
In society, nobody genuinely cares about others			0.772
Interpersonal relationships are purely ones of interest			0.715
People nowadays pursue self-interest at the expense of credit; this is understandable			0.644
Eigenvalue	3.127	2.228	1.012
Cumulative common factor variance (%)	26.059	44.628	53.063

a. Factor extraction method: principal component analysis method; rotation method; orthogonal rotation based on the Varimax method

assessment factor. In other words, the more an individual participates politically, the more he tends to consider the people of the entire society honest and reliable. This positive influence manifests itself especially clearly for it not only affects reliability assessment. Indeed, those rural residents who participate in more political activities also tend to believe all individuals of society are not utilitarian and not interest-driven people. Similarly, participation in everyday private activities will also enhance the universal trust of the individual. Such participation can positively influence the utilitarian assessment of the individual on others; what's more, the more frequently one participates in these activities, the easier one will establish trust ties. The influence of religious participation is very complex. For the urban resident, religious participation does not enhance the individual's universal trust in the entire society. On the contrary, those who frequently participate in religious activities hold others as not so trustworthy and as displaying more selfish propensities. This phenomenon might be attributable to the fact that religious activities reinforce the identification and trust within the religious community while weakening interactions between people outside the religious community. On this point, the rural resident displays the exact opposite tendency. The more the individual participates in religious activities, the more he tends to believe the entire society

Table 6.12 Influence of social capital on universal trust[a]

	Reliability assessment		*(Not) selfishness assessment*		*(Not) utilitarian assessment*	
	City	*Countryside*	*City*	*Countryside*	*City*	*Countryside*
Formal-organisation participation	0.018	0.035	−0.020	0.030	−0.044*	−0.047
Internet participation	−0.030	0.011	−0.046	−0.027	0.011	−0.002
Political participation	0.081***	0.072**	0.034	0.020	−0.020	0.109***
Religious participation	0.020	−0.090***	−0.050*	0.077**	0.012	0.013
Participation in everyday activities	0.030	0.038	−0.037	−0.022	0.053*	0.055*
Participation in social activities	–	0.055*	–	0.009	–	−0.034
Relational trust	0.184***	0.199***	0.051*	0.025	−0.028	0.009
Instrumental trust	0.130***	0.110***	0.093***	0.093***	−0.007	0.041
Genetic-relational trust	0.121***	0.203***	−0.067**	−0.141***	0.010	−0.008
Business-relational trust	0.201***	–	0.042*	–	0.069**	–

a. Figures shown in the table are standardised regression coefficients
The control variables are gender, age, marital status, educational background, vocation, annual income level, type of household registration, political status, and religious belief. The first half placed all factors of interpersonal trust on control in addition to the said control variable in exploring the influence of social participation; the second half placed all factors of social participation on control in addition to the regular control variables.

b. *** $p < 0.001$, ** $p < 0.01$, * $p < 0.05$

to be selfless and kind, and the easier he finds it to enter mutual trust relationships. However, typical of individual social capital representation, formal-organisation participation fails to play any role in improving the individual's universal trust.

In what follows, we will analyse the influence of differential interpersonal relationships on universal trust. Generally, interpersonal trust and universal trust move in the same direction. That is to say, the higher the level of interpersonal trust in a society, the higher the level of universal trust across it. Universal trust may thus be viewed as a continuous accumulation and superimposition of individual interpersonal trust. Besides, such universal trust benefits more from the individual's establishment of trust networks outside blood ties. In other words, the trust forged by the individual with people other than family develops and affects universal trust to a great extent, while the power of blood-related trust may actually weaken universal trust. Indeed, it might alter the individual's appraisal of the selfishness of others. Enhancing blood-related trust strengthens mutual trust inside the family, which in turn encourages the individual to regard individuals outside the family as selfish and may weaken the individual's sense of universal trust. This effect manifests itself not only in the city but also in the countryside. What's more, to rural residents, the contradiction is more obvious. That is, the higher degree of genetic trust, the more universal trust the individual displays; however, it also often leads the individual to perceive the selfishness of outsiders, which weakens universal trust in turn.

It should be acknowledged that, theoretically, social capital and universal trust stand in a very close relationship. Furthermore, to some scholars, universal trust should be viewed as the social capital of the intermediate or macro level. The level of its development indicates the closeness of the social bonds of the whole society, simplifying the operational procedures of that society and reversely affecting the individual's everyday life. However, according to the findings of the present study, in Chinese society, the individual's social capital cannot be effectively transformed into the social capital of the whole society. The individual's participation in social organisations or social activities cannot, for example, improve the universal trust of the individual; this effect will be restricted even when the cumulative interpersonal trust between individuals gets transformed into universal trust. The appearance of such a phenomenon may, on the one hand, be attributed to the relatively low degree of social participation by the Chinese. Especially in some voluntary societies, formal organisations, and social interactions featuring social capital, the overall participation of the population is quite low, for the everyday activities of most people are focused on friends and relations. On the other hand, the pattern of Chinese interpersonal trust makes most people maintain a relatively high sense of trust towards individuals with whom they have blood/genetic relationships and marriage relationships, and a relatively low sense of trust towards "outsiders" who do not bear such characteristics. In fact, it is exactly the latter that plays an important role in forging, or not forging, a sense of universal trust in Chinese society. Most people in society are "outsiders" to the individual; therefore, the differential pattern of trust noted above will to some degree weaken the birth of universal trust in Chinese society.

6.5 Social Capital and Trust in Government by the Urban and Rural Residents

We have employed the Likert Sum Scale to gauge the trust in government. The sum of the five indicators of the level of trust in government are 18.305 for urban residents and 20.103 for rural residents, which indicates the trust level of urban residents is lower than that of their rural counterparts. From Table 6.13, we can find that there are similar trends in government trust from both urban and rural residents. This trust dwindles level by level from the central government to the grassroots subdistrict office; that is to say, trust in government by rural and urban residents cascades lower level by level from the central government to the grassroots level government, while doubt thereof increases level by level.

This pattern differs radically from the state of trust displayed in the various levels of Western governments. In studies by Western scholars, this type of trust shows an inverse proportion, for it grows along with a cascading level of governments. For instance, Frederickson points out in a study that Americans trust government agencies in their immediate environment but consider more remote government agencies untrustworthy.[17] Studies by other scholars have arrived at similar conclusions; that is, the situation of trust towards various levels of government agencies run counter to their Chinese counterparts. Compared with the local government, the federal government stands at the lowest level of trust with the state government next. In other words, as the government level decreases, the level of trust from the people increases.[18] These conclusions diametrically oppose the situation of trust for Chinese governments. In past studies, peasant trust in governmental agencies at various levels cascade down along with the levels of government.[19] In the present study, even for urban residents, this trend remains: the closer government agencies are to the everyday life of urban residents, the lower their level of trust is.

In what follows, we will analyse the influence of social capital on the trust in government by urban and rural residents. In past studies, studying trust in government from the perspective of social capital has been a research paradigm of expounding on the source of political trust. Most Western scholars attempt to verify the relationship between interpersonal trust and political trust and believe that the two stand in a more obvious correlation: interpersonal trust affords a micro-level explanation of how trust in government is generated.[20] Besides, social participation

Table 6.13 Trust in government by the rural and urban residents[a]

	The city	*The countryside*
Trust in the central government	4.09	4.47
Trust in provincial governments	3.81	4.21
Trust in prefectural-level governments	3.61	3.95
Trust in district- and county-level governments	3.44	3.83
Trust in grassroots subdistrict office/township governments	3.36	3.64
Trust in government	18.305	20.103

a. All numbers shown in the table indicate average values

is also considered a factor having an important influence on political trust; some scholars believe that active participation plays an active role in the development of political life and democracy.[21] However, there are also scholars who believe that participation and trust should stand in paradoxical correlation. A higher degree of democracy usually predicts distrust, and a high degree of trust does not necessarily bring forth active democratic participation.[22] Political trust and political participation stand in negative correlation: the higher the degree of political trust, the lower the degree of political participation and vice versa.[23] Nevertheless, Chinese scholars hold that there is a high degree of correlation between political trust and awareness of political participation[24] and point out that participation in business organisations and public affairs has a significant impact on trust in government.[25]

In the present study, we have also analysed two aspects of social capital that affect trust in government: interpersonal trust and social participation. From Table 6.14, we find that, in general, interpersonal trust stands in a relatively close relationship with trust in government; that is, its effects on the latter are significantly positive. Social participation, on the other hand, has a more limited impact on trust in government. Only phenomena like online participation, political participation, everyday-activity participation, and social-activity participation make a significant impact. What's more, the results of these impacts are varied.

Five to six factors are extracted from social participation: namely, formal-organisation participation, online participation, political participation, religious

Table 6.14 Impact of social capital on the trust in government[a]

	Trust in government		*Trust in government*	
	The city	*The countryside*	*The city*	*The countryside*
Formal-organisation participation	0.035	0.024		
Online participation	**−0.053***	**−0.073****		
Political participation	**0.120*****	**0.134*****		
Religious-activity participation	−0.018	−0.019		
Everyday-activity participation	**0.049***	0.017		
Social-activity participation	–	**0.069****		
Relational trust			**0.097*****	**0.200*****
Instrumental trust			**0.120*****	**0.218*****
Genetic-relational trust			**0.117*****	**0.194*****
Business-relational trust			**0.255*****	–

a. The numbers shown in the table indicate standardised regression coefficients.
Control variables are gender, age, marital status, education background, vocation, annual income, type of household registration, political status, and religious beliefs, respectively. All factors of interpersonal trust are placed in an additional control group when exploring the impact of social participation in the first half, and all factors of social participation are also placed in an additional control group when exploring the impact of interpersonal trust in the second half.

b. $^{***}p < 0.001$, $^{**}p < 0.01$, $^{*}p < 0.05$

participation, and everyday-activity participation (the factor of social participation is added to the rural study). Of these, political participation displays a significant positive impact on trust in government, indicating that the higher the degree of political participation of rural and urban residents, the stronger their confidence in the entire government institution. This finding is consistent with research conclusions by many domestic scholars, again proving the relationship between the two. In addition to political participation, everyday-activity participation also has a positive impact on urban residents' trust in government. In other words, active participation of the individual in friend-and-family interactional activities, various classmate get-together activities, and everyday-hobby activities can all help to improve trust in government. Though these activities do not involve politics, they effectively strengthen the connection of the individual with others in private domains, which in turn creates strong and weak "bonds" between the individual and society. The indirect result of this process is a political one. This phenomenon is consistent with the position expounded by the social capital theory: The growth of an individual's social capital in social life can alter his view of the political system. What is more, social-activity participation has a similar influence on rural residents' trust in government.

However, comparatively speaking, formal-organisation participation featuring publicity fails to improve trust in government. That is to say, regardless of how residents identify with a formal organisation, their trust in government remains unaffected. Another point also merits attention. Everyday-activity participation and formal-organisation participation can be viewed as two very different kinds of social participation. Compared with the former, the latter displays more publicity, thus approximating more closely what Western scholars call "social capital." However, this form of participation, which effectively strengthens "social capital," fails to have an effect on trust in government. Quite the opposite: Everyday-interactional activities featuring more privacy bring forth improvements in political trust. Based on the foregoing findings, we believe that Chinese society differs from Western society in its mode of composition: The "incorporation" tradition or social-constitution feature is absent from (urban) Chinese society. In other words, the "self-organised" nature of Chinese society and the main basis thereof differ from its Western counterparts. The growth of individual social capital depends on private associations or on pan-blood relationships derived from the family; the growth of such capital is not organised by a common goal or value outside the family, as observed by Western scholars. Therefore, on the one hand, formal-organisation participation has long been weak in Chinese society, with the life of many people being built on participation in everyday activities. Therefore, it is not hard to identify why formal-organisation participation in China is so weak. On the other hand, everyday-activity participation has a positive impact on trust in government, which seems to suggest that the "social capital" of (urban) Chinese society differs somewhat from the Western concept of social capital. Hence, there remain issues of applicability and explanatory power when using such a theoretical framework to account for social participation and the impact thereof on the political system of Chinese society.

The other aspect of social participation, namely, online participation, has a negative impact on trust in government. Compared with traditional media, such as television and newspapers, as an emerging new medium, the internet brings forth a change in information communication while also implying a weakening of information control. Online information features great quantity, wide coverage, and fast propagation. Information relating to the political system that might otherwise fade from public view, especially negative information screened after a filtering process, may now resurface and enter public view due to the emergence of online media. This phenomenon has given rise to debates and has even led to group behaviours in real life (for instance, the South China tiger and the hide-and-seek incident both originated on the internet). The negative impact of online participation on trust in government exactly reflects how the mode of interaction and the expression of the individual have been changed by this emerging technology. On the internet, the massive quantity of information and its quick, real-time transmission indirectly weakens the government's control of information, while the internet's pluralistic modes of expression can involve all individuals in the discussion of government topics. This type of negative impact reflects a change in the individual's modes of expression and social-information exchange after the introduction of the internet into public life.

In what follows, we will analyse the influence of interpersonal trust. We have constructed the structure of interpersonal trust through factor analysis, including four types of trust that are mutually independent: namely, relational trust, instrumental trust, genetic trust, and business-relational trust (the last factor is absent from the rural samples). In general, interpersonal trust of any type can affect in a positive way the trust of the individual in governmental agencies. In other words, interpersonal interaction often gives rise to a sense of trust and prompts the individual to have more faith in the government. Trust in government and interpersonal trust are closely related to the trust that contains elements of purposive social exchange. In this type of purposive social interaction, the more faith the individual has in the consistency between an expectation of the attainment of a material or emotional objective and an actual situation, the more faith he will have in the operation of the government. Business-relational trust exerts a similarly significant, positive influence on urban residents. In the interpersonal-trust structure, business-relational trust is a type of trust in a special environment, a "unit" environment whose structure and rules resemble those of the political system. What's more, interaction with unit superiors or colleagues is often based on hierarchy, role, and norms of conduct, all of which teem with purpose and utilitarian exchange. Therefore, the more one lets one's guard down in interpersonal interaction in the "unit" domain, the less one guards against others. Relational trust and genetic-relational trust, which feature more emotional interaction, also manifest a positive influence on trust in government. That is to say, the sense of trust built by the individual through interaction with friends, acquaintances, and neighbours can improve his faith in political institutions. In conclusion, the particular interpersonal trust of the Chinese also points to and consolidates the real possibility of a universal institutional trust.

6.6 From Social Capital back to "Relation"

Doubtless, in the study of social capital and trust that intertwine with and complement each other, the birth of social capital theory provides a brand-new theoretical perspective for the study of trust, while trust also plays an important role in the conceptual framework of social capital. The appearance of social capital theory explains that the mechanism for sound social operation requires not only government and formal institutions, but also the need for public domains, community awareness, and citizen participation. The research framework of social capital, active participation of the individual in public affairs, and universal trust (social capital) brings the idea of political trust, which generates the slogan "social participation – social trust – political trust." Therefore, discussion of the relationships between social capital, universal trust, and trust in government should be placed in a continuum. We thus set trust in government as the foundation of this continuum so as to carry out our analysis of the influence of social capital on Chinese society.

Western political thought based on social contract theory considers government the result of "authorisation – agency." On such a presupposition, the political system is always related to the voluntary surrender of rights by the people. Therefore, Thomas Hobbes considered the despotic "leviathan," established on the basis of uniqueness, as the effective source of order that had obtained a contractual surrender of rights from all people. This social contract then acquired absolute trust and absolute obedience from all people.[26] However, the fact that such a despotic trust had no alternative choice brought practical risks. Firstly, there is information asymmetry between the trust agent and trust object. The government, which should be the defender of interests, brings interest damage to both parties, the client and the agent. Secondly, the government, as the agent, violates contractual provisions and the moral code due to information asymmetry, harming the client's interest deliberately. These two risks reflect not only the inadequacy of the political system but also the potential loss of morality.[27] Therefore, the democratic supervision of the political system itself becomes the focus of Western political scholars, and an institutional design that guarantees the legality and efficacy of power becomes the crux of political trust. Over the same period, the discussion of political trust mainly focused on the democratic supervision of power and the "technical excellence" attained by the bureaucratic system. Political democracy guarantees the legitimacy of the source and the exercise of power by the government; meanwhile, the bureaucratic system attains the object of maintaining order by ensuring the technical optimisation of government behaviour through professional division, duty stratification, procedure standardisation, and impersonalisation. However, the trust in democracy here focuses more on the political system itself, and, in fact, it neglects the important role of the common folk as the client in the existence and continuation of political trust. This is also what the social capital theory intends to supplement.

In writing *Democracy in America*, Tocqueville admired the environment of American society "where regardless of age, position, aspiration, Americans are forever organising societies."[28] He believed that only through universally enfranchising people and making them gradually learn how to utilise their political rights can nations make robust citizens who are mutually supportive and zealous in public affairs out of modern individuals who are inclined towards mutual estrangement and pursuing self-interest.[29] In this way, a social order based on "democracy–trust" may be built. Therefore, following the mental route of Tocqueville, based on an empirical study he conducted himself in Italian communities, Putnam officially advanced the social capital theory, defined as "the folk participation network of the regular citizen, and the mutually beneficial and trust norms embodied in such covenants."[30] He regarded social trust and social participation as the two interrelated core elements and believed that they ultimately prompted the operations of democracy, bringing into existence democratic order across the whole society. Therefore, the sense of trust and the degree of participation have become an unavoidable part of the discussion in social capital theory, and they have also become important variables affecting political trust from the social capital perspective. Social participation is considered active participation in social organisations such as religious organisations, clubs, and business organisations, while social trust not only includes interpersonal trust in social cooperation but, more importantly, the universal trust that permeates the social network through such participation. According to social capital theory, interpersonal cooperation and the universal trust arising therefrom promotes the civic spirit and, in turn, nurtures trust in the political system. As observed by Keele,

> Trust is not the result of how the public thinks of the leaders, but is manifested in to what extent the public participates in civic life, and the trust and mutually beneficial attitudes resulting from civic activities. When the citizens seldom participate in civic life and lack mutually beneficial experience, it would be difficult for them to have faith in institutions constraining political life.[31]

In other words, the existence and continuation of political trust rely on the closeness of association among average people and the degree of their involvement in public affairs as well as the mutually beneficial attitudes that arise therefrom.

Be it social trust or social participation, social capital theory presupposes, first, respect for individuality, for individuals who feature wholeness, independence, personality, and rights are crucial to social capital creation; it also presupposes, second, an active citizenry, with individuals who participate in social organisations voluntarily and actively out of rational considerations and who engage in cooperation based on mutual trust. Social capital theory also presupposes, finally, that the result of active participation and trustful cooperation highlights the values or objectives of the entire social organisation. In other words,

> social capital includes the institutional relationships teeming with the life of civic society, networks from the extended family to the neighborhood, from community organizations to religious organizations, from youth clubs to parent-teacher associations, from local business organizations to local

> public-service institutions, from kindergarten game groups to patrolling police and so on; they are all incorporated on the basis of individual and positive citizen rights. The core of such civic society are values including charity, empathy, trust, and participation.[32]

However, if we are to treat the existence and continuation of China's political trust from the perspective of social capital, the theoretical assumption instituted in Western social capital theory does not sound so solid anymore. The supremacy of the individual and the worship of rationality does not seem to accord with Chinese society's mode of composition. Chinese society often places more value on human relationships, the idea that "who you are is not important, who you know is." Respect for both reason and sentiment originating in family life replaces the emphasis on reason by Western society. The only way of handling matters acceptably according to the Chinese is a way that accords with both "reason and sense," while the significance and value of the family are somewhat imprinted on Chinese group cooperation. These aspects of Chinese society provide social capital with different traits that manifest different effects on political trust. We will break down these differences in the following analysis.

Firstly, we should examine social trust. Western scholars perceive social trust as an attitude of trust towards most people in society, a sense of universal trust. However, in his study of Chinese religions, Weber observed that the Chinese idea of social trust is a special one formed and sustained by family advantages such as the blood-relationship community and the bond of clan;[33] similarly, having compared different trust societies, Fukuyama further noted that "the Chinese people tend to strongly trust only those whom they are related to through blood, and do not trust people outside the family or non-relations."[34] Hence, to those other people outside blood and family relationships, the Chinese display their distrust by way of the term "stranger." Therefore, Fukuyama deems China a society with a low degree of trust. However, the sense of social trust in China is far from that simple. To those ascribed blood relationships of family, which are unalterable, trust is absolutely natural; however, to those people outside such relationships, the Chinese can still extend and generalise the trust of blood and genetic relationships to "outsiders" without the ascribed relationships through activities that include entering into nominal kinships, into brethren relationships, through cottoning up, and by offering favour. Thus, trust relationships with differential patterns came into being, extending trust from the insiders of a family outside and giving rise to trust based on relationships. Such trust may have a different pattern, but still, blood relationships are at its core.

So, is there really no "universal trust" in Chinese society in the sense advanced by Western scholars? Rather, along with the deepening of modernity, the force of such universal trust incrementally shows its strength. It actually hints at the possibility of interaction under the risk of unfamiliarity. An important contribution of modernity is the functional division of the whole society. Many professional institutions and vocations have replaced the social function originally assumed by the family; therefore, the individual has to enter relationships with many unfamiliar individuals, and he faces the choice of trust in all such interactions. This efficient and complex way of interaction gradually deprives the forming of trust from "relational" traits, which makes trust more and more a question of rational selection based on identity symbols in fast or even real-time interactions. Thus, the trust of differential patterns ceases to be powerful, while another trust based on the balance of "selfishness" and "profit" gradually becomes the other force dominating trust in Chinese society. Such trust may be regarded as purely rational, a judgement that maximises personal interests after a selfish and pragmatic evaluation.

So far, the power of social trust has similarly manifested a positive impact on the establishment of political trust among Chinese people. However, social trust in modern China also becomes more and more complex, which brings forth a constant impact on the political trust closely related thereto. Firstly, the blood-relationship trust with family at its core remains an indestructible force in Chinese society. Trust in "family" and distrust in the "outsider" still make a great difference, while the trust built on strong blood relationships will strengthen the reliance on family members. This factor indirectly limits interaction with individuals from outside the family and hinders the forging of trust outside the family, undermining the universal trust on which political trust depends. This is also the reason that blood-relational trust tends to weaken the performance of political trust in our study; secondly, relational trust built on extended blood relationships is usually accompanied by frequent interactions and personal favours that "cannot be paid up." Though in fact this kind of "relationship" may bring about interactions between strangers, the core of its trust remains linked up by acquaintance relationship, so it does not shed its identity as trust of a different pattern. What's more, such relational trust usually points to individuals. It is a personal relationship instead of an interpersonal one, which makes it difficult to form general rules on its basis and thus tends towards situational modes of behaviour. Lastly, we should acknowledge that the universal trust on which political trust depends seeks change under the impact of modernity; ever-growing social division makes universal trust with vocation at its core the inseparable buttress for political trust. It is especially affected by factors including urbanisation, marketisation, and the one-child policy. The profit-seeking tendency and shrinking family size make it necessary for the Chinese to rebuild trust in markets, though this may be a long way off.

As to social participation, in the study of Putnam, the reason that social capital can make democracy work is the fact that it can effectively organise the individual into social groups, enhancing the voluntary and active cooperation of individuals and highlighting the value and objectives of such cooperation. Such social participation, which amounts to the degree of involvement in public affairs by the individual, is an important aspect of social civic spirit. What it brings about is the "self-organisedness" of American society so highly praised by Tocqueville and the idea of democracy as a way of life, which may benefit the political system. However, it is not difficult to perceive that this power of social participation is totally based on the division of "public" and "private" that modernity brought to Western society, according to Giddens. By contrast, Chinese society has mostly lacked this basis for organisation and participation. On the macro level, there are differences between "in the establishment" and "outside the establishment" in the

Chinese division of vocations, with those outside the establishment usually lacking channels of participation. What is more, even those inside the establishment may lack the voluntary and active motive for participation explored by social capital theory. Such participation is somewhat like "protective participation" in the eyes of Putnam: "what pushes and constrains people in political participation is the personalised protective affiliation net, instead of principled cognition of public affairs," while "in those areas that feature a high degree of citizen participation, the citizens generally tend to concern themselves with public affairs."[35] Besides, Chinese social participation is often based on "relationships." And the object of participation tends to evolve into permanent and organised relationships between individuals in order to generate an effective means of identifying "those of one's own side" and "personal favour" and "face." These social dynamics, based on relationships, undermine an emphasis on the "public nature" of social capital. Instead, they tend to effect less desirable traits associated with "entering social groups," "setting up social circles," and "pulling strings," though the Chinese government has been working hard to eliminate such tendencies.

Notes

1 Pierre Bourdieu, *An Invitation to Reflexive Sociology*, translated by Li Meng, Central Party Literature Press, 1998, p. 368.
2 Ibid., p. 134.
3 P. Bourdieu, The Forms of Capital. In J. Richardson (Ed.), *Handbook of Theory and Research for the Sociology of Education*, p. 248. Greenwood Press, 1986.
4 James Coleman, *Foundations of Social Capital*, translated by Deng Fang, Social Science Literature Press, 1992, p. 333.
5 Robert D. Putnam, *Making Democracy Work: Civic Traditions of Modern Italy*, translated by Wang Lie, Lai Hairong, Jiangxi People's Publishing House, 2001, p. 195.
6 Putnam, *Making Democracy Work*, Prologue to the Chinese Translation.
7 Putnam, *Making Democracy Work*, p. 208.
8 See Chapter 7 Table 7.1, Table 7.3.
9 Max Weber, *Confucianism and Taoism*, translated by Hong Tianfu, Jiangsu People's Publishing House, 1995; Yang Zhongfang, Peng Siqing, Conceptualization of the Interpersonal Trust of the Chinese People: An Opinion on Interpersonal Relationship, *Sociological Studies* 1999(2), 1–21.
10 Putnam, *Making Democracy Work.*
11 Francis Fukuyama, *The Great Disruption: Human Nature and the Reconstitution of Social Order*, translated by Liu Bangli et al., China Social Sciences Press, 2002.
12 Weber, *Confucianism and Taoism.*
13 Zheng Boxun, Familism and Leader Conduct. Yang Zhongfang, Gao Shangyi. Chinese – A Heart of China [M], Taiwan Guiguan Book Company, 1991; Zhang Jianxin, Peng Maike, Specific Character Object-Pointing Interpersonal Trust: A Cross-Cultural Comparison and the Cognitive Model Thereof. *Acta Psychologica Sinica* 1993(2), 164–172; Wang Feixue, Toshio Yamagishi, Comparative Study of Trust between China, Japan and America. *Sociological Studies* 1999(2), 67–82.
14 Marc J. Hetherington, The Political Relevance of Political Trust, *American Political Science Review*, 1998(92)4, 791–808; W. Mishler, R. Rose, What are the Origins of Political Trust: Testing Institutional and Cultural Theories in Post-Communist Societies, *Comparative Political Studies* 2001(34)1, 30–62; Shi Tianjian, Culture Values and Political Trust: A Comparison of the People's Republic of China and Taiwan,

Comparative Politics 2001(33)4, 401–419; Jenney Job, How is Trust in Government Created? It Begins at Home, but Ends in the Parliament, *Australian Review of Public Affairs*, 2005 6, 1–23; Keele Luke, Social Capital and the Dynamics of Trust in Government, *American Journal of Political Science* 2007(51)2, 241–254; David Easton, *A System Analysis of Political Life*, translated by Wang Puqu et al., Huaxia Publishing House, 1999; Hu Rong, Peasant Petition and the Erosion of Political Trust, *Sociological Studies* 2007(3), 39–55.

15 Luhmann, *Trust: A Simplification Mechanism of Social Complexity*.

16 Putnam, *Making Democracy Work*.

17 H. G. Frederickson, *The Spirit of Public Administration*, Jossey-Bass, 1997.

18 Tyler Schario, David Konisky, *Trust and Responsiveness*, Public Confidence in Government, 2009.

19 Li Lianjiang, Kevin J. O' Brien, Villagers and Popular Resistance in Contemporary China, *Modern China*, 1996(22)1, 40–55; Li Lianjiang, Political Trust in Rural China, *Modern China* 2004(30)2, 228–258; Hu Rong, Peasant Petition and the Erosion of Political Trust, pp. 39–55; Xie Zhiju, *Village Economic Type and Villager Political Trust – a Comparative Study of Village L of Guizhou and Village Y of Jiangsu*, *China Rural Survey* 2011(6), 83–91.

20 John Brehm, Rahn Wendy, Individual Level Evidence for the Causes and Consequences of Social Capital, *American Journal of Political Science* 1997,(41)(October), 999–1023; Robert P. Putnam, *Bowling Alone*, Simon & Schuster, 2000.

21 Gabriel A. Almond, Sidney Verba, *The Civic Culture: Political Attitudes and Democracy in Five Nations*, translated by Ma Dianjun, Zhejiang People's Publishing House, 1989.

22 See related discussions in Chapters 17, 18, and 19.

23 Max Kaase, Interpersonal Trust, Political Trust, and Non-Institutionalised Political Participation in Western Europe. *West European Politics* 1999 (22)3.

24 Yu Mingjiang, Liang Ying, Empirical Analysis of the Intrinsic Connection between Trust in Government and Citizen Participation Awareness: Illustrated with Nanjing, *Chinese Public Administration* 2008(8), pp. 121-125.

25 Hu Rong, Hu Kang, Wen Yingying, Social Capital, Government Performance and Trust in Government by Urban Residents, *Sociological Studies* 2011(1), 96–117.

26 See Thomas Hobbes, *Leviathan*, translated by Li Sifu, Li Tingbi, 1985.

27 Zhang Xiaoting, The Political Constructs of Modern Social Order – Democracy Based on Trust, *Qilu Journal* 2012(6), 64–69.

28 Alexis de Tocqueville, *Democracy in America*, translated by Dong Guoliang, Commercial Press, 1988, p. 653.

29 Ni Yuzhen. The Unique Angle Tocqueville Viewed Democracy: Democracy as a "Social Condition." *Sociological Studies* 2008(3), 90.

30 Putnam, *Making Democracy Work*, p. 1.

31 Luke, Social Capital and the Dynamics of Trust in Government, p. 241.

32 Fred Powell, *State, Welfare and Civil Societ.* Appeared in *Out of the Prisoners' Dilemma – Social Capital and Institution Analysis.* Compiled by Cao Rongxiang, Shanghai SDX Bookstore, 2003, p. 101.

33 See Weber, *Confucianism and Taoism*.

34 Francis Fukuyama, *Trust: The Social Virtues and the Creation of Prosperity*, translated by Peng Zhihua, Hainan Publishing House, 2001, p. 74.

35 Putnam, *Making Democracy Work*, p. 100.

References

Bourdieu, P. (1986). The forms of capital. In J. Richardson (Ed.), *Handbook of theory and research for the sociology of education*. Greenwood Press, pp. 241–258.

Bourdieu, P. (1998). *An invitation to reflexive sociology* (M. Li, Trans.). Central Party Literature Press.

Brehm, J., & Wendy, R. (1997). Individual level evidence for the causes and consequences of social capital. *American Journal of Political Science*, *41*(3), 999–1023.

Coleman, J. (1999). *Foundations of social theory* (F. Deng, Trans.). Academic Press.

de Tocqueville, A. (1988). *Democracy in America* (G. Dong, Trans.). Commercial Press.

Easton, D. (1999). *A system analysis of political life* (P. Wang et al., Trans.). Huaxia Publishing House.

Frederickson, H. G. (1997). *The spirit of public administration*. Jossey-Bass.

Fukuyama, F. (2001). *Trust: The social virtues and the creation of prosperity* (Z. Peng, Trans.). Hainan Publishing House.

Fukuyama, F. (2002). *The great disruption: Human nature and the reconstitution of social order* (B. Liu et al., Trans.). China Social Sciences Press.

Gabriel, A. A., & Sidney, V. (1989). *The civic culture: Political attitudes and democracy in five nations* (D. Ma, Trans.). Zhejiang People's Publishing House.

Hetherington, M. J. (1998). The political relevance of political trust. *American Political Science Review*, *92*(4), 791–808.

Hobbes, T. (1985). *Leviathan*. China Commercial Press.

Hu, R. (2007). Peasant petition and the erosion of political trust. *Sociological Studies*, *3*, 39–55.

Hu, R., Hu, K., & Wen, Y. (2011). Social capital, government performance and trust in government by urban residents. *Sociological Studies*, *1*, 96–117+224. https://doi.org/10.19934/j.cnki.shxyj.2011.01.004

Job, J. (2005). How is trust in government created? It begins at home, but ends in the parliament. *Australian Review of Public Affairs*, *6*, 1–23.

Kaase, M. (1999). Interpersonal trust, political trust, and non-institutionalised political participation in Western Europe. *West European Politics*, *22*(3), 1–21.

Li, L. (2004). Political trust in rural China. *Modern China*, *30*(2), 228–258.

Li, L., & O' Brien, K. J. (1996). Villagers and popular resistance in contemporary China. *Modern China*, *22*(1), 40–55.

Luhmann, N. (2005). *Trust: The reduction mechanism of social complexity* (T. Qu & Q. Li, Trans.). Shanghai People's Publishing House.

Luke, K. (2007). Social capital and the dynamics of trust in government. *American Journal of Political Science*, *51*(2), 241–254.

Mishler, W., & Rose, R. (2001). What are the origins of political trust: Testing institutional and cultural theories in post-communist societies. *Comparative Political Studies*, *34*(1), 30–62.

Ni, Y. (2008). The unique angle Tocqueville viewed democracy: Democracy as a social condition. *Sociological Studies*, *3*, 79–91+244.

Powell, F. (2003). *State, welfare and civil society. Appeared in out of the prisoners' dilemma – Social capital and institution analysis* (C. Rongxiang, Comp.). Shanghai SDX Bookstore.

Putnam, R. D. (2001). *Making democracy work: Civic traditions of modern Italy* (L. Wang & H. Lai, Trans.). Jiangxi People's Publishing House.

Putnam, R. P. (2000). *Bowling alone*. Simon & Schuster.

Schario, T., & Konisky, D. (2009). *Trust and responsiveness*. Public Confidence in Government.

Shi, T. (2001). Culture values and political trust: A comparison of the People's Republic of China and Taiwan. *Comparative Politics*, *33*(4), 401–419.

Wang, F., & Yamagishi, T. (1999). Comparative study of trust between China, Japan and America. *Sociological Studies*, *2*. https://doi.org/10.19934/j.cnki.shxyj.1999.02.005

Weber, M. (1995). *Confucianism and Taoism* (T. Hong, Trans.). Jiangsu People's Publishing House.

Xie, Z. (2011). Village economic type and villager political trust: A comparative study of village L of Guizhou and village Y of Jiangsu. *China Rural Survey*, *6*, 83–91.

Yang, Z., & Peng, S. (1999). Conceptualization of the interpersonal trust of the Chinese people: An opinion on interpersonal relationship. *Sociological Studies*, *2*, 1–21.

Yu, M., & Liang, Y. (2008). Empirical analysis of the intrinsic connection between trust in government and citizen participation awareness: Illustrated with Nanjing. *Chinese Public Administration*, *8*, 121–125.

Zhang, J., & Maike, P. (1993). Specific character object-pointing interpersonal trust: A cross-cultural comparison and the cognitive model thereof. *Acta Psychologica Sinica*, *2*, 164–172.

Zhang, X. (2012). The political constructs of modern social order: Democracy based on trust. *Qilu Journal*, *6*, 64–69.

Zheng, B. (1991). Familism and leader conduct. In Y. Zhongfang & G. Shangyi (Eds.), *Chinese – A heart of China [M]*. Taiwan Guiguan Book Company, 306–407.

7 Social Credit in China in the Internet Era

Since the internet entered China in the 1990s, Chinese society has thoroughly entered the era of internet communication, and many Chinese people have developed an internet-centred lifestyle. The internet's breakthrough in the space-time dimension has brought new interpersonal connections, communication methods, channels, and content, thus also changing the establishment of the social-trust system. At that time, social trust based on certainty began to decline, and uncertainty became the central issue of online trust. In the internet era, familiar trust, social-system trust, and local-network trust encountered, collided, and even clashed with political, economic, cultural, and consumer fields on the internet, thus representing the trust of the whole society as a dynamic, contingency-filled, pluralistic, and complex state. The rise of the internet, to a large extent, both amplified social credibility and brought about a credibility crisis. These events likely ushered in the question of credit reconstruction.

7.1 Fragmentation of Social Trust under Uncertainty

7.1.1 Uncertainty in the Internet Era

Before the emergence of the internet, human social interactions all occurred in temporal and spatial dimensions. That is, when looking back at the composition of society in terms of space and time, all kinds of human interactions can be categorised in space and time. The temporal dimension refers to the perceived "transience" or "permanence" of the interactions between interactors in a society. The longer the interaction, the more stable the relationship and the more difficult it is to create trustlessness. The spatial dimension refers to the mobility status of a person throughout his or her life. If a person is in the same space throughout his or her life, the objects of his or her interactions are fixed and rarely selective; if a person is frequently mobile, the objects of his or her interactions expand infinitely and the selectivity of his or her interactions increases significantly. The characteristics of Chinese relationships originate from blood and geography and reflect fixed interactions in the same territory, which are characterised by "permanence" and "non-selectivity." This is the logical starting point of Chinese social interactions, which also constitutes the above-mentioned traditional way of social-trust construction and the characteristics of such trust.

DOI: 10.4324/9781003375579-9

The change and development of modern society have brought about a spatial and temporal change in interpersonal interactions, which is mainly reflected in the concept of "disembedding"[1] proposed by Giddens. "Disembedding" is a modern sociological concept of space, which refers to people's social relations transcending from a specific territory to a trust in expert systems, and thus to institutional trust. And with the advent of the internet, such disembedding is further generalised. The generalisation of decontextualisation occurs from the role played by internet technology. With mobile internet technology, people can meet and chat, exchange information, and enjoy relative goods and services across time and space wherever they can get a signal.

The technological progress of the internet has led to faster and cheaper information transmission. The boundaries of internet society do not coincide with the boundaries of real society. The internet's influence can spread to any part of the world, and the way people focus is not on a real neighbourhood or town or country, but more likely lies in interest, attention, and browsing. Since information exchange can happen at any time on the internet, any individual's needs can theoretically be known and satisfied by the individuals, organisations, advertisements, or commodities covered by the network.

The internet society, as a new social form, has undergone substantial changes, from productivity to production relations, from economic foundation to superstructure, and its more obvious "decoupling" has led to a large number of falsehoods or information asymmetries transpiring in the process of interaction and transaction, thus bringing uncertainty and risk in the area of social credit.

7.1.2 Information, Reputation, and Internet Trust

Before we can identify internet trust, we need to clarify several related concepts, namely information, reputation, confidence, and their relationships with online trust.

When we analysed the relationship between the concepts of integrity, trust, and credit in the previous sections, we pointed out that integrity and credit basically have different emphases on the continuum of Xin. From the perspective of the "individual-relationship-institution" continuum, integrity is oriented to the internal moral quality of individuals, trust reflects the state of social relationships, and credit emphasises the stable state associated with structural factors such as organisational systems and culture. In other words, in Chinese culture, "integrity, trust, and credit can correspond to individuals, relationships, and institutions, respectively, and refer to morality, interactions, and overall operational results." So, what is reputation? Simply put, reputation is the accumulation of various focuses on this continuum, including the accumulation of honesty, trust, or credit. Reputation is usually an evaluation, divided into positive and negative evaluations. If trust is gained to get a positive reputation, then the continuation of the interaction between the two parties or the subsequent engagement is established; conversely, if a person is not reputable, either his or her character is denied or the subsequent transaction has to be terminated and brings negative effects to his or her social reputation.

Sometimes, reputation exists more as the potential capital of a person, a group, a regulatory organisation (especially governments and enterprises), etc., that is, they do not necessarily manifest themselves directly, but through such things as the words and actions of a legal person, a product, an event, or an advertising spokesperson, such as the organiser of a social group, the leader of a business, a government or other social organisation, a quality product or service, the endorsement of a public figure (such as a celebrity), a well-established brand image, a powerful advertising slogan, etc., and will lead to the establishment of reputation, even if there is no good reputation behind this symbol. Therefore, discussing the meaning of "reputation" is actually a way to discuss the operation of integrity, trust, and credit. Moreover, this concept tells us that the accumulation of "reputation" is consistent, and it faces a lot of questions and tests in the time dimension. The accumulation of reputation includes information content, communication channels, and communication methods. These all affect people's judgement and acceptance of a certain reputation.

The internet society is formed with computers, mobile communication, and network platforms. The information it generates is not just data, but the society formed by the data. Internet trust is the interaction formed on the basis of online information. Under its auspices, people's trust is not based on dependence and mutual familiarity, but on the screening and judgement of constantly updated information. Since the speed and coverage of communication have been enlarged far too many times compared with that of real society, it leads to tremendous complexity in the network communication environment and a diversity of communication channels (information). This means that any attempt to maintain a consistent reputation becomes more difficult, such that a person, group, or organisation is constantly challenged with threats to reputation.

7.1.3 Diversification of Trust in the Internet Era

The trust network established by the agrarian culture was itself self-contained. People did not emphasise the importance of faith, not because they did not have any, but because it was pre-existing. If there was a breach of trust, the cost was much higher than the cost of keeping trust, and the maintenance mechanism mainly depended on local opinion and the culture of shame. At that time, it was impossible to flee home because of a breach of trust or deception. In a local society connected by relationships, one could not avoid closely related others even after running away; as the old Chinese saying has it, a monk cannot run away from the temple. In the era of the planned economy, the government adopted a household registration system with a binary division between urban and rural areas, which fixed the rural-born population in their hometowns, while the urban-born residents belonged to urban Hukou, and most of them were incorporated into state-run units or large or small collective households for management. Each one of them started to build a personal record since school that stayed with the person for the rest of his or her life. The rewards or punishments received or the growth and performance of the person were recorded in the file, which played an important role in the promotion or transfer of the person. Such an approach was very different from that of the agrarian era, but in terms of space and time, there was little difference: They both achieved the stability of institutional constraints in the same place, only the latter was controlled, while the former was free. Alternatively, we can see that credit control in the planned economy was an extension of the credit of rural society, whose commonality was achieved by means of the immobility of the population.

After the reform and opening up, social relationships that had been predictable and stable began to be replaced by unpredictable and loose interactions with strangers. Industrialisation and urbanisation broke up the communal life of traditional Chinese society and the trust network built up by it. In particular, as the population of large cities exploded and hundreds of millions of peasants entered the cities to work, most interactions were with strangers, leading to the virtual disappearance of stable social networks unless people returned to their hometowns or maintained classmate or neighbourhood relationships, without the establishment of a functioning credit system to match. Since the internet officially entered China in 1995, its use has expanded rapidly. More and more people of different ages, classes, and professions have begun to establish new connections with society through electronic devices such as personal computers, cell phones, and tablets, and many Chinese people (especially the younger generation) have developed a lifestyle centred on the internet (including mobile networks). The emergence and prevalence of virtual societies have brought new interpersonal connections, communication methods, channels, and content, thus also changing the foundations on which social-trust systems are built. The trust system based on local networks and the acquaintance society has suffered a large impact, and social credibility needs a new way to fortify itself under a brand-new communication environment. Since the communication characteristics of the internet are not continuous, the "longevity" and "non-selectivity" of a society of familiars must be transformed in accord with the transient and click-based, loose relationships of the internet. This means that the kind of self-restraint previously limited by social or local relations, especially acquaintances and family members, has been eliminated all at once, and the anonymity, temporality, and physical absence of communication subverts the habitual establishment of human interaction.

Although the virtual society is very different from real society, as long as people's minds are not blank when they enter this platform, they will definitely bring the customs, beliefs, and trust habits that have been formed in different fields. As long as the virtual society is not a kind of robot designed to interact, it can only be an extension of human interaction, an extension of real society. Furthermore, interaction on the internet does not take place in an independent space closed by electronic technology; instead, it has always been part of a real social environment that exists to meet people's realistic wishes or wishes that cannot be met in the real world. These characteristics show that the internet is not only a technology invented for the rapid dissemination and distribution of information but also a real social force. This power is also manifest in the content of its information, which both comes from and informs society. This content has changed society in an unprecedented way of connection. People in real society are very much in need of a specific time and space. For example, powerful movements may converge in downtown squares or on important traffic roads. However, the social forces of the internet directly influence people's opinions and attitudes, thus affecting and changing society. The information on the internet also differs from the information of the past. Traditional media information has designated collectors (journalists), preparation (screening), review methods (control), and other processes, but these protocols were broken by the internet. A large amount of information began to surge, both good and bad. The public may not have the ability to distinguish the good from the bad but is more likely to face this cascade of information with confusion. Consequently, credit building in this new, virtual society needs to be considered and studied in this environment.

7.2 Credit Crisis in the Internet Era

7.2.1 Online and Offline Credibility Disputes: A Look Back at Some Online Public Events

In the era of mainstream media such as radio, television, movies, and newspapers, all aspects of information in Chinese society were strictly controlled and managed, and this contributed to a consistently high level of credibility and social image for the government at all levels of the country. With the breakthrough of the internet and the popularity of the internet, a digital and networked information revolution has taken place in the media field, and more traditional media have been involved on the internet. The innovation and transformation of media technology have led to the original issue of social credibility being greatly complicated. In China today, there are objectively two public opinion arenas. One is the party and government newspapers, state TV stations, state news agencies, etc. As mainstream media, they faithfully propagate the policies of the party and the government and spread core socialist values; the other is private opinion that relies on self-media. At first, people discussed current affairs, criticised society and government on blogs, microblogs, BBS, QQ, and other platforms, but now they have turned to various self-media and gradually constituted a competitive relationship with the official media. As a result, the internet has become a distribution centre for ideological and cultural information and an amplifier of social opinion, rewriting the new pattern of public opinion guidance. In a standoff situation where positive reports and negative events are pitted against each other, the internet presents an amplified social credibility and a credibility crisis at the same time.

Many originally private, local events (most of them negative), through the large-scale publicity and proliferation of websites, netizens, and other media, quickly become public events of concern to the whole network, the whole society, and even the whole world. The powerful atmosphere of public opinion created in the virtual world also creates great psychological pressure, questions, and challenges for people involved in the real world. Although in some respects, traditional official media still maintain a positive propaganda role and consolidate the credibility of society, in many places the spread of untrustworthy, counterfeit, and malicious events through the internet can spill over into public discourse about the image of the state or its ability to govern. In addition, the internet's extensive reporting and reconstruction of such incidents can also serve as a hint and a demonstration. Due to the anonymity feature of the internet, many similar negative reports also make it difficult to distinguish whether the incident is true or false, or whether someone has deliberately spread rumours to grab people's attention. Nowadays, the most common phrase we hear is that the internet is not a place in which rules do not apply, meaning that people should also obey the law in a virtual society. But perhaps the rule of communication that emerged from the internet is that traffic is money: So very often, a variety of true and false news is flying all over the place, in a sense dissipating the seriousness of events. So, there is a tendency to entertain it. In the meantime, there are also more and more cases of lawsuits interrogating individuals' or organisations' credit or reputation.

On the whole, news dissemination in the internet era has caused the development and evolution of "from point to point," "from local to national," and "from small to big events," resulting in a change in the meaning of credibility and making it difficult for society to return to the possibility of forming a consensus.

7.2.2 The Credibility Crisis of Official Media and Civil Media

Below we use our survey data to reflect the changes in social credit in the internet era.

7.2.2.1 Crisis of Social Credibility of Official Media and the Underlying Reasons

Let's first understand the change of channels for urban and rural residents to learn about current affairs. Although traditional media with TV as the core still occupies the main position (rural areas are more dependent on traditional media than urban areas), channels such as portals, online forums, and cell phone subscriptions have shown a significant increase (this is more obvious in urban areas), increasingly crowding out the communication position of traditional media (see Tables 7.1 and Table 7.2).

On the other hand, the emergence of multiple news channels has led to a breakdown in the prestige of the official media. For example, when urban respondents

Table 7.1 The first channel for urban residents to learn about current affairs (N = 3138)

		Frequency	*Percentage*
Valid	TV	1582	50.4
	internet portals such as Sina, Sohu, etc.	429	13.7
	Online forums (such as BBS, Weibo, etc.)	353	11.2
	Cell phone subscription	239	7.6
	Newspaper, magazine	208	6.6
	Radio	156	5.0
	Private channels such as friends, familiars, etc.	125	4.0
	Others	10	.3
	Total	3102	98.9
Missing	System	36	1.1
Total		3138	100.0

Table 7.2 The first channel for rural residents to learn about current affairs (N = 2158)

		Frequency	*Percentage*
Valid	TV	1512	70.1
	Cell phone subscription	157	7.3
	Private channels such as friends, familiars, etc.	135	6.3
	Radio	89	4.1
	Online forums (such as BBS, Weibo, etc.)	61	2.8
	Newspaper, magazine	51	2.4
	internet portals such as Sina, Sohu, etc.	45	2.1
	Total	2050	95.0
Missing	System	108	5.0
Total		2158	100.0

were asked, "Which of the following sources do you think is the most credible source of information about the effects of nuclear radiation in Japan?" 48.6% of urban residents still chose to believe the official news released by the government, but 11.7% also chose to believe the information released by independent media, 11.1% believed the information released by experts and scholars, 9.6% chose to believe the information released by internet uses, and less than 10% chose to believe the information released by foreign media and other sources. In another survey on the credibility of the reports of the July 23 rear-end accident, the percentage of respondents who believed the government dropped even further to 42.1%, while the percentage of those who believed information released by independent media and internet users rose to 16.8% and 14.8%, and the percentage of those who believed authority figures dropped to 8.4%. Furthermore, when we take the data of those urban residents who are accustomed to using online channels such as portals, online forums, and cell phone subscriptions (N = 1019) and analysed them separately, we get a clearer answer to the above two questions: Only 32.3% of urban netizens believed the government's reports on Japanese nuclear radiation coverage, while those who believed independent-media surveys, overseas media, internet releases, and information released by authoritative figures. Only 23.8% of urban netizens believed the official news about the accident released by the government, while the percentage of those believing independent media, internet users, overseas media, and authoritative figures were 23.8%, 22.6%, and 8.9%, respectively (see Figures 7.1 and 7.2).

Although the trust of Chinese residents, especially urban residents and rural citizens, in different media and objects varies when facing different news events and social situations, in general the authority and credibility of traditional official media and websites are gradually decreasing along with the increased popularity of the internet and the diversification of media information. However, it should be noted that the official media and official opinion field led by governments at all levels still maintain high credibility, and the credibility of TV, newspapers, radio, and official websites is also higher than that of related private media such as the internet and cell phones, in which internet users are active.[2]

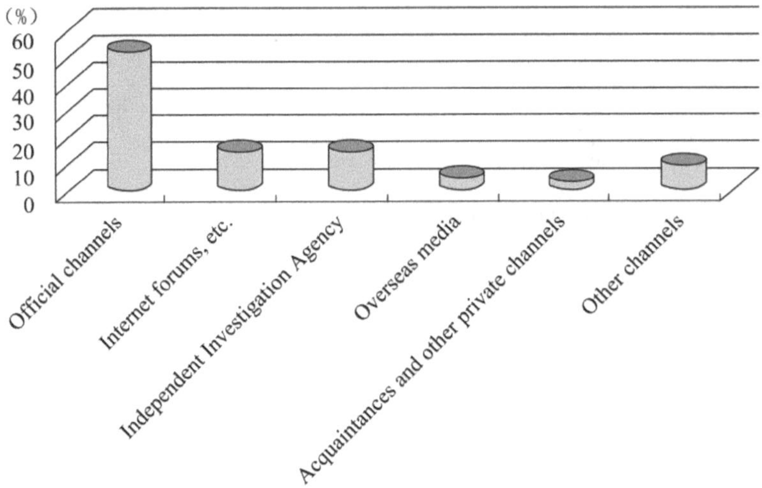

Figure 7.1 The most credible information channel on the Japanese nuclear radiation incident

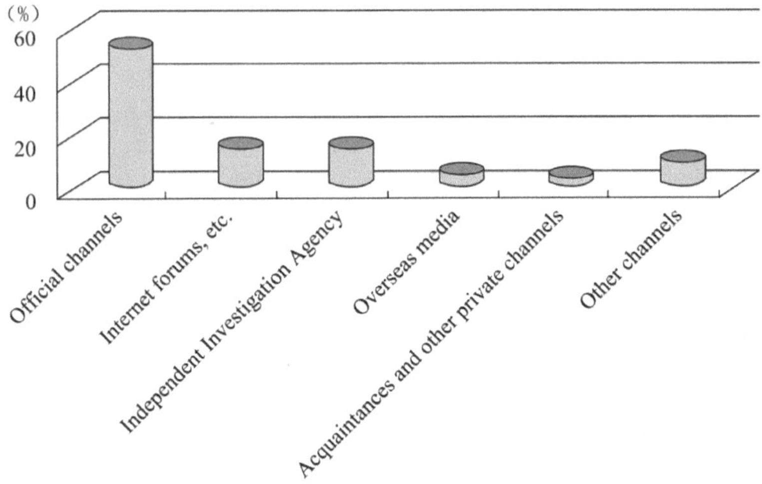

Figure 7.2 The most credible information channel on the July 23 rear-end accident

7.2.2.2 The Social Credibility of Civil Media and the Underlying Reasons

The shift in the focus of communication media has a more complex impact on the civil media and civil-opinion field, which, while providing many opportunities for their own credibility building, have in many cases also led the credibility crisis themselves.

On the one hand, the popularity of the internet has, to a certain extent, expanded the influence and reach of the civil media and enhanced their social credibility. More and more internet users choose to obtain various news information from unofficial channels on the internet. From the survey data of this project, 32.5% of urban residents and 12.2% of rural residents already tend to use web portals, online forums, cell phone subscriptions, and other online civil channels to learn about current affairs. In addition, consulting the latest statistical report on the development of China's internet (see Table 7.3), the number of users of instant messaging, search engines, online news, and blogs/personal spaces, which are the main unofficial media, has since the second half of 2013 accounted for 70% of the total number of Chinese internet users and has shown a further upward trend. The number of users of other civil-media platforms such as microblogs, emails, social-networking sites, and forums/BBS is all above 100 million, although the proportion of users is slightly smaller and each has its own increase or decrease.

However, the credibility of netizens as a special opinion field is itself limited. According to the results of this survey, 38.6% of urban residents chose a negative attitude when asked whether the information provided by unofficial organisations such as online forums or independent media is true and reliable, while only 21.3% answered in the affirmative and 39.8% were ambiguous. When asked, "If the internet is full of negative comments about a product, I will lose confidence in that product," 43.9% of urban residents answered in the affirmative, while only 24.1% answered "no" and 31.9% "can't tell." It can be seen that urban residents' trust in online information varies depending on the social context and content of events. When faced with some positive reports from online civil media, the public's trust in them is low, but when faced with some negative comments, the public's trust in them is higher. This result shows that the general public has a highly sceptical and wary attitude toward the social credibility of online civil media, but this attitude is miraculously weakened in negative reports. This actually reflects another aspect of the decline of the authority of official media, the impossibility of pluralism to make a single civil credibility dominant, and the ensuing pluralism of news reporting making the authenticity of information more questionable. At this time, the public tends to be torn between the official media and the mass media, and of course tends to believe in official media when there are conflicts and conflicting views, although new research also proves that there are differences in access and age groups between the north and south.

In conclusion, in different online events and the social contexts in which they occur, we cannot simply understand them theoretically as a collective voice of online public opinion, and we cannot ignore the complexity, plurality, and heterogeneity of their internal composition. Conflicting interests, emotional venting, entertainment satisfaction, and rumour spreading among internet users may affect the social value orientation, a phenomenon not found in the era of traditional media.

7.2.2.3 Dimensional Adjustment of Credit in Modern Society

The first decade or so of the internet's entry into China caused a complication of social opinion and the emergence of additional voices in the original public

Table 7.3 December 2013–June 2014 utilisation rate of various internet applications among Chinese internet users

Application	*June 2014*		*December 2013*		*Semi-annual growth rate*
	User Scale (10,000)	*Utilisation rate of internet users*	*User scale (10,000)*	*Utilisation rate of internet users*	
Instant messaging	56423	89.3%	53215	86.2%	6.0%
Search engine	50749	80.3%	48966	79.3%	3.6%
Online news	50316	79.6%	49132	79.6%	2.4%
Blog/Personal space	44430	70.3%	43658	70.7%	1.8%
Weibo	27535	43.6%	28078	45.5%	−1.9%
E-mail	26867	42.5%	25921	42.0%	3.6%
Social-networking sites	25722	40.7%	27769	45.0%	−7.4%
Forum/BBS	12407	19.6%	12046	19.5%	3.0%

Source: Abridged from China internet Development Statistics Report, July 2014, P26, www.cnnic.net.cn/hlwfzyj/hlwxzbg/hlwtjbg/201407/P020140721507223212132.pdf.

opinion. In the last decade or so, however, the internet has become more closely bound to real society, and of course, its modes of expression are still evolving. The understanding of this point requires shifting our original research framework that focused on the transition from traditional to modern to a comparative study of the communication of public opinion in the modernity of society itself.

The Chinese character "信," which consists of "人" and "言," actually reveals the two layers of meaning of the Chinese word for "信." The first layer of meaning concerns the person himself, including his moral character and ability; the other layer concerns the matter, mainly the truth or falsity of the information. Of course, these two directions are not completely separate, so in Chinese "personnel" combines concepts, indicating that no matter what things have to be done by someone, no matter what information has to be conveyed by people, they are ultimately combined in "信." The reasoning is that people are different. With the same character, their ability may be different; with the same ability, their relationship may be different; if the relationship is different, the intelligence and information that can be obtained from them may also be different. Therefore, to get reliable information, first of all, one must be reliable, and the relationship must be reliable. But from the theory of credit building itself, "people" and "things" are not always combined. For example, once a person has faith or believes in a doctrine, he will automatically block unfavourable information, or even reject certain facts, etc.; or there are times when we are more concerned about the truth, regardless of who said it. Thus, depending on how people and things fit or don't fit in terms of credit, we divide the credit dimension into person-based expressive credit and matter-based factual credit.

The theoretical question we need to deal with now is this: According to the above division between person- and matter-based credit, does its social operation matter in terms of the expressiveness of the person or the actuality of the matter?

In the 1950s, American social psychologists C. L. Hovland and W. Weiss showed through a series of experiments that credibility is based on the source of information and professionalism. The source of information involves the accumulation of the communicator's character or reputation, such as honesty, impartiality, objectivity, etc., while professionalism lies in whether the person who publishes the information is an authority on the subject. Another study by Kellman and Hovland shows that the authority of experts diminishes over time, while the persuasive power of non-authority increases because people remember more about the content of the information as time passes. That is, there is a "dormant" effect between trust in the authority and content relationship.[3]

Judging by Hovland's research as well as common sense, it is of course people who matter, because things are done by people. This is also why our previous thinking and research on 信 always dwelt on the concepts of integrity, trust, credibility, and credit: These concepts involve various human characters and behaviours, and in turn, people and scholars alike tend to think that the problem of "信" is in fact the solution to the problem of people, especially the problem of moral character. Once the problem of the human being is brought to the fore, the importance of the way in which the human being itself is constituted emerges. Accordingly, in order to ensure the division of labour and the resolution of political, social, educational, and physical commissions and contracts, as well as the exchange of economic, social, cultural, and symbolic capital, various social organisations have been created, and various events have taken place in them, which together form a huge and complex society.

In order for this complex society to function in an orderly manner, the society is designed into a hierarchical structure, and social organisations, large and small, are assembled into this structure in a hierarchical manner, with hierarchies of positions and functions and corresponding levels of power, at which point the social trust we originally discussed is more nested in the various power relations. The hierarchy of power is important because it is used to maintain the normal functioning of society. The structure of power actually touches on the way modern society is constituted, i.e., the hierarchical system, also called bureaucracy. In other words, trust based on "facts" has the same vertical character as the way people are organised. Of course, vertical transmission of information is important and reasonable in itself, but it is only because it is dependent on people, and it is complicated by the complexity of people.

However, the advent of the internet era has triggered a separate emergence of actuality trust. In other words, with the emergence of the internet, the information flowing in it expresses a strong urge to try to get rid of expressive trust. At this moment, actual trust began to be decoupled from expressive trust.

Why is this so? This is determined by the characteristics of the internet itself. As a platform for information dissemination, the internet itself is incapable of establishing its hierarchical relationships. It is flat, or, by and large, network-like matters that lack hierarchy; correspondingly, only organisation-like matters have a hierarchy. Sociology likes to discuss concepts such as nodes, strong and weak relationships, information bridges, structural holes, or small worlds when studying social networks because the structural problems of networks are not vertical and controllable, but diffusive.

This is not to say, of course, that there is no centre or priority in network communication. In fact, whether it is an information bridge, a structural hole, etc., the meaning of these concepts is to discuss the problem of connectivity at the nodes. What the connection at the node wants to show is that information only has a chance to spread out if it is connected to an information distribution centre. Accordingly, it also follows that if a central point publishes more important, peculiar, or attractive information, it is more likely to receive attention and more likely to attract other central points to connect, leading to an increase in its position in the network. But the prominence of the network's central point cannot be considered hierarchical, but only as a powerful point brought about by its attractiveness. This effect expresses the degree of attention received, just like a web celebrity who can be said to receive a high degree of attention without having any necessary authority. Therefore, even if a website provides important information, this does not mean that it is an authoritative organisation. With today's explosive emergence of self-media, non-authoritative institutions of all sorts and sizes have also exploded.

After factual trust was detached from expressive trust, we were surprised to find that many people who gave information on internet platforms did not emphasise their identity and status; they either kept their names anonymous and used only a web name to express sometimes important and sometimes trashy news and opinions; or they consciously published only information or comments without revealing themselves for fear of liability. For the hierarchical system, the advent of the internet has never meant the decay of its authority. As long as there is a hierarchy, the control of information will become a topic that must be taken into account, and thus the tension between expressive and factual trust, which were originally combined, emerges. It is the trust model above that has changed (see Figure 7.3).

The dotted line extended by the authority dimension indicates that with the development of internet technology, the current focus of social trust is no longer on getting people to pay attention to what information, anecdotes, and opinions come from which people, organisations, and institutions. Many people no longer care about authoritative information as much as they did before but are more concerned about what is happening, what comments are being made, what the social repercussions are, etc. Driven by this impetus, many online writers are mobilised, and their economic drive comes more from increasing retweets, likes, and clicks. Ultimately, the flattening of internet communication has led to a delicate balance between power-dependent expressive trust and internet-dependent factual trust. Traditional media no longer occupy the central position of information distribution as they did in the past, and a certain degree of competition has emerged between them and the new self-media. The chain reaction of the emergence of this relationship is the division of people's trust, with some people insisting that authoritative trust is necessary and others believing that what is passed on the internet is true,

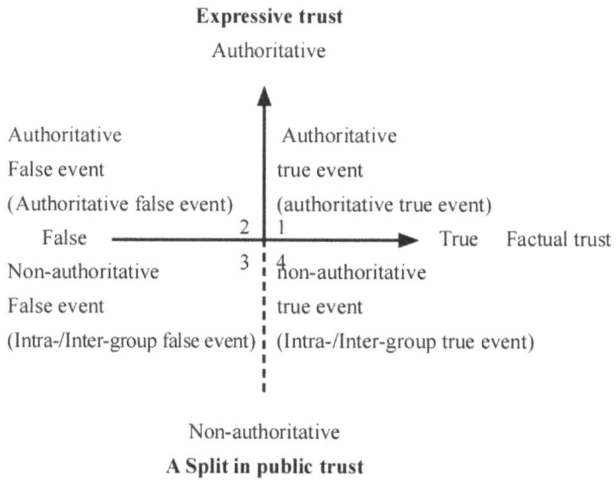

Figure 7.3 Trust model in the internet era

which in turn may express doubts about information from authoritative institutions. The traditional media, in order to change this situation, will also be actively involved in the establishment of internet platforms, insisting on the daily release of a variety of important authoritative information.

The framework of trust analysis for an ideal type of trust in modern society is due to the emergence of the internet.

Importantly, this model is only used for analytical research and not for personal understanding of one's real situation. People in a certain vector do not necessarily recognise themselves as being in that dimension, or at least they do not believe the information they receive is false. For scholars, what we see is that in a hierarchical and at the same time internet-enabled information society, two dimensions of trust have developed. Among them, the core of expressive trust is the question of authority, which can be divided into two kinds of pointers: Authoritative and non-authoritative; the core of factual trust is the question of the truth or falsity of a situation. The split relationship between them leads to four different combinations, each of which represents an ideal type of social trust. Accordingly, the issues of integrity, trust, credibility, and credit in major emergencies can be discussed.

7.3 The Mobile Internet and Business Credit: A Case Study of Group-Buying Groups

With the emergence of the internet, business transactions have expanded from real transactions to network transactions. The most important feature of online transactions is that they are not limited by time and space. One of the most immediate consequences of this expanded decentralisation is the disappearance of market locality and the re-integration of goods and customers. This means that the customer base of merchants is increasing and the profit potential is increasing, but the impact of reputation evaluation is also increasing, and with it, the risk of reputation is increasing. As a result, given these characteristics, successful internet companies, with strong incentives to make profits and maintain their reputation, are innovating ways to proactively empower consumers to increase their confidence in the transaction. For example, Jingdong shows the sincerity of self-restraint through the display and control of physical quality, Taobao guarantees the transaction funds through third-party escrow to ensure that there are no problems with the transaction credit, and other online shopping companies influence consumers' purchasing preferences through the evaluation system, which of course does not exclude seeking false positive reviews from their own people or pressuring customers with negative reviews. Overall, these are all forms of empowerment by merchants, and consumers are passive recipients of their empowerment. Of course, such innovation does solve many credit problems in real transactions, but there are also some loopholes: One is the credit problem between fragmented consumers. Because they are only a group of strangers temporarily grouped together based on a certain shopping intention, whether they believe the various comments published online may still have a significant meaning. For example, if someone buys something, has an extremely poor experience, and gives the seller a negative review, it is not clear whether that will affect the credit of the merchant if more than 70% of the other comments are positive. Of course, the consumer may trust the third party and the evaluation system despite all their problems. For example, a merchant may hire someone to post a review in his favour to boost the positive rating, or the merchant may remove the bad rating rate through improper means. Clearly, there is a necessary governance cost here if the integrity of the evaluation system and of the third-party intermediary is to be preserved.

The above loopholes have led to a new form of shopping, namely "marketing" by building groups in WeChat. This kind of marketing is different from simple online shopping, although it is derived from online shopping. Its characteristics are to build a network space with the real space, to realise the interaction between "online" and "offline," to evaluate the real and the extended, and to empower the group purchase to consumers. This is the group-buying transaction model.

7.3.1 The Establishment of Group Buying

The group purchase is an emerging transaction model formed by the building of WeChat groups in communities, and our focus at this time is, first, whether and how community residents can form an integrated force sufficient to counterbalance the merchants; second, how to build a credit chain between customers and merchants to reach cooperative behaviour; and third, what role mobile internet technology plays in the group purchase and how participants can unleash their own initiative to utilise the technology so as to make it play a greater role in promoting credit. Here we take the example of a WeChat group purchase in a community in Nanjing to explore the pattern, formation, and influential factors of such credit.

With the outbreak of the pandemic in early 2020, the country entered a state of epidemic prevention and control, with grassroots communities (urban residential neighbourhoods) under closed management, online shopping and courier services halted, public places closed, food-service industries temporarily shut down, and supermarkets open for limited hours. The general public, in such a closed and isolated state, was most worried about how to maintain its daily life. In particular, the public was worried about getting the usual food, getting alcohol for disinfection, getting masks, and so on. While the local government had no time to take care of these details, the residents quickly found a way to help themselves by initiating group buying on their own with the help of the WeChat group platform. As the epidemic eased, such a shopping mode was not as popular as it was during the severe period of the epidemic, but it became a regular mode of shopping for community residents.

Group purchase groups can develop in scale on WeChat due to various life needs. That is to say, due to different life needs, there are various types of businesses stationed in the group purchase groups: There are shopping malls, hotels, and restaurants; there are general breakfast stores and dessert houses; there are also farms, vegetable farms, and orchards. Operators may be community-based or foreign merchants; some may be relatively long-established while others are recently established. Due to the growing number of people joining the groups, management has conveniently divided them into Group 1, Group 2, and Group 3, and it can extend these groups according to the needs of the residential district or of the participants involved. In addition, members of different groups may overlap.

The effective development of the community WeChat group-buying model also increases the power of the buyers. Community members are integrated as buyers through the WeChat platform, instead of facing merchants as scattered individuals. If internet technology has the potential to both enhance credit and dismantle the foundation of credit construction (such as the loopholes mentioned above), then the community WeChat group-buying model combines mobile internet technology and the Chinese "circle culture" factor. Based on some common interests, through the interactive platform provided by the "WeChat group," the two-way influence of social interactions and the two-way transformation of social networks are realised online and offline, allowing weak relationships in physical space to interact more frequently in cyberspace. The basic sociological view was that only real social interactions form strong relationships, but we found in our research that the expansion of group-buying groups also helps to enhance intimacy, forming a new form of interaction that integrates online and offline.

The prevalence of WeChat groups in China in fact invariably fits into the Chinese tradition of trust, i.e., forming circles because of proximity. Such a manoeuvre is a key step for Chinese people to build trust. This is particularly evident in the group-buying model. Specifically:

From the formation of the group-buying group, the group members are composed of community residents who live in a stable residential space and have the basis of a real network with each other, rather than being strangers who have no interactions at all, not to mention that some of them were previously familiar with each other. In other words, this network is no longer passive in accepting rights, but self-empowered, and its autonomy and dynamism are stronger than those of consumers in general online commodity transactions, because of the emergence of group consciousness in the relationship between group owners and their trust relationship with merchants.

From the process of group purchase trust construction, the participants need to elect a group administrator, who will assume the function of commission and agency to find cooperative merchants for the group members. On the one hand, the group administrator acts as an information intermediary, selects suitable merchants, guides merchants into the group transaction, and passes information between merchants and members; on the other hand, he acts as an executive intermediary, coordinates and solves the conflicts between buyers and sellers, and encourages, supervises, or disciplines merchants' behaviour. As a result, members of the group establish trust in the merchant through trust in the group administrator, and further test their trust in the merchant through their own shopping experience and through group comments and questions. The merchant will show its credibility through its responses, eventually forming a stable credit relationship. Even though the group is gradually expanding in size as more people join in, its credit system tends to be stable.

7.3.2 Credit Maintenance in Group-Buying Groups

The power presented by the group-buying groups reflects the credit maintenance mechanism in forming mutual stimulus and motivation among group members, group administrators, and merchants. Specifically, this mechanism is manifest in the following ways.

First is the establishment of reputation constraints. The group members choose to elect the group administrator independently. The trust relationship between group members and the group administrator starts from the neighbourhood relationship in real space and the common concept of online shopping, and the group members entrust the group administrator to find a merchant with good quality and a low price, and the group administrator charges the service fee (administration cost) provided by the resident merchant. If the merchant provides goods in line with the needs of the group members, the better the reputation of the group administrator. The more the group members trust the group administrator, the more they trust the merchant, the more goods they buy, and the more the resident merchant is motivated to provide goods. The more service commissions the group administrator gets, the more he is motivated to find a better-quality merchant, making the group members, the group administrator, and the merchant form a favourable credit chain. To reduce the cost of administration, group administrators are also motivated to make effective rules to ensure orderly group-buying action and to avoid the possible crisis of trust due to the lack of third-party supervision. Of course, if a group administrator or merchant has a single breach of trust or fraudulent behaviour, then it may lead to a collective boycott by group members, resulting in a total loss of credit. If the group administrator's reputation in the community is damaged, the merchant must terminate the transaction behaviour and quit the group shopping group. This is the reputation mechanism generated by the WeChat shopping group.

Second is the change of empowerment mechanism. Due to the advantages of high efficiency, low cost, and no delay in the storage and dissemination of information in WeChat groups, members can be the first to evaluate and get feedback on each business, and scattered consumers can instantly combine to form a consensus, thus reducing the repetition of games between buyers and sellers and greatly reducing the possibility of individuals being swindled. The many technologies in the mobile internet era enable individual buyers to highlight, gather, evaluate, and resist their needs, thus empowering them in ways that they were not (or are not) in traditional society. The relationship structure and power established in the WeChat group-buying model is both similar to and different from that of general online transactions (e.g., successful internet companies like Jingdong, Taobao, etc.). The similarity is that both have evaluation systems, but the difference is that buyers are empowered in general online transactions, and once sellers or third parties are unwilling to empower them, trust risk arises. In the community group-buying model, sellers are not facing scattered individuals, but a group integrated through the WeChat platform, with mutual trust among group members and highly bundled interests, enabling members of the network to implement collective resistance to violations, resulting in lost business for the merchant. The buyer is no longer an individual, but always a group. Group-buying groups not only ensure the quality of goods through mutual interests but also supervise merchants through comments. At this point, the seller no longer has the ability to bribe the evaluator, and it is impossible to ignore a small number of negative comments, creating an invisible monitoring mechanism. As can be seen, the credit relationship maintained in the group-buying model is closely related to the overall effect of changing the empowerment of buyers from passive to active in its relationship structure, all of which is brought about by evaluation.

Third is the spread of dissemination. Merchants are by nature rational actors whose actions are intrinsically motivated by profit. After the outbreak, merchants (especially in the service and catering industries) faced a severe sales crisis, and WeChat groups gave them a good opportunity to sell and profit, i.e., a chance to find a large and stable group of quality customers again. Since merchants see great business benefits in this, they will naturally seek to make a strong demonstration of their credibility. If a merchant's quality or credibility is not up to standard, the merchant will face not just the loss of casual customers, but of an up-scale customer base. The latter is often built on the speed of information delivery, low cost, and the convenience of the network connection method triggered by mobile internet technology. Moreover, once the communication subject projects a personal, emotional evaluation to each "WeChat group" or "circle of friends," this evaluation is forwarded through the "circle of friends" layer by layer. Imagine: If a merchant loses trust, he loses not only a shopping group but a large community of customers, resulting in incalculable losses.

The group-buying model in a WeChat group makes us realise that it has obvious differences with the credit process of internet merchants.

First, the empowering and empowered subjects are different. The carrier of credit generation in the group-buying model comes from the fact that the relationship among group members, group administrators, and sellers may form closer interests than those of the general shopper relationship. Once the relationship is close, the evaluation of a certain commodity will be more effective than the evaluation sent by scattered customers from all directions. Usually, the evaluation of scattered customers is reflected by a percentage; for example, there may be three negative reviews out of one hundred reviews, but this means there are ninety-seven positive reviews, which constitutes a huge majority of positive reviews. The members in the group-buying groups have both offline interaction and online evaluation, and they often have similar emotions and common consumption perceptions, which will form a consistent evaluation if they have a predetermined trust relationship with each other. From the trust relationship construction of group-buying groups, we also found that individual members' introductions and evaluations also showed extremely strong initiative and autonomy. Group members are likely to promote what they want and block what they do not want, which is a kind of buyer-oriented empowerment.

Second, the boundary of the group is not some kind of organisation in real society. The group has a stable structure but also scalability and duplicity. This means that if the merchant dares to deceive the group members, that information will be easily passed among the potential consumers the merchant wishes to reach, and the opinions associated with the members of the group will be potentially organised to achieve a kind of cognitive preparation, either love or denial, which is the reputation building mechanism in transaction governance (i.e., as the saying goes, "good things don't go unnoticed, bad things spread"). This can in turn lead the merchant to lose buyers and to lose his competition with other merchants. Such a dynamic inadvertently enhances the power of group members to discipline merchants.

Third, the success of the group-buying model also lies in the fact that from the traditional Chinese trust-building to the emergence of commodity transactions on the internet, intermediaries have been essential, unless the self-owned family group could exempt the third party. However, the group-buying model breaks through this point and is closer to the node problem discussed in social capital theory. The group administrator is elected by members' own choice, which is actually a structural hole,[4] and he creatively realises the replacement of the third-party intermediary. The familiarity and mutual benefit among group members and the group administrator make the group administrator doubly entrusted. The profit motive also contributes to the fact that the group administrator, as an important link between group members and merchants, has an incentive to adjust the credit relationship among group members and merchants and promote fair trade. At the same time, a series of rules set by the group administrator supplants the formal order (law) and the third-party intermediary, solving the credit crisis that may exist due to the lack of third-party supervision, thus saving considerable governance costs.

7.3.3 Reconstruction of Social Credit in the Mobile Internet Era

While elements such as formal legal norms and institutions are crucial in business relationships, it is not impossible to construct credit relationships despite less-than-ideal conditions. The group purchasing model is a mode of autonomous transaction governance reached by group members without the constraints of external forces. The informal power on which the group governance relies depends mainly on the trust network of the group as well as the mutual trust embedded in the network of mutual interests with elements of information transparency and common ideas. This coordinated action of buyers and sellers facilitated by reputation mechanisms is a continuation of traditional local-network reputation constraints on the one hand and a new form of internet transaction on the other.

Technological advances have the potential both to deconstruct trust and to rebuild it through the empowerment of individuals. With the internet, buyers who were in a retail state are connected by the integration of WeChat groups, constituting a kind of network group with common needs. Their presence in the marketplace has led to a corresponding change in the trading strategies of merchants, constituting a new credit relationship between them.

In the mobile internet era, the shopping experience of individuals has also fundamentally changed, as they are integrated into groups of varying sizes for various reasons and in various ways. They have grown in their rights and increased their ability to make demands in their interactions with merchants. Even if there is a temporary lack of corresponding institutional regulation on the operation of society, community residents can creatively solve the problem of a breach of trust in the process.

The study of group-buying groups may be a special case of commercial credit research in the internet era. There may be much to think about and learn from in terms of the difficult governance problems faced in community building, such as insufficient participation of residents in community affairs, inefficient but exhausted grassroots staff, and ineffective community governance with high costs. Our concern at this point is no longer to emphasise the establishment of institutions at the macro level (e.g., through legislation), but to try to examine how communities now use mobile networks to mobilise the motivation and creativity of multiple subjects. One thing noteworthy about the success of the community group is that its rules are often self-created by group administrators, which is very different from previous systems where leadership made the rules and subordinates implemented them.

Community WeChat groups seem to be built on the basis of digital media, but people's communication online and offline has always perpetuated the tradition of building trust in real society and has always had a philosophy and interest collusion different from that established by kinship and geo-relationship. This suggests that the social credit of the internet era, along with that of the previous era, has not been fractured but has been continuous and evolving.

For society as a whole, the advent of the internet era will give rise to a credit approach that is in line with the characteristics of this era. Compared to the previous era's face-to-face or organisation-to-organisation credit characteristics, the internet's coverage spans a specific field and makes the issue of reputation more prominent. This point can bring two new possibilities for social credit: First, a system for searching information on the internet; second, network technology for tracking the mobility of individuals. But this work is only peripheral. Such a convenient query technology should be used to prevent breaches of trust. It will not make social credit better; its significance is to keep the bottom line. But society still requires a moral bottom line. Consider how modern people judge where it feels safe to live. They care about more than anti-theft devices and the quality of anti-theft locks. They also care about all the things that go into a favourable social climate.

Trust in itself is important, trust in the quality and binding nature of its own composition is important, and trust in the confidence of future expectations is all-important to us. A high degree of control supports more than just a reduction in the phenomenon of breach of trust. Though all the pretty data on the reduction of breach of trust may be supplied to praise some technical innovation, society is really built on the hearts and minds of the people.

Notes

1 Giddens, *The Consequences of Modernity*, p. 18.
2 For more detailed findings, see Zhang Hongzhong, *Chinese Media Credibility in Transition*, Nanjing Normal University Press, 2013.
3 C. L. Hovland, W. Weiss, The Influence of Source Credibility on Effectiveness. *Public Opinion Quarterly* 1951(15), pp. 635–650.
4 Ronald Burt, *Structural Holes*, translated by Min Ren, Lu Li, Hong Lin, Gezhi Press-Shanghai People's Publishing House, 2008 edition, pp. 16–20.

References

Burt, R. (2008). *Structural holes* (R. Min, L. Lu & L. Hong, Trans.). Gezhi Press, Shanghai People's Publishing House.

Giddens, A. (2011). *The consequences of modernity* (H. Tian, Trans.). Yilin Press.

Hovland, C. L., & Weiss, W. (1951). The influence of source credibility on effectiveness. *Public Opinion Quarterly*, *15*, 635–650.

Zhong, H. (2013). *Chinese media credibility in transition*. Nanjing Normal University Press.

8 Funnelling Theory

The reason for the ineffectiveness of the current credit building in Chinese society is that the overall and complex nature of China's credit problem has been overlooked, with only partial responses to it being made that are ineffective and extremely costly. In order to curb the problem of credit failure as a whole, we propose the idea of "funnelling theory." "Funnelling theory" is a prevention-oriented concept, not an improvement of the system. As a concept, we believe credit education, the construction of credit files and evaluation systems, and the shaping of honest and trustworthy behaviour for minors are important while changing the norms of different industries or increasing the number of provisions at the legislative level also help.

8.1 Effectiveness of the Implementation of the Existing Social Credit System in China and Its Problems

8.1.1 The Construction History of China's Social Credit System

An institutionalised social credit system first occurs in the quality of goods and counterfeiting and then gradually evolves to all fields of society. At the national level, with the gradual progress of reform and opening up, market development has put forward higher credit requirements for the government, enterprises, and individuals. During the social transformation that started in 1978, the market-economy system, which was born from the traditional planned economy, did not raise the issue of credit in the initial stage because of the government's compulsory allocation of economic resources and the fact that the main body of the market was state-owned enterprises, and its social credit was concentrated in the state system itself. At this time, credit as an auxiliary resource allocation was concentrated in the financial field and was evaluated and used by the national banks. Its closed information did not receive much attention. However, in the late 1980s and early 1990s, when the market was liberalised and the individual economy developed, various problems of product quality and counterfeiting began to emerge, driven by the interests of various market entities. Thus, in the 1990s, the "China Quality Walk" was one of the most influential social activities in China. The event was co-sponsored by the major news organisations in the capital and supported by the State Council. The content and purpose are reflected in the explanation of its name:

DOI: 10.4324/9781003375579-10

"Quality Miles" "China's quality work" is facing a journey of a thousand miles, a journey of ten thousand miles; And Chinese journalists, in order to publicize and report on quality issues, will do a journey of a thousand miles, a journey of ten thousand miles. In August 1992, the Publicity Department of the Central Committee of the Communist Party of China, the State Press and Publication Administration, the Chinese Journalists Association, and the Organizing Committee of the China Quality Walk jointly held a concluding meeting of the first year's activities. Its message was a combination of news and market that supplemented the national economic development with news reports. Some researchers pointed out that since the founding of the country, the country had always attached importance to quality work but had suffered from lacking a good way to implement this work. China Quality Miles found a good way to promote quality work. One way to promote this work came from the perspective of journalism, and the other came from the perspective of economics; the two combined could be seen as a comprehensive evaluation of China Quality Miles activities. With a large number of counterfeit cases exposed in the news media and a large number of brand enterprises and famous products supported and promoted, the confidence of domestic and foreign consumers and traders in China's market environment was greatly restored. Needless to say, the impact of this activity was far-reaching. It not only reversed the chaotic situation of China's credit order in the short term, but also played a significant role in promoting the development and improvement of the legal system, the establishment and strengthening of national quality awareness, and the enhancement of Chinese enterprises' investment in quality work.[1]

In the economic field, the State Council issued the "Notice on the Nationwide Launching of the Work of Clearing 'Triangular Debt'" on 2 April 1990 to clear the problem of "triangular debt," which was a prelude to the systemic project of the social credit system construction.[7] The circular sought to standardise the business behaviours and issues of related economic order. However, in the end, these vigorous "credit-rectification campaigns" had trouble achieving their original purpose due to the unsoundness of relevant laws and regulations. In addition to the fanfare surrounding the "triangular debt" clean-up, the "fight against counterfeiting" also became a prominent credit-building "symbol" during that historical period. Since the overall market environment at that time was still chaotic, various counterfeiting practices not only disrupted the normal economic development of the country and brought great trouble to people's lives, but were also a great hindrance to China's important national development plans, such as the introduction of foreign investment and accession to the WTO. Therefore, the Chinese government needed to take practical actions to show the world that we had the ability and confidence to "create a consumer environment that satisfie[d] consumers, a market environment that allow[ed] enterprises to compete fairly, and an investment environment that ma[de] foreign investors feel safe."[2] In this context, a joint anti-counterfeiting action whose purposes were to fight counterfeiting, to support excellence, to regulate the market, to guide consumption, and to serve enterprises gained great momentum.

However, this credit-building model, which relies on short-term forceful raids, cannot solve the root problem after all. In the absence of supporting laws and regulations, the social-governance effect brought by the "Quality Miles" campaign soon became a "flash in the pan." In the development stages after the 1990s, the cross-border development of market transactions put forward higher requirements for credit construction, while the absence of relevant laws and regulations or lagging legislation, unclear division of functions of credit-management agencies, or contradictory coverage, became constraints to the development process. Therefore, the subsequent construction of the social credit system was expected to be more systematic, mainly involving three levels of content:[3] basic credit with market traders as the main body, institutional credit through the legal system, international practice with business customs as the main body, and supervisory credit with government supervision as the main body. More specifically, this new system would involve credit legislation; the collection and use of credit data and the establishment of a credit database; and the establishment and regulation of credit intermediaries.

Although there was progress in the construction of a social credit system in the above areas, it was not until the promulgation of the Regulations on Credit Industry Management on 26 December 2012 that the unified supervision of the credit industry, including credit reporting, credit scoring and credit rating, was basically completed, and the construction of the social credit system at the national level reached a more finished stage.

While the state actively promoted and led the construction of the credit system, various regions and localities also joined the construction of the regional credit system. At the beginning of the 21st century, cities and provinces such as Shanghai, Shenzhen, Beijing, Hangzhou, Gansu, Zhejiang, and Guangdong have taken the lead in taking practical steps to develop local credit regulations and build credit data platforms.[4] In general, the construction work in different regions has been tailored to local conditions and different characteristics, resulting in the "Shanghai Model," "Zhejiang Model," "Shenzhen Model," and "Wenzhou Model." In general, this kind of pilot exploration in different regions is beneficial to the overall construction of China's social credit system, but there are still various problems, such as contradictions between central and local initiatives, the unbalanced degree of credit collection among different regions, the mutually beneficial symbiotic relationship between the government and the market, competition and cooperation between industries, etc.

8.1.2 Ideas for Building China's Social Credit System

Compared with the credit model in Europe and the United States, which is based on endogenous contractual relations, China's credit system, which was originally built up by "relations" and population immobility, is obviously unable to fix the problems that have erupted in the market economy. These problems cannot be solved by the market economy itself but require a transformation of the whole society. In this context, the construction of China's social credit system was destined from its inception to choose a different development path from that of Western countries. The negotiation between the state, the market, and society in this process reflects both the uniqueness of the Chinese experience and the commonality of economic and cultural integration driven by the historical trend of globalisation.

For example, the opinions of the "General Office of the State Council on the construction of the social-credit system" clearly pointed out that

> the construction of the social-credit system should be based on the legal system, taking the credit system as its core, to improve issues of credit, taxes, contract performance, product quality, and credit records, adhering to the principles of "integrated planning, classified guidance with orderly governmental promotion, improving regulations with strict supervision, orderly opening, and maintaining security", to establish a credit-agency system with distinctive service features such that nationwide credit-collection agencies may coexist with social-credit agencies. Ultimately, what needed to be established was a basic framework of the social-credit system and an operating mechanism with a clear division of labor, efficient operations, and strong supervision.

From the opinions, it can be seen that the idea behind the construction of China's social credit system was to achieve joint control of such a system through the joint forces of all parties under the promotion of the government and through market-oriented operations and the industry association's self-discipline. This idea was reasonable as it fits the current situation of China's credit problem with linkage effects that broaden outwards. China's credit problem is not a single, local problem of the market or the financial field, but involves various fields like politics, economics, culture, and education, as well as individuals, organisations, and society.

The aforementioned design idea for a social credit system is obviously meant to learn as much as possible from foreign models based on the national conditions of China, so that a peculiarly Chinese credit system may be worked out.

However, despite the good intention of this design, there are many problems in the construction process. The fundamental problem is that the main body of social credit construction is unclear. From the General Office of the State Council, we see rather vague statements about "governmental promotion and market cultivation." These statements contain two contradictory meanings: First, if the main body is a market-oriented operation, the government's driving force should be emphasised; second, if the government's driving force is the primary motivation, it should be clear that the social-credit construction system is not a government-controlled system or a government project.[5] This contradiction reflects a Chinese problem-solving mindset: The government, market, and society cannot be separated from each other but can be integrated and extended, and all solution strategies, if traced back to their roots, can only originate from the government's leadership and promotion. The formation of the "strong government" social pattern has a certain historical continuity, for it did play a strong mobilising role in dealing with overall social problems in the early years after the founding of the country, and the use of this pattern is even more inertial when a better development path has not been found. According to the scholars and experts who devised this idea, the Chinese model is firstly a "practical model" to solve the bottleneck of China's credit development, and secondly a "technical model" to catch up with developed countries.[6] The so-called "practical model" is problem-oriented, regardless of its market orientation or its focus on public management, as long as it can have the effect of "setting things right" by achieving "immediate results" in the short term. But in the long run, the difficulty of reconciling the dual-track system of "government" and "market" or "state" and "society" remains a major challenge. The General Office is still unclear on how to reconcile the two forces.

The arduousness of the aforementioned plan for building China's social credit system implies that the government-led "dual-track system" pattern may lead to several consequences. First, it may lead to the government's interference with market behaviour and the market's dependence on the government. The government's strong involvement in the market has to a certain extent inhibited the play of market forces and social forces and has also made it easy for the franchised credit agencies to form monopolies, contrary to the laws of fair competition in the market operation. At the same time, the government's customary social-movement-type approach is likely to cause local governments to focus on image rather than actual performance, which is not conducive to stable market operation. In addition, the market's development is not yet mature. Without government investment, policy support, open-information sources, and institutional satisfaction of credit demands, the survival of the credit agencies becomes problematic. Second, the involvement of market behaviour in the process of building public-credit systems tends to breed corruption unless there are legal protections in place. The government's dual role as the credit regulator and the consumer may lead to bribery and other malfeasance, not only causing regulatory failure but also damaging the government's credibility.

In conclusion, although the idea of building China's social credit system is to a certain extent in line with national conditions (i.e., China's weak credit foundation), it still has many problems in a comprehensive view. These are clearly pointed out in the Notice on the Issuance of the Outline of the Social Credit System Construction Plan (2014–2020) issued by the State Council in June 2014: "Although the construction of China's social credit system has made some progress, the contradictions that do not match, coordinate, and adapt to the level of economic development and the stage of social development are still prominent." Therefore, over the next five years, the construction of the social credit system needs to "accelerate the construction of government integrity," "promote the construction of business integrity," "comprehensively promote the construction of social integrity," "vigorously promote the construction of judicial credibility," and "strengthen the construction of integrity education and integrity culture."[7]

8.1.3 Problems in the Implementation of China's Social Credit System

At present, the establishment of China's social credit system is characterised by both its early and late start of construction, its obvious administrative colouring, its non-uniform credit-collection standards, and its inconsistent and non-uniform content coverage. Specific manifestations are as follows.

First, credit legislation. Since the planning of China's economic development path is still under exploration, the central government is obviously cautious in establishing and implementing credit-management laws and regulations based on developed countries, and it is difficult to establish basic laws directly related to the credit industry. In the past two decades, there have been no stable and unified basic and core legal provisions in the field of social credit at the national level. Instead, various Notices, Regulations, and Ordinances have been issued one after another according to the changing market situation. Although in the short term these regulations can play a role in regulating market credit, in the long term there is neither a basic guidance nor a principled basis for credit issues, and there are conflicting regulations that overwhelm credit agencies and consumers and that also provide an opportunity for some enterprises and individuals to "exploit loopholes" and "find loopholes." As a result, the implementation of these regulations becomes a task, a formality that only deepens the original problem. Compared with the more mature market economies in Europe and the United States, the capital market in China's transitional society has not yet matured, and credit issues are more complex, making it very difficult to establish a stable "standard," but this implies the necessity of a stable "standard." In December 2012, the State Council promulgated the official "Regulations on Credit Industry Management" (hereafter referred to as "the Regulations"),[8] which provides a certain institutional standard and regulatory basis for the construction of the credit market, but whether it has a "fundamental" status for social-credit construction remains to be seen in time.[9]

Second, the collection and use of credit data and the establishment of a credit database. The important content of this construction is to establish the basic database of enterprise and personal credit information to provide a reference for the regulation and restriction of credit behaviour, which involves subjects that include the government, enterprises, and individuals, and not only affects many departments but also has complicated and sensitive contents. This makes the joint credit-collection work very difficult; it progresses very slowly in terms of compulsory disclosure of information, restricted disclosure of information, and protection of commercial secrets and personal privacy, etc. Today's social-credit problems are "comprehensive." The linkage effect makes the construction of the credit database itself multi-departmental and multi-regional to achieve its maximum effectiveness, otherwise, the duplication of construction in each region will become ineffective, and the inconsistency or contradiction in the content and degree of credit collection in different regions will hinder the construction of the credit system. Therefore, in addition, the monopoly of credit-management agencies with access to the credit market and business scope has created a certain operating space for the privatisation of public power, resulting in the corruption of sectoral-interest units and individuals, while the unequal rights and obligations stipulated by credit agencies and information subjects have created the hidden agenda of illegally acquiring citizens' information and making profits, damaging the rights and interests of information subjects.

Third, in terms of the choice of a credit-management-agency formation model, at this stage, China has mainly adopted a government-led model for credit construction in various industry sectors. Compared with foreign countries, which rely more on independent third-party, corporate-credit intermediaries to provide credit guarantees and evaluation services, China has mainly adopted a credit-intermediary development model led and promoted by national government departments such as the State Economic and Trade Commission, the Ministry of Finance, and the People's Bank of China, and it has gradually adjusted its institutional settings according to market demand. This model emphasises that the governmental agencies combine the functions of legislation, law enforcement, and supervision, and the credit-management and intermediary agencies they set up enjoy absolute control over other credit assessment and credit implementation agencies. This "monopolar" model is beneficial to China's immature market system, underdeveloped social capital, and weak credit foundation, but there are substantial problems with the government's complete control of the "credit discourse." This is because, first of all, the social transformation brought about by the economic transformation has made the government incompetent to work in an "omnipotent" mode, and its control over the market and society is to a certain extent lacking the corresponding hard and soft conditions such as technology, capital, and human resources to support it; second, the loopholes in the government's internal management system make it difficult for the government to effectively perform its role as a credit-management agency. The identity of the government is difficult to effectively fulfil, and the division of departmental functions, duplication of settings, and opaque operations cause its supervision of the credit market often to lag behind or be weak; what's more, the government has multiple identities as "legislator," "enforcer," and even "supervisor." This factor not only creates a certain "vacuum" in legal regulation but also causes a large amount of public information to be blocked by administrative power, which hinders the flow of credit information. In addition, the existing government functions are based on the government's credibility, which is a credit field that needs to be systematically built and managed, because it is formed by the government over time by the long-term performance of its duties, and is manifest in its authority, influence, and appeal among the public, as well as by the embodiment of the government's legitimacy.[10] Therefore, once the credibility of the government is lacking, its credit-management agencies will not only fail to perform their functions properly but will intersect with the government's behaviour, leading the government itself to be widely questioned and making its efficacy weaker.

In a sense, the problems in the implementation of the credit system are merely a reflection of China's consistent regional segmentation strategy of social governance. This governance strategy attempts to gradually enact relevant laws and regulations in different industries and fields in a "piecemeal," localised manner to complete the overall standardisation of society and eventually achieve the overall credit enhancement of the country. However, the whole is greater than the sum of the parts, and it involves different levels of credit problems. On the surface, this seems to fit the current situation of China's vast territory, large population, complex social stratification, and different social problems, but in essence, it only catalyses the "headache and foot pain" of specific areas and levels of institutional remedies, which cannot fundamentally realise the integrity consciousness (moral level) and credit level of the whole society. On the contrary, it has given rise to more "policies from above and countermeasures from below" solutions outside the system. Although, according to the existing credit-system-construction pilot, Shanghai, Shenzhen, Nanjing, and other economically developed major cities have played a certain pilot and demonstration role, other cities and provinces, especially economically underdeveloped areas, still have many complex problems, either because the credit-construction work requires a lot of long-term investment in human and material resources, making it difficult to achieve immediate results due to the inherent lack of motivation, or the credit-system construction does not work due to greed and impracticality. Moreover, there are even some areas that face excessive competition for investment due to the pressure of performance assessment, artificially hindering credit-system construction,[11] which results in the suffering of market order caused by the loss of trust on the one hand and the reluctance to give up short-term economic benefits brought about by the loss of trust on the other.

8.2 The Proposal of "Funnelling Theory"

Compared to the localised credit problems in Western developed countries, the credit problems in Chinese society are "holistic and comprehensive."[12] Therefore, if we only consider the problem from the top down, relying on policies, regulations, designations, and enforcement, without thinking about how to curb the credit crisis at the source, we will be caught in a passive response to the various kinds of mistrust and misbehaviour, but we will never make the substantial progress needed for the overall improvement of social credit.

In fact, the credit problem in Chinese society is to a large extent closely related to the inherent characteristics of Chinese society, and in a sense reflects certain important features of the traditional culture and institutional structure of Chinese society. According to our previous theoretical assumptions:

> Homogeneous and heterogeneous societies are different directions of development for understanding modern societies. Revisiting the data and cases presented by different dimensions and aspects of Chinese society with this pair of concepts reveals that the law of competition, embodied by the localisation of social evolution since China's modernisation, is commonly shared by the Chinese population in terms of ways of thinking, values, and behaviour, resulting in the loss of identification of Chinese society in terms of the differentiation and purity of the quality or qualities of social units. The way to change the characteristics of a comparatively heterogeneous society lies in enhancing the discriminatory power of social units by any means.

According to this understanding, when money becomes the most important criterion for measuring success, the proliferation of money and power in all walks of life causes the nihilization of various industry norms and standards, which may be regarded as the root of social-credit problems.[13]

In this regard, the cultivation and improvement of social credit is undoubtedly a long-term cultural project. The current lack of social credit basically reflects the extreme, utilitarian way of thinking that dominates China today. Hence, the solution to problems of trust and credit in China is fundamentally a matter of the indoctrination of the "human heart."

Therefore, from a sociological standpoint, we are considering how to find a way to cover as wide a range of people as possible and to help them establish moral indoctrination in order to realise the most basic sense of social-credit operation. This approach can be referred to as the "funnelling theory."

The so-called "funnelling" is actually a figurative metaphor. In a sociological sense, in modern civilised society, every individual's socialisation process goes through an optimal formalisation and standardisation process, which is also the process of forming his values. This process usually takes place before he enters society, thus establishing a moral foundation for dealing with complex social problems in the future.

The reason for such an idea is that society, as a form of interaction that is both ephemeral and co-occurrent, is characterised by two dimensions. Vertically, the continuation of society is accomplished by the intergenerational change of countless individuals, and the influence of the times in which people are born and grow up will be continued in their social consciousness and social behaviour afterwards. Therefore, although the process of social problems appears to be both coherent and new, the renewal of values can also find an opportunity to intervene in the intergenerational break and policy making. For example, the terms "post-70s," "post-80s," "post-90s," and even "post-00s," which are widely used in online contexts, are indicative of the fact that different generational groups have different perceptions of social issues and therefore different characteristics as groups, yet the many policies implemented since the reform and opening up began at one point in time. Horizontally, the collection of different individuals in the same space-time conditions based on common rules becomes a social fact external to the individuals, and this social fact (collective consciousness) is implicitly coercive for individuals. That is, if they internalise the norms and values required by society, they can consciously and voluntarily comply with those norms, but if they are unwilling to accept the guidance of social values or even violate them, they will be subject to formal (punishment or arrest) or informal (public opinion ridicule or reproach) constraints. In this way, it is possible to follow the above basic concept.[14] According to the above, we can do the following for social credit construction: Take a certain period of life as an entry point, shape the concepts of honesty and trustworthiness and train the behaviour, so that the credit problems can be curbed from a certain point and put on some benign development track. This is the essence of "funnelling," that is, to educate the population of a certain age in an operational way, so as to train them before they enter society in terms of concepts and behaviours.

In terms of the target group, we believe the most logical stage for this approach is the group of students without occupational class distinctions, specifically, students in secondary education such as general high school, vocational-technical high school, specialised secondary education, and technical schools. The importance and rationale of choosing this specific group for the point of implementation of the "funnelling" are as follows.

First, in terms of the educational status of the youth population, the number of students at the high-school level accounts for a large proportion of the youth population. Compared with primary and junior high school, high school is the bridge and link between the nine-year compulsory education and higher education, and plays an important role in improving the basic quality and social and cultural literacy of workers, and in providing higher education with available talents.[15] According to the Statistical Analysis Report on Youth Development in China (2005), in 2003, 11,086 million students were enrolled in general higher-education schools, while 96,138 million students were enrolled in general secondary schools, including 5,024 million students in general secondary specialised schools, 85,832 million students in general middle schools (high schools), and 19,648 million students in high schools.[16] At the same time, considering the 60.2% rate of junior-high-school graduates, more than half of the junior-high-school students are going to continue their education in senior high school, so the total number of people receiving senior-high-school education is about 59 million. According to the fifth national census in 2000, the total population of youths aged 15–19 is more than 103 million, and the final proportion of high-school students is about 60%. This proves that high-school education plays a very important role in the overall educational status of our youth population.

Second, in terms of social mobility, the high-school level is the minimum educational limit for the civilian class to move to the elite class of the country. According to the analysis of sociologists Blau and Duncan on the occupational structure of American society,[17] the phenomenon of social class is influenced by both innate and self-induced factors, and the level of education of individuals as one of the latter factors is crucial to the formation of social class, so it is very important to find the minimum educational limit to promote the formation of a national elite class and to cultivate it. According to the survey, about 25% and 26% of the managerial class,[18] including cadres of party and government organs and institutions at all levels, as well as directors and managers of enterprises, have higher education and high-school education, respectively. Especially for cadres, the education level plays an advantageous role in obtaining elite professional and technical positions, one of the important manifestations of which is that the state hires cadres or civil servants and other state employees according to the development needs of specific periods by means of examinations, which generally require a university education level or above.[19] From the data of China's sixth census, it can be concluded that 8.93% of the total population is educated at the university level (including college) or above, and 22.96% of the total population is educated at the high-school level or above,[20] with the beginning of the former stage is based on the completion of the latter stage, so the high-school stage is used as the behaviour training for credit "funnelling." In this way, the participation and demonstration of integrity by the national elite will have a "weathervane" effect on China's overall social credit, which will not only help establish integrity norms for the general public and promote the construction of the social credit system but will also ensure the basic quality of national civil servants, research-institute staff, urban and rural managers, most of the middle class, owners of large and medium-sized enterprises, and white-collar workers.

Third, students at the high-school level do not yet have occupational stratification differences, which allows for centralised management and implementation of integrity education. In today's social-transition period, the complexity of China's social-credit problem is to some extent rooted in the change in the social stratification structure, which promotes further division of interests of different social groups or even conflicts.[21] Thus the solution to the credit problem involves coordinating the collective action of different social groups based on the objective stratification structure, but it is difficult to implement such a solution under the existing structure. Different occupations require different group behaviours and individual quality levels, which further promotes the formation of similar values and interests within the group; therefore, occupational stratification is both an objective manifestation of the social stratification structure and a major way to form social stratification. In order to reduce the differences in occupational stratification and create a basis for a common social consciousness, social-credit indoctrination should be given to all individuals at the time they are about to enter the occupational field. Although a part of the youth population starts to work after graduating from junior high school, due to the limited level of knowledge and skills taught in compulsory education, the occupational fields they are exposed to are relatively homogeneous, such as agriculture, forestry and fishing, manufacturing, wholesale and retail trade, and catering, which are relatively less technically demanding.[22] As the starting point of non-compulsory education, high school not only improves the cultural knowledge and operational skills of future workers to a greater extent but also lays the foundation for individuals to enter higher education and engage in occupations with greater class differences in the future. At the same time, compared to the more relaxed and less constrained environment of college, high-school students have a more standardised curriculum, and because they are maturing mentally, they are able to develop a deeper understanding and more active awareness of the social issues they will be exposed to than junior-high-school students.

Fourth, in terms of its effectiveness in regulating and disciplining human nature, school as a place of education is more influential and far-reaching than the workplace. As a form of social reproduction, the essence of education is to internalise the dominant ideology of society into individuals and to produce the type of individuals needed by society. As a place of education, the school itself is "an institution invented to maintain, disseminate, and inculcate the cultural norms of a society,"[23] so education can "provide not only the transmission of technical knowledge and skills, but also the socialisation of people to fit particular cultural traditions." In this way, "power and knowledge are directly mutually inclusive."[24] That is, the power of social control and regulation will be exercised by a new generation of workers who will acquire specialised knowledge of credit and norms of credit behaviour, i.e., as "authorities" in the field of credit to regulate and influence more members of society. If credit education and practice are implemented in schools before students graduate, all individuals will acquire the right values before the social division associated with labour, and they will all experience rewards and punishments on their assignments, and exams and in their moral lives, and they will all be shaped into what society expects, which will ultimately reduce the occurrence of credit crises.

In contrast to the suitability of credit "funnelling" measures for high-school students, the highly socialised adult population has a variety of complexities that make effective control difficult. On the one hand, the adult population is huge, accounting for about three-quarters of the country's 1.33 billion people, according to 2010 statistics,[25] and has remained at around 1.4 billion since then, requiring huge social resources for any institutional measures. On the other hand, with the transformation of the economic system, China's social stratification has been gradually divided from the "two camps" in the era of the planned economy to the "ten classes" after the reform and opening up,[26] whose respective economic interests, social needs, value judgements, and political demands have all shown a diversified trend. From the perspective of the distribution of occupational structure, the number, gender-and-age composition, education level, and professional skills required by different occupations are different due to the influence of industrial structure, technological progress, labour resources, economic system, etc. This makes the understanding and acceptance of "social credit" by adult individuals vary. The level of credit behaviour varies greatly. In addition, different industries require different standards of credit practice: First, the social influence of the industry is different; second, the degree of overlap between the professional ethics required by the industry and the personal integrity of the employees is also different. For example, the credit construction of special industries such as education and medical care is closely related to the practitioners' own quality, as the content of their industries cannot be measured by explicit credit standards one by one, and the existing credit system only regulates the relevant personnel's qualifications such as education and professional level, and cannot predict their moral quality. This is why it is difficult to implement a credit system in China.

Another approach that differs from funnelling theory is to advance credit education before high school (prior to their entry into society) in elementary or middle school. We believe the best time for honest indoctrination should accompany the growth of children, i.e., the earlier the better. However, due to the complexity of Chinese society and culture, especially the continuation of traditions and market-oriented results on the level of values, such an idea is unrealistic and cannot be realised, which means a family's educational atmosphere cannot solve this problem. The solution relies on schools. However, it is also impossible for elementary and junior-high schools to attempt to offer such a course, and usually all that can be done is to accompany the integrity requirements that should accompany daily performance, including homework, exams, and classroom group activities. One problem that cannot be ignored, however, is that Chinese children are subject to test-based education, formalism, and the interdependence embodied in a relational society from kindergarten through later secondary-school studies, where many children's homework and work are done by their parents. In such a culture, these events are seen as commonplace. And the most serious cases are that the winning entries of youth science and technology competitions held in some parts of China are also done by parents. So, the first issue that needs to be addressed, from children to parents, and to schools, is to create awareness of having social credit. This requires a special curriculum that incorporates cases, laws, etc., and that allows them to become trustworthy citizens through education and practice before they enter society and give up their daily habits of taking things for granted.

In light of the above, we believe that the "funnelling" initiative is probably best implemented at the high-school level.

8.3 The Implementation Strategies of "Funnelling"

At present, with the issuance of a series of relevant important documents such as "Several Opinions of the Central Committee of the Communist Party of China and the State Council on Further Strengthening and Improving the Ideological and Moral Construction of Minors," "Outline for the Implementation of Civic Moral Construction," and "Notice on Further Strengthening Integrity Education in Primary and Secondary Schools," integrity education in primary and secondary schools has received unprecedented attention from the central to local levels and has been gradually implemented in schools in many places. However, in line with the implementation results, this education has not achieved the expected purpose because, first, it does not have a good understanding of the essential connotation of integrity education and its position in the socialisation of students. From the central to the local level, including some experts and scholars who specialise in how to carry out integrity education in primary and secondary schools, it is regarded as a kind of value education,[27] i.e., as a component of the moral education of primary and secondary students. In the education system where the "college-entrance examination" is the baton, students' integrity behaviour is not a mandatory criterion and therefore does not receive due attention. Second, in the process of implementation, the most effective paths have not been well explored. Ideological and moral education in Chinese schools is rather formal. Much of the content is highly abstract and vague and difficult to implement at the institutional level, leading students to take these contents as answers to exams but not to implement them into their own actions. They are even less likely to manifest them in daily behavioural norms, resulting in a disconnection between classroom knowledge education and practical experience.

In contrast, the purpose of the "Funnelling" initiative is to make minors in the process of receiving school education have to practice honest behaviour, and actually experience the consequences of not speaking honestly, so that the word "integrity" is no longer a piece of paper, but becomes the actual code of conduct for each individual. "Funnelling theory" is a measure to learn and practice the knowledge of high-school students through the transfer of knowledge, the regulation of words and actions, and the setting of punishment mechanisms. This is manifested in the following areas.

First of all, integrity education should be incorporated into academic education at the high-school level. The status of civic education should be raised in the subject setting of high school, and it should be made a compulsory subject for high school students. The rationale is that if a person is dishonest, all his thoughts and behavioural expressions become slogans, lies, misrepresentations, or simply a mechanism for coping with exams, making civic education lose its foundation. In the process of knowledge transfer, the mental characteristics of high-school students should be combined, and the indoctrination of abstract ideas and opinions should be abandoned and replaced by the teaching of integrity virtues, i.e., regulations and knowledge that can be understood and accepted by students and supplemented by a corresponding platform of practicable experiences. We believe that an important part of implementing integrity education is to make students aware of the national credit system and norms by reforming the relevant curriculum and developing teaching materials. Depending on the level of students' understanding, the textbooks can be based on the establishment and development of the personal credit system, and the content can be arranged with examples from social life – especially in relation to the future career and life of the individual – to teach students about personal credit and its importance. For example, on the one hand, students will understand that malicious purchase loans, student loans, credit card overdrafts, cell phone bills, and falsified personal data (including data of actual work experience, study, training, education, etc.) are all bad credit records,[28] and these phenomena have seriously damaged the order of economic and social life in China. With the gradual improvement of China's credit law, reckless "credit stains" will make the life and work of individuals punished by laws and regulations chaotic and unpredictable, "all over the place." When students realise this, combined with legal knowledge, they will recognise the importance of credit in social, political, economic, cultural, educational, and daily life. On the other hand, teachers should help students to establish a strong sense of social responsibility and civic consciousness, especially to understand the professional ethics and conduct required in important industries like education, medical care, administration, finance, science and technology, etc., which have a bearing on the people's livelihood.

Secondly, integrity education should not only stay at the level of theoretical knowledge but should pay more attention to the practice and operation of credit, which means that the main content of students' learning and life is incorporated into the credit assessment system so that they can feel the huge cost of breaking credit rules or not complying with the credit system. Integrity education in secondary schools should be considered a process implementation system. The main area of practice is school performance, curriculum learning, and the assessment of high-school students. This education assessment is used not only to identify, evaluate, and measure the level of students' morals, knowledge, and skills, but also to evaluate the quality of a school's education and its evaluation of talents. However, in the current examination-based education system, where the assessment method is relatively singular, the impact of assessment results on students' life growth is not progressive but abrupt. That is to say, the various tests students take in the ordinary learning process do not play a substantial screening role, and their further education or employment is always determined by graduation examinations such as the college-entrance examinations. For the sake of maintaining personal interests, students may disregard their 'credit' and use various tricks or even cheating methods to obtain good test scores. Therefore, we believe we should incorporate all the high-school students' academic life since their enrolment in credit education, and strictly formulate and implement punitive measures against untoward behaviours such as cheating on exams, plagiarising assignments, lying, and daily disciplinary violations. The implementation of this "process" credit practice system requires the school to establish more comprehensive and complex credit files for each individual student, in which cheating will be recorded and important exams will be recorded in the student's file if he cheats. On the other hand, daily disciplinary violations will be included in the cumulative portion of the credit assessment, and here unfavourable credit records can be recorded in different ways through, for example, an observation period, an elimination period, or a permanent retention period. Most importantly, linking these credit records to students' immediate interests such as admission to college-entrance exams and hiring opportunities makes it imperative that schools be responsible in recording the files and that independent third-party educational assessment agencies report students' personal credit files to higher-education institutions or social enterprises and institutions. Two other potential issues need to be addressed: First, personal credit files must be given the same importance as later personnel files; and second, the rating of schools and their administrators themselves cannot be measured by mere promotion rates. Both of these issues need to be addressed at the level of national-education institutions so that they take on the social pressure and responsibility rather than just the secondary-education schools. Otherwise, the credit-punishment system, no matter how strict, will still be regarded as a piece of paper by schools, students, and their parents under the guidance of the "baton" of the college-entrance examination.

Finally, it is clear that the main subjects of credit-education implementation are schools, educators, and the construction of schools' own credit systems and credit practices. The reason why schools should be both implementers and objects of credit construction is that credit construction as an education and a practice actually represents the concept of the national training of talents and the development of social-dominance consciousness. This concept should be actively imposed on the citizens to make them understand it and accept it consciously. Therefore, when implementing credit education and practice for high-school students, school administrators should invest appropriate human and material resources for teacher instruction and retraining so that educators and frontline teachers can keep their credit knowledge and practical experience up to date. In addition, teachers and education administrators, as adults, are subject to the complex operation of multiple social factors in the accumulation of their personal credit. They may also have instances of breaches of trust in their own records, making it unfeasible to rely solely on their personal ethics. Hence, there is a need for institutional assessments, like qualification reviews and awards for honours, to be included in the scope of their work to ensure that teachers set good examples of trustworthiness for their students.

In conclusion, the development of social credit and its practice by students is a basic requirement of modern civilisation. As a "national strategy," it should be included in core educational thinking. A real and effective practice of the principle of honesty and integrity in education will be a warm-up and preview for the systemic construction of social credit, instead of always hoping to solve the social-credit crisis by punishing afterwards or mending the fold. We believe that the only way to effectively reduce many of the social problems that are currently occurring is to both learn, practice in advance, and further improve the relevant systems when striving to build a more perfect credit system for Chinese society.

Notes

1 Baidu Encyclopedia. China Quality Miles. http://baike.baidu.com/view/891669.htm?fr=aladdin.
2 Legal Network Laws and Regulations Database: "Notice of the State Council on the Nationwide Work of Cleaning Up "Triangular Debt"". Legal Network, 26 March 1990. http://law.legaldaily.com.cn/law_content.php?law_id=0a97e4f47718632c556e9ac591d5f3c29953&key_word=
Director of "Anti-counterfeiting Office": China has the Ability to Solve the Counterfeit Problem". Sina.com, 16 November 2000. http://finance.sina.com.cn/2000-11-16/22838.html.
3 Liu Jianzhou, Social Credit System Construction: Connotation, Model and Path Choice, *Journal of the Party School of the Central Committee of the Communist Party of China* 2011, 15(3), pp50-53.
4 Zhao Zhiling, Shanghai, Zhejiang, Shenzhen Social Credit System Construction Model and its Inspiration, *Modern Economic Discussion* 2007, No.310(10), pp45-49.
5 The central government has renamed the "National Credit Management System" as "Social Credit System." According to the rumours, there are two explanations: One is that it accepted the suggestion of economist Professor Wu Jinglian; the other is that it wants to emphasise that the system corresponds to the "social security system," because the two systems are equally important for the market economy.
6 Lin Junyue, Social Credit System: A Model for the Efficient Establishment of a Credit System in China, *Credit* 2011(2).
7 State Council: "Notice of the State Council on the Issuance of the Outline of the Social Credit System Construction Plan (2014–2020)," Central People's Government of the People' s Republic of China Portal, 14 June 2014, www.gov.cn/zhengce/content/2014-06/27/ content_8913.htm.
8 Ibid.
9 Zhao Feng, Review of the Regulation on the Credit Industry, *Credit* 2013(4).
10 Zhou Jun, Special Five Government Credibility, *People's Daily Online*, 21 October 2011, http://edu.people.com.cn/GB/ 8216/232418/232666/15979073.html.
11 Xiaobo Xie, Jiong Huang, A Study on the Excessive Competitive Behavior of Local Governments in the Yangtze River Delta in Attracting Investment, *Technology Economics* 2005(8).
12 Zhai Xuewei, The Social Roots of the Credit Crisis, *Jiangsu Social Sciences* (1), 2014, No.272(01), pp. 85–96.
13 Ibid.
14 Zhou Xiaohong, *The History and System of Western Sociology, Vol. 1)*, Shanghai People's Publishing House, 2002, pp. 245–246.
15 Hou Jiawei, Liu Junyan, Statistical Data Analysis Report on China's Youth Development Situation, *China Youth Studies* 2006(1).

16 State Council Population Census Office and Department of Population and Employment Statistics, National Bureau of Statistics, China, 2000 National Population Census Information, National Bureau of Statistics of the People's Republic of China website, 2000, www.stats.gov.cn/tjsj/pcsj/rkpc/5rp/index.htm. Note: Because of the lack of 2003 data, the exact total population of youth aged 15–19 is missing, so the 2000 national census data are used here for projection.
17 Yi Zhou, After the Blau-Duncan Model: Transformation or Challenge, *Sociological Research* 2009(6).
18 Liu Jingming, Education and the Changing Structure of Social Stratification – An Analysis on the Middle and Senior White Collar Professional Classes, *Journal of Renmin University of China* 2001(2).
19 Yu Yang, From elite nationalization to state elitism: A historical survey of China's cadre recruitment system, *Society* 2010(6).
20 Population Census Office of the State Council and Department of Population and Employment Statistics of the National Bureau of Statistics, eds. 2010 Population Census of China, website of the National Bureau of Statistics of the People's Republic of China, 2010, www.stats.gov.cn/tjsj/pcsj/rkpc/6rp/indexch.htm.
21 Liu Jingming, Li Lulu, Stratification: Living Space, Lifestyle, Social Interaction and Class Identity – An Empirical Study on Social Stratification in China's Urban Areas, *Sociological Research*, 2005(3).
22 Hou Jiawei, Liu Junyan, Statistical Data Analysis Report on China's Youth Development Situation," *China Youth Studies* 2006(1).
23 David Swartz, *Culture and Power: The Sociology of Bourdieu*, translated by Tao Dongfeng, Shanghai Translation Press, 2012, p. 219.
24 Dennis Long, *Theory of Power*, translated by Lu Zhenlun, Zheng Mingzhe, China Social Science Press, 2001, p. 16.
25 Population Census Office of the State Council and Department of Population and Employment Statistics of the National Bureau of Statistics, eds. 2010 Population Census of China, website of the National Bureau of Statistics of the People's Republic of China, 2010, www.stats.gov.cn/tjsj/pcsj/rkpc/6rp/indexch.htm.
26 Liang Lai, Social Stratification and Social Mobility: Reality, Problems and Prospects for Development, *Leadership* 2014(1). Specifically, the "two camps" refer to the "people's inner circle" and a small group of "class enemies," the former of which can also be divided into "unit workers" and "commune members" according to urban and rural areas. The former can be divided into "unit workers" and "commune members." The "ten classes" include state and social managers, managers, private entrepreneurs, professionals, clerks, self-employed, commercial and service employees, industrial workers, agricultural laborers, and the jobless, unemployed, and semi-unemployed in urban and rural areas. (See also Lu Xueyi, *Research Report on Social Class in China*, Social Science Literature Press, 2002.)
27 Guan Li, Vigorously Strengthening Integrity Education in Primary and Secondary Schools, *People's Education* 2004(10).
28 Deng Tianjiang, Zhang Xu, Legal Reflections on the Establishment of China's Personal Credit System – A Perspective of Learning from the U.S. Personal Credit System, *China Lawyer*, 24 June 2013, www.acla.org.cn/lvshiwushi/9306.jhtml.

References

Baidu Encyclopedia. (n.d.). *China quality miles*. http://baike.baidu.com/view/891669.htm?fr=aladdin

Deng, T., & Zhang, X. (2013, June 24). Legal reflections on the establishment of China's personal credit system: A Perspective of learning from the U.S. personal credit system. *China Lawyer*. http://www.acla.org.cn/lvshiwushi/9306.jhtml

Director of "anti-counterfeiting office": China has the ability to solve the counterfeit problem. (2000). http://finance.sina.com.cn/2000-11-16/22838.html
Guan, L. (2004). Vigorously strengthening integrity education in primary and secondary schools. *People's Education*, *10*, 14–15.
Hou, J., & Liu, J. (2006). Statistical data analysis report on China's youth development situation. *China Youth Studies*, *1*, 56–64. https://doi.org/10.19633/j.cnki.11-2579/d.2006.01.015
Legal Network Laws and Regulations Database. (1990). *Notice of the state council on the nationwide work of cleaning up "triangular debt"*. http://law.legaldaily.com.cn/law_content.php?law_id=0a97e4f47718632c556e9ac591d5f3c29953&key_word=
Liang, L. (2014). Social stratification and social mobility: Reality, problems and prospects for development. *Leadership*, *2*, 7–22. https://doi.org/10.13533/j.cnki.ldwc.2014.02.013
Lin, J. (2011). Social credit system: A model for the efficient establishment of a credit system in China. *Credit*, 29(2), 1–7.
Liu, J. (2001). Education and the changing structure of social stratification: An analysis on the middle and senior white collar professional classes. *Journal of Renmin University of China*, *2*, 21–25.
Liu, J. (2011). Social credit system construction: Connotation, model and path choice. *Journal of the Party School of the Central Committee of the Communist Party of China*, 15(03), 50–53.
Liu, J., & Li, L. (2005). Stratification: Living space, lifestyle, social interaction and class identity - An empirical study on social stratification in China's urban areas. *Sociological Research*, *3*, 52–81+243. https://doi.org/10.19934/j.cnki.shxyj.2005.03.003
Long, D. (2001). *Theory of power* (Z. Lu & M. Zheng, Trans.). China Social Science Press.
Lu, X. (2002). *Research report on social class in China*. Social Science Literature Press.
Swartz, D. (2012). *Culture and power: The sociology of Bourdieu* (D. Tao, Trans.). Shanghai Translation Press.
Xie, X., & Huang, J. (2005). A study on the excessive competitive behavior of local governments in the Yangtze River Delta in attracting investment. *Technology Economics*, *8*, 70–72.
Yi, Z. (2009). After the Blau-Duncan model: Transformation or challenge. *Sociological Research*, *6*, 206–225+246. https://doi.org/10.19934/j.cnki.shxyj.2009.06.010
Yu, Y. (2010). From elite nationalization to state elitism: A historical survey of China's cadre recruitment system. *Society*, *6*, 41–64. https://doi.org/10.15992/j.cnki.31-1123/c.2010.06.002
Zhai, X. The social roots of the credit crisis. *Jiangsu Social Sciences*, *1*, 85–96. https://doi.org/10.13858/j.cnki.cn32-1312/c.2014.01.030
Zhao, F. (2013). Review of the regulation on the credit industry. *Credit*, 31(04), 51–53.
Zhao, Z. (2007). Shanghai, Zhejiang, Shenzhen social credit system construction model and its inspiration. *Modern Economic Discussion*, 319(10), 45–49.
Zhou, J. (2011, October 21). Special five government credibility. *People's Daily*. http://www.gov.cn/zhengce/content/2014-06/27/content_8913.htm.
Zhou, X. (2002). *The history and system of western sociology, vol. 1*. Shanghai People's Publishing House.

Afterword

This book is a simplified version of the final report of the National Social Science Foundation major bidding project "Research on China's Social Credit System" (China Social Science Press, 2017), which I edited. At that time, the total length of this report was about 600,000 words, but now has been simplified to 150,000 words for translation and publication.

In this rewrite, we first removed many statistical tables to increase readability, and we also removed some events and case studies that had been treated as hot topics in Chinese society, considering the specific background and context in which they were understood.

In Chinese writing, the word "信" is very old and is one of the most discussed core concepts by Chinese sages, and this concept has been broken down into many meanings in modern society, such as integrity, trust, credibility, credit, and so on. In addition, there are many combinations of the Chinese word for "信," such as confidence, letter, etc. The most commonly used software on cell phones, WeChat, also has the word "信"in it. These circumstances show that the study of Chinese social credit has its own cultural lineage, and I am aware of the difficulty of translating it into English. The easiest way to overcome this difficulty is to adopt a suitable English word to express it, but this is not simply a translation technique but changes the cultural preconceptions behind it, which will result in bias and misunderstanding of Chinese social credit, and in the end, we have to follow the Western trust theory in academic terms. So, I think it is very important for our understanding of Chinese society to be aware of the social differences that are reflected in the way words are used. Another relevant reason for doing so is to construct a perspective and framework for the study of credit from Chinese culture in today's social science research, in which readers can see that this concept operates in human societies with both universal and specific meanings. Another issue that has to be mentioned is that the data in this book are also somewhat outdated. Since data in the relevant fields of sociology are different from data in economics, and their tracking requires a lot of human and material resources, this makes the empirical research I can conduct confined to a certain period of time, and since many behaviours in today's society are more often reflected on the internet, the latest changes in social credit supported by new data are not yet available. But years of research have also convinced me that this situation is inevitable in most sociological studies, yet it

DOI: 10.4324/9781003375579-11

does reflect to some extent the general look of a society. If societies change, then the data presented here reflect a cross-section of that change and can be used as a comparison of new forms of society. What I value more is the theoretical thinking that comes out of it.

Finally, I would like to thank the panellists who contributed to the research in this book. I would especially like to thank Gao Xuede of Lanzhou University for his statistical contributions, Wang Huogen of Nanchang Aerospace University for combing through the historical literature, and Hou Mengting of Jiangsu Academy of Social Sciences for her painstaking efforts in the questionnaire design and survey.

Xuewei Zhai
6 August 2021

Appendix 1

Questionnaire for the “Study of China’s social credit system” (city version)

No.:__________

Area code:__________

Interview Date: ________ Month ______Day

Dear Residents.

Hello!

We are conducting a nationwide survey in order to understand the current situation of social credit in China and to provide a reference basis for relevant government decisions. We would like to know your opinion on these questions below, which may take you a little time. According to the Statistics Law of the People’s Republic of China, all your answers will be used for statistical analysis only, and your personal information will not be disclosed, so you do not need to have any concerns. The answers to this survey are not right or wrong, so please tick the answer to each question according to your actual situation, and there is only one answer to each question without special instructions.

We will offer you a small gift, as a souvenir for your participation.

Thank you very much for your support and cooperation!

Research Group of "Study on Social Credit System in China"

Head: Prof. Xuewei Zhai

School of Social Sciences, Nanjing University, 210093, China

Contact email:

September 2011

Interviewer name_______________

Supervisor name _____________ **Remarks**___________________________

Name of the first examiner_______________ **Date of the first examination:**_______**Year**______**Month**_______**Date**

Name of the second examiner_______________ **Date of the second examination:**_______**Year**______**Month**_______**Date**

1. Gender: 1) Male 2) Female
2. Age: __________
3. Marital status: 1) Married 2) Unmarried 3) Widowed 4) Divorced
4. Ethnicity: 1) Han 2) Ethnic Minority
5. Current Hukou: 1) Agricultural household 2) Non-agricultural household
6. Religious belief:

   1) Christianity 2) Catholicism 3) Islam 4) Buddhism 5) Taoism

   6) Folk beliefs such as worship of gods 7) None 8) Others______
7. Educational level:

   1) Basically illiterate 2) Primary school 3) Junior high school

   4) High school (including junior college, technical school)

   5) Vocational university 6) Undergraduate 7) Postgraduate
8. Your occupation five years ago_______; Your current occupation________:

   <u>(If you are retired, please fill in the "Your current occupation" column with your occupation before retirement)</u>

   1) State and social administration 2) Business management

   3) Professional and technical staff

   4) Clerical staff 5) Self-employed 6) Business services staff

   7) Industrial working class 8) Agricultural working class

   9) Urban unemployed

   10) Student 11) Military 12) Others (Please specify) _________

9. Your father's occupation_________; Your mother's occupation _________:
   (If your parents are retired, please fill in "_______" with their occupation before retirement)
   1) State and social administration 2) Business management
   3) Professional and technical staff
   4) Clerical staff 5) Self-employed 6) Business services staff
   7) Industrial working class 8) Agricultural working class
   9) Urban unemployed
   10) Military 11) Others (Please specify)
10. Your current political status:
    1) CCP member 2) Non-communist parties 3) Youth League member
    4) General public 5) Others________
11. Your annual income last year was about _________Yuan (including basic salaries, bonuses, and other income)
12. You think your social status is:
    1) Upper level 2) Upper-middle level 3) Middle level 4) Lower-middle level 5) Lower level
13. Is your current place of residence different from that of five years ago?
    1) Yes 2) No
14. Do you own your own home (with equity))
    1) Yes 2) No (skip question 15)
15. What is the total square metres of your current home? _________ square metres

16–27. Where do you fit into the following groups?

Group type	*Core*	*Activists*	*General members*	*No participation*
16. Hometown associations				
17. Reunion				
18. Comradeship clubs				
19. Various QQ groups				
20. Internet forums				
21. Folklore groups				
22. Religious groups				
23. Academic groups				
24. Industry associations				
25. Community owners committee				
26. Public charity organisations				
27. Workers union				

28–42. Do you take part in the following social activities?

	Often	*Sometimes*	*Occasionally*	*Never*
28. Spending time with good friends and relatives				
29. Various reunions among classmates				
30. Daily hobby activities, such as card playing, chess, etc.				
31. Sports and recreational activities organised by the unit				
32. Cultural and sports activities organised by the community committee				
33. Community owners' committee election campaign				
34. Various political elections (e.g., election of NPC deputies)				
35. Various democratic appraisal activities related to party and government work				
36. Participate in activities such as making suggestions to government departments (including participating in opinion consultations on government websites)				
37. Online participation in hot social discussions (e.g. microblogs, forums)				
38. Spontaneous exchange activities for parishioners				
39. Participate in religious activities organised by temples or churches				
40. Voluntary participation in public welfare activities, such as caring for the elderly				
41. Spontaneous participation in various charitable donation activities				
42. Participate in various blood donation activities (including organ donation)				

43. In your daily life, do you pay attention to all kinds of current affairs?

    1) Very much 2) Relatively 3) Generally 4) Less concerned

    5) Not at all (skip question 44)

44. Through which of the following channels do you usually learn about current affairs? (please select three and rank them in order of frequency of use)

    ________>________>________

    1) Mobile subscription 2) Private channels such as friends and acquaintances 3) Radio

    4) TV 5) Various online forums (e.g., BBS, Weibo, etc.) 6) Newspapers and magazines 7) Sina, Sohu, and other such portals 8) Others_________

45. Through which of the following channels do you usually learn about product quality? (Please select three and rank them in order of frequency of use)

    ________>________>________

    1) Radio 2) TV 3) The internet 4) Mobile subscription

    5) Circle of acquaintances 6) Newspapers and magazines

    7) Others_________

46. Which of the following sources do you think is the most credible source of information about the effects of nuclear radiation in Japan? (single choice only)

    1) Official government release 2) Information posted by netizens on the internet

    3) Information from independent media surveys 4) Information released by experts, scholars, and other authorities

    5) CNN, BBC and other foreign media 6) Private channels such as friends and acquaintances

    7) I do not understand this matter 8) Other information sources ___________

47. Which of the following sources do you think is the most credible source of information about the 7/23 train accident? (single choice only)

    1) Official government release 2) Information posted by netizens on the internet

    3) Information from independent media surveys 4) Information released by experts, scholars, and other authorities

    5) CNN, BBC and other foreign media 6) Private channels such as friends and acquaintances

    7) I do not understand this matter 8) Other information sources ___________

48. Which of the following charitable organisations are you aware of? (multiple answers allowed)

    1) China Charity Federation 2) China Disabled Persons' Federation

    3) China Youth Foundation

    4) China Foundation for Poverty Alleviation 5) China Women's Development Foundation 6) China Red Cross Society

    7) China Environmental Protection Fund 8) Song Qingling Foundation

    9) China Society for Promotion of the Guangcai Program

    10) China Foundation for Justice and Courage 11) None of them

    12) Other charities you know _______

49. Which of the following views do you agree with most about celebrities doing charity?

    1) Can play a very good role of demonstration and guidance 2) Is worth encouraging 3) Just show

    4) Just to make more money 5) No comment

50. Which of the following donation methods do you think is the most reliable?

    1) Direct deduction from salary by the unit 2) Organisational and spontaneous donations by the unit

    3) Donation through the donation methods announced by official charity organisations 4) Searching for private charity organisations to donate by yourself

    5) Donation directly or through volunteers to the recipients

    6) Other _______

51–70. Please make a judgement on the following statements:

	Totally agree	*Generally agree*	*Not sure*	*Generally disagree*	*Totally disagree*
51. The quality of most products is reliable					
52. Most companies keep their after-sales service promise					
53. When choosing goods I have not bought, I prefer to choose goods with established brands					
54. When there is a choice, international brand products are more reassuring to me					
55. I believe more in products with celebrity endorsement					

	Totally agree	*Generally agree*	*Not sure*	*Generally disagree*	*Totally disagree*
56. The product information provided by TV shopping is true and credible					
57. Information provided by unofficial organisations such as online forums or independent media is true and credible					
58. If the network is full of negative comments about a product, I will lose confidence in that product					
59. When buying large items, I believe in all kinds of promotional ads for products					
60. Qualifications or diplomas that reflect a person's special competence in a particular area					
61. When buying similar products, I prefer to trust the products with national quality certification or food safety certification					
62. The pursuit of a good reputation is more important than the pursuit of profit					
63. Contracts, agreements, and other documents can ensure that my interests are not compromised					
64. Only if the state increases the investment and management of public transportation, its safety can be better					
65. I take advice from experts (professors, doctors, lawyers, etc.) on anything I don't know					
66. I am relieved that the government has invested in public transportation facilities					

	Totally agree	*Generally agree*	*Not sure*	*Generally disagree*	*Totally disagree*
67. Government spokespersons are truthful and credible in their explanations of various types of traffic accidents					
68. Only full marketisation of public transportation can ensure safety and improve service quality					
69. I believe that the donations will be delivered to the recipients					
70. I believe that the operation process of all kinds of charities is open and transparent					

71. Do you know the bank's personal credit report?

    1) Don't know 2) Yes, and have inquired 3) Yes, but have not inquired

72. When someone borrows money from you and a large amount of money is involved, which of the following factors do you look for most in the other person?

    (Please select three and rank them in order of importance) ________>________>________

    1) Whether there is an acquaintance guarantee 2) The other party's official unit status 3) The other party's ability to repay 4) Whether to write IOU or sign a contract 5) Moral quality of the other party 6) The relationship with me

    7) Whether there is interest in return 8) Others

73. Do you use credit cards to make purchases?

    1) Yes, I use it often 2) Yes, I use it occasionally

    3) I have a credit card but never use it 4) I don't have a credit card

74. Many merchants use pre-paid spending in their promotions; when you encounter this situation, your choice is

    1) Very well, I tend to choose the pre-paid consumption

    2) Only for some merchants with good reputation, I will choose this way

    3) Not good, but if the discount is large enough, I will also choose this way

    4) Not good, there is a risk of being cheated by the merchant, even if the discount is large, I will not choose this way

    5) Not sure

75. Have you ever had a dispute with a seller over a purchase?

    1) Has happened, only a few times 2) Has happened, and the frequency is very high

    3) Never happened (skip questions 76 and 77 and take question 78)

76. What is the reason for your dispute with the merchant? (multiple choice possible)

    1) Product quality defects 2) Price fraud 3) Poor after-sales service

    4) Others

77. How are these disputes usually resolved? (multiple choice, three at most)

    1) Negotiate and solve the problem by yourself 2) Seek help from the media and coordinate through the media

    3) Find a consumer association to protect my legal rights 4) Through personal connections, find someone to settle

    (5) Obtain compensation even through lawsuits (6) Depending on the situation of other similar victims

    7) Consider yourself unlucky 8) Not sure

78–81. Please comment on the effectiveness of the following market supervision and management departments:

	Very satisfied	*Generally satisfied*	*Generally dissatisfied*	*Very dissatisfied*	*Doesn't matter*	*Don't know*
78. Government agencies at all levels						
79. Various news media						
80. Consumer associations						
81. Corporate autonomous industry associations						

82–95. To what extent do you think the following types of people are trustworthy?

	Very trustful	*Generally trustful*	*Doesn't matter*	*Generally distrustful*	*Very distrustful*
82. Core family members					
83. Immediate family members					
84. Other relatives					
85. Intimate friends					
86. General friends					
87. Neighbours					
88. General acquaintances					
89. Hometown fellows					

	Very trustful	*Generally trustful*	*Doesn't matter*	*Generally distrustful*	*Very distrustful*
90. Leaders in your department					
91. Colleagues in your department					
92. Online friends					
93. Manufacturers					
94. Sellers					
95. Strangers					

96–106. How much trust do you have in the government and other social service workers?

	Very trustful	*Generally trustful*	*Doesn't matter*	*Generally distrustful*	*Very distrustful*
96. Public servants					
97. Urban management and law enforcement officers					
98. Judges					
99. Police officers					
100. PLA soldiers					
101. Journalists					
102. Expert professors					
103. Medical and nursing staff					
104. Primary and secondary school teachers					
105. Lawyers					
106. Enterprise technical staff					

107–118. How much trust do you have in the following organisations?

	Very trustful	*Generally trustful*	*Doesn't matter*	*Generally distrustful*	*Very distrustful*
107. Central government					
108. Provincial government					
109. Local municipalities					
110. District and county government					
111. Grassroots street office					
112. Courts					
113. Army					
114. Public security					
115. NPC institutions					
116. Party organisations at all levels					
117. Official charity organisations (e.g., China Charity Federation)					
118. Other charity organisations					

119–137. Please make a judgement on the following statements:

	Totally agree	*Generally agree*	*Not sure*	*Generally disagree*	*Totally disagree*
119. We are all brothers in the world					
120. Good intentions have good rewards					
121. One must guard against people					
122. If a major accident occurs, I will protect my family from harm first, no matter what, and then consider others					
123. Even if you can get benefits, you can't fail to keep your word					
124. Now, it's understandable to be untrustworthy for your own benefit					
125. If I treat people with sincerity, they will treat me with sincerity					
126. Most people are honest and trustworthy					
127. The vast majority of people are willing to help others					
128. People put personal interests ahead of other interests					
129. People are selfish					
130. In the current society if you do not stay alert, others will take advantage of you					
131. In this society, no one really cares about others					
132. The relationship between people is purely of interest					
133. People are good at heart					
134. No matter what, when I see someone in need of help, I will do my best					
135. I am willing to sacrifice myself for the benefit of others					
136. Helping others does not require a return of favour					
137. Evil has its rewards					

138–149. Please comment on the following important functions or institutional development in various areas of government:

	Very satisfied	*Generally satisfied*	*Not sure*	*Generally dissatisfied*	*Very dissatisfied*
138. Food supervision					
139. Earthquake relief					
140. Environmental protection					
141. Compulsory education					
142. Employment					
143. Charity					
144. Judicial system					
145. Household registration system					
146. Pension system					
147. Medical insurance system					
148. Social assistance system					
149. Affordable housing					

150–167. Your judgement on the following statements about the current situation of our government is:

	Totally agree	*Generally agree*	*Not sure*	*Generally disagree*	*Totally disagree*
150. The government can make policies that represent the interests of the majority of people					
151. Some policies could be changed from time to time					
152. The government work report is true and credible					
153. The government's price hearings are just a formality					
154. Government spending is in accordance with the government's budget and well spent					
155. The civil service selection process is fraught with foul play					
156. The abuse of power by a few officials can greatly affect the positive image of the government					
157. Most government officials are servants of the people					
158. Government officials are often only concerned with their own performance					
159. The law enforcers are simply not administering according to the law					

160. Most officials are corrupt
161. The current economic development situation of the country is relatively good
162. The current situation of democracy building in the country is relatively good
163. Current government corruption governance is more effective
164. The people's democratic dictatorship is still the best
165. Generally speaking, what our government officials do is right
166. The head of the government is like the head of the family and we should obey their decisions
167. It is up to the government to decide what topics can be discussed in the community

---

The Questionnaire ends here, thank you for your cooperation!

Index

Note: Page locators in *italics* refer to figures and **bold** refer to tables. Locators followed by 'n' refer to notes.

abstract credit system 71
acquaintance network 121
acquaintance relationship network 36
acquaintance society 122–123
agricultural economy 48
agricultural social credit 49
agricultural society 2, 24, 26, 27, 29, 45, 46
Alexis de Tocqueville, A.: *Democracy in America* 153–154
Analects of Confucius 103
Anhui merchants 52, 63, 64; birth and operation mechanisms of 55–57
autonomous folk-governance mechanism 59–60

Bao-Jia system 51
Becker, Gary 127
Benedict, Ruth 124
benevolence 34, 103, 104, 106–109
Bergere, Marie-Claire 60
Blau, Michael 191
blood-relationship trust 156
Bourdieu, Pierre 128
brand credit 87, **88**
business credit 45, 174–180
business-operation activities, Anhui and Shanxi merchants 55
business-relational trust 138, 152

Cai Dong 56
charity credit 71, 88, *89*
China: agricultural society 26; credit problem 22; dishonest conduct in real economy 7; disintegration acquaintance society 27; domestic and foreign consumers and traders in 183; economy 4; lopsided development of economy 8–9; marketisation process of 5; pre-liberation modern period of 47; problem and problem awareness 4–6; secular philosophy 29–32; social characteristics of 22; social credit evolution 24–29; socio-economic foundation of 48; "system of XIN" 23; traditional business activities of 56; traditional culture and social structure 9; transitional period 8; urban population of migrant workers 121; WeChat groups in 176
China Quality Miles 183, 184
China Quality Walk 182, 183
Chinese folk society 48
Chinese merchants, characteristics of 45
Chinese society: civilisation process of 32; construction of 106; credit problem in 189; government credit 9; intermediary 47; network of relationships in 53; social capital on 153; social credit of 24; transformational features of 5; transformation of 65; unit quality in 37; universal trust in 148, 155
Christianity 106
civil media, social credibility of 168–169, **170**
clan community 48, 49, 56, 57
close-door enrolment 40
Coleman, J. S. 116, 128, 129
collective expulsion 51
commercial activities 49
Commercial Bank of China 58
commercial society 47, 49
commodity economy 47
Communist Party of China (CPC) 5
community group-buying model 179
competition of species 30
Confucianism 17, 27, 31, 108

Confucianists 17, 20, 22, 26, 29, 33, 34, 103, 105, 108, 122, 123; social development of 114
Confucianist thought 105–109, 116, 122, 124
Confucius 17, 34, 103, 104, 106
"connotation of reputation" 124
contemporary Chinese credit system 122
contemporary Chinese society 9, 35, 86
contemporary credit 10–12
continuous perspective 22
cooperative relationships 102
credibility crisis: of official media and civil media 166–174; online and offline 165–166
credit: assumption on human nature 101–106; social-control mechanism of 123; treatment in China 118
credit assessment system/credit reference system 7
credit-building model 184
credit-constraining mode 48
credit crisis 4, 19
credit crisis, in internet era: credibility crisis of official media and civil media 166–174; online and offline credibility disputes 165–166
credit data, collection and use of 187
credit database, establishment of 187
credit economy 7
credit legislation 187
credit-management agency 188
credit-management-agency formation model 188
credit-punishment system 196
credit-rectification campaigns 183
credit-system construction 189

daily activity participation 135
Darwin, Charles 30
data collection method 73
decontextualisation 162
Democracy in America (Tocqueville) 153–154
disembedding 162
"Drawing Sword" campaign 38
duality 131
Duncan, Otis Dudley 191
Durkheim, E. 49, 96

economic punishment 50–51
employment guarantee system 64
everyday-activity participation 151
expert system credit 71, 85

factual trust 173
faithfulness 16, 17
fake certificates 39, 118
Fei Tsao Tung 49, 112, 113
fellow-countrymen groups 59–60, 63
financial industry 58, 59
fleecing acquaintance 36
folk covenants: functions of 45–47; use of 46
folk-credit governance, intermediary participation in 52–53
folk society autonomous governance 64
formal-organisation participation 133, 136, 151
"four feelings" 104
Frederickson, H. G. 149
Fukuyama, F. 143, 155
"funnelling theory" 182; implementation strategies of 194–197; proposal of 189–194

Gao Xuede 201
genetic relation trust 138
genetic trust 152
Giddens, A. 110, 114, 156, 162
governmental agencies 120
government credit 8
government-led "dual-track system" pattern 186
government trust 144
grander trust 111
group-buying groups 174–176; credit maintenance in 177–179; establishment of 175–176; social credit reconstruction in mobile internet era 179–180
group-buying transaction model 175
group purchase trust construction 176
guarantee system 55, 64

Han dynasty 52
Hanfeizi (Master Han Fei) 34, 105
Hawthorne Experiment 115
heaven 106
heterogeneity 37, 38, 42
homogeneity 36–39, 41, 42
homogeneous society 96–100
Hovland, C. I. 171
Huang Zongzhi 53
human capital 127–128
humanity 105; benevolent nature of 104
humanity assumption 114–115, 122; Western culture's hierarchy of 116; in Western society and culture 115

human nature: comparison between East and West 106–109; effectiveness in regulating and disciplining 192; good in 106
human-nature assumption 102, 109
Hu Shih 30
Huxley, T. H. 29–31
"hypothesis of social man" 115

immobile agricultural society 46–47
import-export business 61–62
individual credit 69
individual–interpersonal credit 71–72
"individual-relationship-institution" continuum 162
industrialisation 164
information 162–163; on internet 165; and professionalism 171; source of 171
information asymmetry 8, 11, 20, 51, 55, 64, 153
information symmetry 20, 62
in-house self-filling questionnaires 73–74
innovation mechanism 61
institutional credit 70
institutionalisation 110
institutionalised distrust 116
institutionalised social credit system 182
institutional trust, in Western society 116
institution credit, average values of 77, *81*
institutions: function of 110; matching cultural presupposition with design 114–119; public ratings of 120; relationship between trust and 110–114, 119; returning to tradition in paradox 119–121
instrumental trust 138, 152
integrity 1, 5, 7, 19, 107
integrity crisis 19, 118
integrity education 195–196
intermediary 52–53
internal informal credit maintenance mechanism 64
internal trust 123
internet-dependent factual trust 173
internet era: credit crisis in 165–174; social credit reconstruction in 179–180; technological progress of 162; trust diversification in 163–165; trust model in *174*; uncertainty in 161–162
internet participation 133, 136
internet trust 162–163
interpersonal credit 72, 90
interpersonal trust 114, 116, 136, 142, 148, 152; in social cooperation 154
interpersonal trust variable: rural sample 139, **141**; urban sample 136, **138**, 138–139, **140**

King Xiaogong 111

Lao Zi 34, 103
Legalists 34, 105, 107, 109
Lin Bao 52
linkage effect 185, 187
litigation-free covenants 46
Luhmann, N. 21, 110, 112, 113
Luke, Keele 154

Making Democracy Work (Putnam) 129
market credit 69, 71; issues 8
market economy 7–9, 41, 45, 123, 182
marketisation process 5, 37
Maslow, Abraham H. 115
May 4th Movement 32
McGregor, Douglas M. 115
mechanical solidarity 96–97
Mencius 26, 104–106
mercantilism 127
merchant communities 54
mobile internet technology 162, 174–180
mobile merchant community 50
modern economy 57
modernisation process 24, 28, 31, 36
modern society 200; change and development of 162; dimensional adjustment of credit in 169, 171–174, *173*
money-shop business 61–62
monopolar model 188
morality 102, 103, 123–124; and external guidance 121–124
moral self-discipline 51
Myao, G. E. 115
myths, demystification of 127

National Financial Work Conference (2007) 5
native perspective 21, 23
Ningbo Business Group 57–62
Ningbo merchants 64; credit generation and operation mechanism of 57–63
Ningbo-Shaoxing business group 60
North, Douglas C. 115

official media: and mass media 169; social credibility crisis of 166–167, **167**, *168*
offline credibility disputes 165–166
Olson, M. 115
online credibility disputes 165–166

on-the-spot settlement transaction mode 45
open-door enrolment 40

participation in religious activity 135
People's Republic of China (PRC) 4, 31, 40
performance appraisal mechanism 8
performance credit 70; effective percentage of 77, **79**; of interviewees, levels of education 77, *78*; of interviewees, political status *80*; of interviewees between city and countryside *80*
personal credit 69, 196; education background on *92*; factor analysis of 90, **91**
personal–interpersonal credit 90, *91*, **91–93**, *92*, 92–93
personnel credit 70–72; effective percentage of 77, 78, *83*, **84**; mean value of *85*
political participation 135, 150, 151, 157
political trust 144, 150, 153–156
politics–government credit 70, 77–78, *78*, **79**, *80–83*, 83, **84–86**, 85–89, *87*, *88*, **88–90**
power: of blood-related trust 148; democratic supervision of 153; institutionalised distrust of 116; legality and efficacy of 153; organisation mode of public power 51; on personal character 28; of social control and regulation 192; of social participation 156; of social trust 156; structure of 172; in WeChat group-buying model 177
power-dependent expressive trust 173
practical model 186
pre-liberation modern times 57
principal-agent relationship 56
principle of joint liability 51–52
private-activity participation 136
product quality credit: crosstabs analysis between education level and *88*; crosstabs analysis between vocation and *87*; crosstabs analysis of *87*
product service credit **88**
The Protestant Ethic and the Spirit of Capitalism (Weber) 119
public-credit systems 186
public interest (collective interest) 115
public trust: in immediate enforcement agencies 120; in institutional enforcement officials 120
Putnam, R. D. 130, 143, 156, 157; *Making Democracy Work* 129

Qing dynasty 52, 53
Qin Kingdom 111–112
questionnaire, for "Study of China's social credit system" 204–215; determination of research variables 69–74; sampling design and implementation of 72–74; social demographic situation of interviewees 74, **74–77**; survey methods 68–69

rationality 2, 6, 70, 102, 116, 155
regional credit system 184
Regulations on Credit Industry Management 184
relational trust 138, 152
relationship network 122, 123
Reliability Assessment Factor 144
religious participation 136, 146
reputation 162–163
reputation constraining mechanism 56
reputation constraints 177, 179
reputation debasement 50–51
research assumption 36–42
righteousness 17, 20, 103, 106
risk-laden business activities 63–64
"rule of virtue" 34
rural social participation 135
rural society 123; characteristics of 120; legality in 53; punishment for contractual default and dishonest conduct 50; reputation constraining mechanism 56

sages 104–105
Sanbei Company 59
Schultz, Theodore W. 127
secular authority, holy sanctity with 53–54
selection by nature 30
Selfishness Assessment Factor 144
self-organisedness 156
"self-realization of man" 115
shame culture 124
Shanghai Business Conference Council 60
Shanghai General Chamber of Commerce 60, 62
Shanghai Money Shop Guild 62
Shang Yang 111–112
Shanxi merchants 52, 63, 64; birth and operation mechanisms of 55–57
Shanzhai products 38–39
Shequ 25
Siming Bank 58, 59
sincerity 17, 33
Sino-foreign trade 62
Smith, Adam 127

social-activity participation 135–136, 151
social capital 99; back to relation 153–157; characteristics of urban and rural residents 139, 141–143; connotations of 127–131, **131**; dimensions of 130, **131**; explorations of 130; forms of 129; interpersonal trust variable 136, **138**, 138–139, **140**; measurement of 132–139; relationship between social credit and 132; relationship between trust and 131; and social credit 143–144; social participation variable 132–133, **133**, **134**, 135–136, **136**, **137**; and trust in government, by urban and rural residents **149**, 149–152, **150**; and universal trust 144–148
social capital theory 129, 130, 153, 154
social contract 153
social control 32–36
social credibility: of civil media 168–169, **170**; crisis of official media 166–167, **166**, **167**, *168*
social-credit construction system 185
social credit crisis 5, 6, 190
social credit system 5, 15, 23; basic forms of 77–96; classification of 69; construction history of 182–184; cultivation and improvement of 190; development of 197; evolution of 24–29; in folk society 65; history of 28, 29; ideas for building 184–186; implementation problems of 186–189; measurement and determination of variables 70–72; reconstruction in mobile internet era 179–180; relationship between social capital and 132; and social capital 143–144; and social control 32–36; of traditional Chinese society 24
Social Darwinism 29
social exchange 102
social group 102
social homogeneity 98
social immobility 51
social-interaction contexts 128
social mobility 191
social networks 128; closeness of 129; two-way transformation of 176
social-organisation participation 93–96, **94–96**
social-organism theory 31
social participation 150–151, 156, 157; social trust and 154
social participation variable: rural sample 135–136, **136**, **137**; urban sample 132–133, **133**, **134**, 135
social-relationship networks 128
social relationships 18, 21, 25, 164
social structure, stability of 129
social-transition period 192
social trust 18, 22–23, 130, 155, 172; fragmentation under uncertainty 161–165; power of 156; and social participation 154
society–market credit 71
socio-economic phenomenon 58
Spencer, Herbert 29, 31; The Principles of Sociology 30
State Public Security 39
supplementary sampling 73
symbol credit 71, **86**

Taoist 103, 109
Taylor, Frederick W. 115
technological innovation 118
theory of evolution 29–32
theory of social resources 102
traditional business culture 57
traditional business-operation activities 56
traditional Chinese society 45, 46; appeal to gains/material benefits 52; business groups in 63; community life of 20; covenant in 47; credit institutions of modern society in 47; gains/material benefits 52; governance of 64; individual credit in 47; "litigation-free" covenants in 46; merchants in 54; modern society in 47; social credit of 24; and trust network 164
traditional credit 48–49
traditional credit, historical inheritance of 54; Anhui and Shanxi merchant groups 55–57; internal logic of 63–65; Ningbo merchants 57–63
traditional credit governance, fundamental principles: combining economic punishment and reputation debasement 50–51; combining holy sanctity with secular authority 53–54; combining moral self-discipline and collective expulsion 51; intermediary participation in folk-credit governance 52–53; principle of joint liability 51–52
traditional media 165, 166, 173
traditional media information 165
traditional money-shop business 58

traditional rural society 56
triangular debt 183
trust 26–27, 101; from abstract systems 111; basic level in society 143; of differential patterns 156; diversification in internet era 163–165; in government, by urban and rural residents **149**, 149–152, **150**; in government agencies, by urban and rural dwellers 77, *82*; in government agencies, levels of education 77, *81*; in government agencies, political status 77, *82*; in institutional enforcement agencies 120; negative impact of online participation 152; in quality and binding nature 180; relationship between institution and 110–114, 119; relationship between social capital and 131; in social relationships **92**, **93**; types of 152; of urban residents and rural citizens 167
trust network 26, 28, 47–50, 123, 163, 164; maintenance of 50
trust zone 35
truthfulness 53, 101, 102, 108
two-layered governance model 64–65

uncertainty 5; in internet era 161–162
universal trust 153, 155; of urban and rural residents 144–146, **145–147**
uprightness 108, 109
urbanisation 164

Wang Anshi 112
Weber, Max: *The Protestant Ethic and the Spirit of Capitalism* 119
WeChat group 175–180, 200
Weiss, W. 171
Wenzhou merchants 54
Western culture: external guidance of traditional 123–124; hierarchy of humanity assumptions 116
Western institutions: analysis of 119; compared with arrangements 120
Western market economy 65
Western religious beliefs 107
Western social capital theory 155
Western social credit systems 6
Western society: humanity assumption in 115; human nature in 102; institutional trust in 116
Western sociological theory 110
Western sociologists 41
Western theory of evolution 31
Wu Jinglian 197n5
Wu Zhihui 32

XIN: cultural explanation of 33; native explanation of 15–17; relevant conceptual relations 18–21; research perspective 21–24
X theory 115
Xunzi 105

Yan Fu 29–31
youth population, educational status of 191–192
Y theory 115
Yu Qiaqing 59

Zhejiang business group 60
Z theory 115